LEISURE SERVICES IN CANADA: An Introduction

Venture Publishing, Inc., 1999 Cato Avenue, State College, PA 16801

Leisure Services in Canada:
An Introduction

By: Mark S. Searle, Ph.D.
and
Russell E. Brayley, Ph.D.

Recreation Studies Degree Programme
The University of Manitoba
Winnipeg, Manitoba
R3T 2N2 Canada

Printed in the United States of America

Library of Congress Cataloging in Publication Data
Authors: Mark S. Searle, Ph.D. and Russell E. Brayley, Ph.D
    Leisure Services in Canada: An Introduction

Production: Bonnie Godbey
Printing and Binding: BookCrafters, Inc.
Manuscript Editing: Michele L. Barbin
Graphic Design: Naomi Q. Gallagher
Cover Design: Sandra Sikorski, Sikorski Design

Library of Congress Catalogue Card Number 93-61300
ISBN 0-910251-64-9

10 9 8 7 6 5 4 3 2 1

Table of Contents

CHAPTER TEN: OUTDOOR EDUCATION AND ETHICAL OUTDOOR LEADERSHIP

CHAPTER ELEVEN: OUTDOOR RECREATION AND MANAGEMENT IN CANADA

DEDICATION

To our families:
Judy, Erin and David; and Renée, Doug, Austin, Erika and Natalie

Chapter One

An Introduction

Does a life of leisure sound appealing? Does a career in helping others satisfy their leisure seem interesting? Is leisure something you have, or is it something you experience? Does leisure involve more than time away from work or school? Does leisure have an economic impact? Is tourism related to leisure? These are just some of the questions we address in the pages that follow. We hope that through reading this text, you will achieve a greater understanding of the full dimension of leisure in our society and of the importance it has within our individual lives.

Over the past hundreds of years, leisure has been embraced as an ideal, discarded as hedonistic, accepted under limited terms, valued, and not valued. It has been in abundance for some, while others may never have experienced leisure, at least as we define it through our culture. Yet no matter how leisure has been viewed, it has been the subject of study for many years and in this century, it has attracted even more attention as early predictions heralded the imminent coming of the "leisure age". We know that such an age is not yet upon us, but public opinion polls show that individuals value leisure more today than at any point earlier in this century. Perhaps it is an issue of supply and demand. We seem to be working harder and longer to sustain our standard of living and as a result, the opportunity for leisure diminishes. As this occurs, our desire for it increases, and thus our increasing valuing of it.

Where Has All The Leisure Gone?

Recent research by Shaw (1990) has suggested that the average work week among Canadians whose employment provides more than 30 hours of work per week has actually increased not decreased. Moreover, Shaw has noted that, with the increase in two career families, the availability of leisure for individuals in such families has decreased. Statistics Canada has also indicated that the availability of leisure time seems to be decreasing. They noted an increase between 1976 and 1984 of persons working 50 hours per week or more. Shaw noted that the average retiree reported having only 11.6 hours per week to experience leisure. These data strongly suggest that, as Canadians, we value work and are not prepared to do away with it. By the same token, we are also reporting greater feelings of being rushed and not being able to take advantage of our leisure opportunities (Shaw, 1990). We ask, as did Shaw, "where has all the leisure gone?"

Leisure: A Growth Industry

It is also quite clear that leisure is growing in importance even if its availability seems to be diminishing. This can be inferred from the extent to which government, not-for-profit and commercial sector organizations promote and facilitate leisure activity. At one point in time, leisure was considered to be a frill or add-on service provided to the public if funds were available. Today, we find leisure services provided by public agencies in all levels of government (e.g., Canadian Parks Service, provincial and municipal recreation departments), not-for-profit agencies (e.g., YM-YWCA, Boys' and Girls' Clubs, and senior centres), and commercial organizations (e.g., Whistler Resort, movie theatres, and shopping malls such as the West Edmonton Mall). Indeed, *leisure expenditures by the federal government alone* have grown from $539.1 million in 1980-81 to $1.5 billion in 1989-90. Annual expenditures on leisure by Canadian families have, according to Statistics Canada, risen by 40.4 percent from 1982 to 1986.

A recent book by Allan Gregg and Michael Posner (1990) has suggested that leisure will become more and more important in the lives of Canadians through the 1990s. This, they say, is reflected in the expressed desire to have a better quality of life and more personally satisfying lifestyles. They claim that "in the 1990s, people will discover that leisure is not simply an end in itself, but a means to a greater end: well-being" (p. 156), and that our aging but relatively healthier population will, as a result, create a demand for new and more challenging leisure experiences. Moreover, Gregg and Posner suggest that this older population will be wealthier and this will allow them to seek more exotic leisure experiences such as mountain climbing in Nepal and photographic safaris to Kenya.

Our health has become a primary focus in the recent years. The dramatic exclusion of smoking as a socially acceptable activity and the changed attitudes toward drinking capture some of this newfound interest in healthier lifestyles. Leisure is a great vehicle for promoting positive lifestyles and activities. Those who provide opportunities for leisure will be at the vanguard of helping Canadians achieve a better level of health. Each provincial government in Canada is faced with a growing debt, a seemingly unrequited demand for health services, and an inability to fund either. As a result, we are witnessing dramatic changes in the health care system in Canada. The emphasis is shifting to community-based care, preventative health, health promotion, and reductions in the number of physicians being trained. Moreover, it may be that the full preventative health aspects of leisure are finally recognized and some funds now invested in acute and chronic care health systems will be redirected toward leisure services.

Leisure and the Environment

Leisure also includes our interactions with, and experiences in, the outdoors. In addition, these outdoor spaces for leisure offer an important support to our ailing environment. Recognition of the need to protect our natural resources and to provide opportunities for Canadians to experience their leisure in natural environments and places of historical significance led to the creation of Banff National Park in 1885 by the Canadian Government. Subsequently, this led to the creation of the national parks system (the largest in the world). It has also led to the systematic protection of historic sites. Similar initiatives by provincial park services make an important contribution to the social fabric of the nation and increasingly to the health of our environment.

We also need to develop an appreciation for the role of the leisure service professional as stewards of our environment and as conservators. In that capacity, leisure service professionals may have to limit some opportunities which, uncontrolled, might inflict damage on the environment. In some circumstances, leisure service professionals must protect some areas by preventing any kind of human intrusion. These protected areas are often referred to as ecological areas, and are essential to sustaining our life as well as our way of life. The controversy in British Columbia concerning the harvesting of old growth trees and the challenge in Quebec to the construction of the second phase of hydroelectric development in the James Bay region are but two examples where resource potential creates a conflict over modern society's needs and the need for life itself.

Leisure as an Instrument of Government

Leisure has been used instrumentally by governments at all levels to contribute to economic growth, promote national unity, and promote a sense of pride among Canadians (we would say promote nationalism, but Canadians do not generally think of themselves as nationals or nationalistic). Leisure was used in World War II as a means to redress the poor physical condition of the recruits that the armed forces were attracting (Westland, 1979) and, more recently economic and nationalistic objectives have been addressed through such activities as the hosting of provincial, national and international multisport events, the giving of support to Canadian athletes, and the extension of support for PARTICIPaction and Active Living '92'. In fact, federal government support was given to an *ad hoc* organization in 1992 to promote neighbourhood "block parties". These were, in part, supposed to contribute to a greater sense of unity among Canadians.

The need for leisure services is not really perceived to be a frill by public policy-makers. Recent research in Nova Scotia revealed that 87 percent of the municipal councillors surveyed believed recreation was an "essential service" in their community. This belief was grounded in the role of leisure as an important instrument for promoting community cohesion and for maintaining a mentally and socially healthy community.

Leisure has been used to achieve objectives associated with the improvement of the quality of life enjoyed by Canadians. This has resulted, as noted earlier, in extensive resources being invested in our leisure service delivery system by all levels of government and by the private and commercial sectors. One of the results of this financial investment has been the need for skilled professionals and technicians to manage the system and for a better understanding of the dynamics of leisure behaviour, systems, and infrastructure planning and development.

Why Study Leisure?

So why study leisure? The field of study is complex. Each individual should have an understanding of the important role leisure plays in our social, physical and psychological development, the role of leisure in our history, and full impact of leisure in our society so that we might better make judgements and decisions as informed citizens. The aspiring leisure service professional must have a sense of the history of leisure and leisure services, a grounding in the behavioural aspects of leisure, understand the different meanings of concepts used in the field such as play, leisure, recreation, and work, and have a thorough understanding of the range and scope of leisure services including how they are and can be provided, to whom they are or might be provided, and the different environments in which leisure may be experienced. Finally, it is critical to apply this information to considerations of the prospects for the future.

The role of leisure in the social fabric of our society is substantive and important to sustaining our quality of life and improving it. Leisure service professionals must be capable of meeting those needs in the community or face the problem of becoming obsolete.

Previewing the Text

The book is divided into fourteen chapters. These can be grouped into four units. The first unit includes Chapters One through Four and covers the history of leisure and leisure services, the important concepts and related issues, and philosophical foundations.

By becoming aware of how leisure was viewed before and during the early days of our country's existence, and by examining how attitudes towards leisure have changed during the last 150 years, we can more fully appreciate the significance attributed to it today. Through an examination of significant events and trends in Canada and the United States we can develop a greater appreciation of the historical perspective of recreation and we can develop a sense of where our modern Canadian society and its institutions are going with respect to this important aspect of our lives.

The concepts *leisure, play, recreation, sport,* and *work* are a major focus in Chapter Two. These concepts are the foundation for understanding behaviour and many associated issues. The final part of Chapter Two reviews many of the more prominent philosophical positions adopted by the professional practice at different times. How those philosophies influenced the development of these conceptual perspectives is also discussed. Finally, we seek to explain why an understanding of these concepts and philosophical foundations is important for leisure service professionals, and how the adoption of different conceptualizations and philosophical positions ultimately influences the leisure services provided.

The final chapter in this first unit is focused on the explanation and elaboration of the following concepts: leisure participation, leisure repertoire, leisure motives, leisure attitudes, and constraints on leisure. The intent is to explain each of the concepts briefly, reflect on some of the principal research conducted in each area, and summarize the main findings as they relate to the leisure service professional.

The second unit of the textbook includes Chapters Five, Six, and Seven. These chapters explain the public, private (voluntary), and commercial subsystems of the leisure service delivery system in Canada. The purpose of Chapter Five is to describe the public recreation system in Canada. It will explore the roles of the federal, provincial and municipal governments in providing and facilitating the provision of publicly funded leisure services. Through this exploration we can develop an appreciation for the extent of public sector involvement in the leisure service industry and begin to understand the nature of public agency involvement in the development of our individual leisure lifestyles.

Chapter Six examines the nature of volunteering, voluntary agencies, and various issues associated with the not-for-profit sector. We examine where Canadians volunteer their time and energy, the kinds of activities they engage in as volunteers, and the role of volunteers in leisure service organizations.

The final chapter of this second unit provides an overview of commercial sector activities in leisure services. As an important part of the community recreation system, commercial recreation enterprises contribute to the economy and to the quality of life enjoyed by Canadians. The purpose of this chapter is to distinguish commercial leisure services from those provided by public and private not-for-profit recreation agencies, and to offer useful background information to individuals who might pursue careers in the commercial recreation field.

Chapters Eight through Twelve form the basis for the third unit in the textbook. These chapters address a range of topics which are important to the leisure service delivery system such as tourism, recreation for persons with special needs, outdoor recreation, environmental ethics, natural resource management, and recreation programming.

The purpose of Chapter Eight is to explore travel and tourism as a leisure experience, and to describe the scope of tourism activity in Canada. It discusses the reasons for which people travel and the benefits they derive therefrom. Also discussed are the impacts of leisure travel on host and guest leisure opportunities and choices.

Chapter Nine provides an introduction to the opportunities which are presently available to persons with special needs related to recreation and leisure, the conceptual foundation for such opportunities, and most importantly, the changes which are necessary to ensure that opportunities for persons with special needs continue to grow.

The philosophical foundations of outdoor education and recreation, a description of some specific programmatic applications of outdoor education, and the connection between outdoor leadership to the larger context of humans' ethical relationship to natural areas are the foci of Chapter Ten.

The purpose of Chapter Eleven is to describe the significance of natural places for outdoor recreation, the components of the outdoor recreation experience, and the policies and structures for managing natural areas for ecological integrity and the outdoor recreation experience.

The final chapter of this unit, Chapter Twelve, has been designed to introduce you to the nature of recreation programming and its significance as part of the services provided by leisure services practitioners. We describe the historical evolution of recreation programming, the emergence of theoretical models to better understand and plan for the recreation program experience, leisure education, and issues facing those involved in providing recreation programs.

The final unit of the textbook includes Chapters Thirteen and Fourteen. These chapters examine the issue of the development of the profession of leisure services and contemporary issues facing those in leisure services. More specifically, Chapter Thirteen provides an overview of the issues associated with the move toward greater professional status for those working in leisure services, we describe some of the principal organizations that exist to promote leisure in Canada and assist those in the field (both volunteer and paid employee). We also briefly describe some of the organizations that exist internationally, and then we review the state of university and college education in leisure.

The purpose of Chapter Fourteen is to focus your attention on circumstances and changes in Canadian society that might affect or be affected by leisure services. It is intended that your consciousness of and concern in matters relating to these issues will be heightened, and that you will view leisure services as being within the range of solutions that are appropriate to specific social problems. In addition, this chapter should stimulate thinking about the future, particularly as it relates to the role of leisure in our lives and the way that leisure services in Canada will be managed and delivered.

Do you need to read the textbook in sequence? We recommend that Chapters Two through Four be read first. The sequence of reading the Chapters Five through Seven is not important but they should be read as a group. Chapters Eight through Twelve may be read in any sequence upon completion of the first unit. We do recommend that Chapters Thirteen and Fourteen be read last as they will fit better contextually at that time.

We have provided a series of study questions at the conclusion of each chapter as well as the references used in that chapter. The ability to answer all of the questions should prepare you to respond well to questions about the material. The references provide a source for you to begin further research in any of the topics discussed.

Summary

We have introduced you to some of the many issues that confront us individually in our leisure and will challenge us as professionals in leisure services. The changing workplace, global politics, economy, relative wealth, average age, and other factors lead us to foresee a dynamic seven year period until the end of the 20th century. Leisure has survived since the time of Ancient Greek civilization and well before then and it is unlikely that the desire or need for leisure will ever abate. Rather, leisure, with its potential to be used as an important developmental tool, has much to offer restructured health care systems, changed economies, and new workplaces and work systems. Leisure has many benefits. Through reading this book, we hope that they become more clear and we hope that you acquire an appreciation of the full range of leisure services and its impact on our Canadian society.

References

Gregg, A. & Posner, M. (1990). *The big picture.* Toronto, ON: Macfarlane, Walter & Ross.

Shaw, S. (1990). Where has all the leisure gone? The distribution and redistribution of leisure. In B. Smale (Ed.) *Proceedings from the Sixth Canadian Congress on Leisure Research* (pp. 1-5). Waterloo, ON: University of Waterloo Press.

Westland, C. (1979). *Fitness and amateur sport in Canada—The federal government's programme: An historical perspective.* Ottawa, ON: Canadian Parks/Recreation Association.

Chapter Two

Perspectives On The Past

Overview

PURPOSE

The purpose of this chapter is to describe the historical development of leisure services in Canada. By becoming aware of how leisure was viewed before and during the early days of our country's existence, and by examining how attitudes towards leisure have changed during the last 150 years, we can more fully appreciate the significance attributed to it today. Through an examination of significant events and trends in Canada and the United States, we can develop a greater appreciation of the historical perspective of recreation and we can develop a sense of where our modern Canadian society and its institutions are going with respect to this important aspect of our lives.

LEARNING OBJECTIVES

At the completion of this chapter, you should be able to:

1. identify the source of many of the ideas that influence the role of leisure services in modern Canadian society,

2. identify changes in Canadian society that have contributed to increased emphasis on, and opportunity for recreation,

3. describe some of the significant events in the history of recreation development in Canada, and

4. drawing from a knowledge of the past, make preliminary conclusions about the future of leisure and recreation development in our society.

Perspectives On The Past

In order for us to fully appreciate the nature and importance of leisure services in modern Canada, it is necessary to turn, for a moment, to the past and examine the historical context of recreation and leisure in western civilization and in the development of Canadian society. We study history not as a purely academic exercise but as a way of learning lessons from those who have gone before us and applying those lessons to the present. We also study history as a means to better understand why things are the way they are today, and how they might be in the future.

In this chapter we will only briefly discuss leisure in ancient times and focus primarily on the social history of Canada and on the social role of leisure and recreation in the years since confederation. In so doing, the temporal development of leisure services in Canada will be traced against the backdrop of several demographic, political, cultural, and technological trends and events that have significantly helped to weave the fabric of modern day Canada.

Leisure in Ancient Times

Our discussion of the history of leisure might begin with an exploration of the way prehistoric man incorporated play and art into daily survival activities and religious practices. It could continue with a look at games as rites, and the development of sports as modified warfare. It could also focus on the use of feasts, dancing and contests in primitive societies for the enhancement of military, political or industrial strength. It will, however, begin with a look at leisure as an ideal pursued by the ancient Greeks.

We choose to begin our history of leisure in the Golden Age of Pericles (from about 500 to 400 B.C.) because of the enduring influence of the philosophers and writers of that time and that society on the development of western civilization and Canadian society. Those philosophers and writers include Socrates, Plato, and Aristotle.

The Socratic view of leisure was dominated by its utilitarian function. Leisure and play were seen as "valued possessions", but only because they provided an atmosphere in which children could "grow up to be well-conducted and virtuous citizens" (Plato). Plato recommended compulsory education for leisure as a means of stabilizing social order and maintaining laws. To Plato's philosopher friends, leisure was an instrument to be used in facilitating good personal and social government.

Aristotle, who was Plato's student, is regarded by most modern scholars as the "Father of Leisure". Obviously, Aristotle did not invent leisure, nor did he author such concepts as free time, pleasurable activity and the contemplative state of mind, but it was Aristotle who championed the view of leisure as an end in itself and documented the Greek pursuit of leisure as an ideal. Aristotle stressed that "the first principle of all action is leisure" and that "leisure is better than occupation and [is] its end" (Ulich, 1950). With this reasoning, the Greeks became very interested (in fact, preoccupied) with *schole*. Schole, to Aristotle's fellow citizens and symposiarchs, was a conscious cessation of obligatory activity and the pursuit of noble and desirable activities done for their own sake. It is the root word for both leisure and school, and refers mainly to the exercise of speculative facilities for purposes of inspiration and enlightenment.

The leisure of ancient Greece was a lifestyle rather than an event, activity or period of time. Ironically, it was a lifestyle of freedom for a few, bought with the enslavement of many. Only the privileged classes were able to obtain leisure and it was this that entitled them to full citizenship.

The glory of Greece was eventually eclipsed by the military might of Rome, and unlike their idealistic neighbours across the Ionian Sea, the pre-meridian Romans pursued a different kind of leisure. They valued physical strength over philosophic prowess and promoted the idea of games and athletic competition as a higher ideal for citizens of Rome. Social classes were technically non-existent in early Rome and citizenship was more widely granted than in Greece. Leisure was considered a right of citizenship and leisure activities other than contemplation and syllogism had to be included in the new "mass leisure".

The masses, however, soon became classes and leisure once again became a distinguishing feature of social stratification. The ruling classes engaged in creative, cultural activities that only they could afford, and the *plebs* (free common people) did what they could with limited resources and excess free time. To palliate social abuses, the ruling classes staged amusements and entertainments for the plebs and gave them a basic subsistence allowance of grain. This policy of "bread and circuses" gave rise to amusive leisure in place of the Greek concept of contemplative leisure. To facilitate amusement and entertainment activities, specialized facilities such as the Colosseum were built and as many as 175 official holidays during the year were proclaimed for theatre, circus, races, combats and festivals (Roberts, 1962).

Roman holidays were characterized by increasingly perverse and morally deficient behaviours, and brutality, corruption and degradation became part of how the Romans experienced their "leisure". This abuse and Roman leadership's inability to deal with mass leisure in a positive way, claim many historians, was the major reason for the downfall of the Roman Empire. This abuse was also the major contributor to the development of official disdain for leisure in the middle ages.

LEISURE IN MEDIEVAL EUROPE

The unifying force of Rome: the Empire crumbled under military defeat, but was later replaced by the unifying force of Rome: the Church. Christianity, as represented in Europe by the Catholic church, had suffered much for the sake of pagan Rome's leisure, and the church was eager to disassociate itself with the hedonistic way of life practised by its early oppressors. Leisure as an ideal ceased to be promoted and the value of work was stressed from the pulpit as well as from the taskmaster's mount. Pleasurable pursuits were considered to be sinful, and the righteous soul was recognized as one that was molded through self-denial, sacrifice and solemnity.

This period, known as the Dark Ages primarily because of the official intolerance of personal and societal development, had little hope to offer the common folk who yearned for education, enlightenment, and relief from daily toil. The Dark Ages were a period of limited leisure, and what little leisure the common people of the time could secure was characterized by crude activities like athletic contests, wrestling, ball games, cockfighting and bull-baiting. Even some of these activities were forbidden by the Church and by harsh feudal lords. Yet, even though they expressed disdain for leisure, the nobility of the time ensured that at least they themselves had ample resources and opportunity for rest, festivity, art, sport, entertainment, and education. They engaged in debate, oration, music, dancing, hunting, gambling, and a wide variety of games including chess, checkers and backgammon. On occasion, some of these leisure experiences were extended to common people but only through festivals, tournaments and events which involved commoners as spectators and noblemen in public demonstrations of physical skill and social superiority.

Progress towards wider enjoyment of leisure was slow, but by the time Christian reformers like John Wycliffe, Martin Luther, and John Calvin arrived on the scene, Europeans were beginning to get a taste for education and for involvement in activities that were designed to do nothing more than provide enjoyment. The loosening of the Catholic grip on cultural evolution in Europe was facilitated by the protestations of these reformers, and part of that cultural evolution included the development of a general appreciation of leisure and the extension of leisure opportunities to the masses.

It should be noted, however, that the Protestant Reformation was not all progressive as far as leisure is concerned. Zealous leaders of fledgling religious sects were eager to break from the control of Rome's church and often went to extremes to differentiate their doctrines and practices and to establish control over their followers. Most protestant churches reviled against the non-labouring Catholic aristocracy by declaring the importance of work for all, and by discounting the fine arts enjoyed by the clergy as wasteful, useless, and often sinful pursuits that have little or no personally or socially redeeming value.

LEISURE IN PRE-CONFEDERATION NORTH AMERICA

Many of the new religious groups that fled European persecution for the protection of North America's isolation held very extreme views about leisure, play, and recreation. The Puritan work ethic was strong and ecclesiastical restrictions on leisure served an important social control function for both church and civic leaders in the new colonies.

Ibrahim (1991) has also suggested that leisure was not highly prized in colonial times because the first settlers had little time to play, and because "building the country was a priority and . . . other activities would have to be postponed" (p. 163). He proposed that, by necessity, pursuit of happiness in colonial life was secondary to pursuit of the new political and economic system.

As the colonies moved towards becoming states into nations and provinces into confederations, the importance of recreation and leisure in society gained wider recognition. Perhaps it was because of a second wave of religious reformation that swept over North America (particularly the United States) in the early 1800s, or maybe it was because the time had arrived for those leisure activities that were postponed only to allow for the taming of the frontier and the building of the nation. Whatever the reason or reasons, North American society moved quickly into what has been referred to by Chubb and Chubb (1981) as the Recreation Renaissance.

Before discussing the events of this renewed interest in recreation, it is necessary to return to the past and comment on the role and development of leisure and recreation among Canada's aboriginal peoples. We must recognize that neither life nor leisure in Canada began with the European settlement (McInnis, 1969). Before Cartier and Cabot, the Inuit population and the native communities of southern Canada hunted, fished and sustained their independent cultures. They also played games, sang songs, played musical instruments, danced, and told stories for entertainment and amusement. Leisure was valued highly by our indigenous societies (Malloy, 1991).

Blanchard and Cheska (1985, p. 142) characterized the Inuit as 'playful' and Ibrahim (1991) described some of their culturally significant games. He wrote that "among their games is *agraoruk*, in which the contestant tries to kick a sealskin dangling from a pole. *Nalukatook* finds them bouncing on a walrus hide held by others, and the object of *ipirautaqurnia* is to flip a whip precisely" (p. 148).

The Algonquians and Iroquois played a game called *baggataway*. This game involved a contest in which players on two teams used a curved netted stick and a ball-like object to score goals. The modern version of the game is Canada's national sport and bears the name given it by French settlers: lacrosse.

Through their games and ceremonies, Canada's native people established social roles, sought diversion from the daily challenges of survival, and related to the gods. While some of their recreations were adopted by European settlers who came later, most native leisure activities and practices fell victim to acculturation (McInnis, 1969).

Leisure in Post-Confederation North America

A renewed enthusiasm for recreation affected European-dominated Canadian society in the period which began in the 1840s and continued through to the 1880s. It was a period in which community resources, structures and values were undergoing significant changes, and the role of social institutions (especially the church) in directing the leisure activities of individuals was being challenged. The Puritan notion that recreation was sinful was beginning to erode, Sabbath observance was becoming unfashionable, and loose social networks that developed around rapidly growing urban settlements were resulting in non-traditional amusements, entertainment, and diversion opportunities. Modern Christianity was changing and doctrines were being reinterpreted or rewritten to give recognition to the importance and value of physical fitness and social recreation. These significant changes in the moral foundation of British North American society cleared the way for participation in an expanding range of 'acceptable' recreation and leisure activities (Cross, 1990; Wright, 1983).

During the period of the recreation renewal, Canadians were celebrating the founding of a nation and were perceiving greater freedom, democratic opportunity and independence (McInnis, 1969). Leisure and recreation became areas in which this sense of celebration could be expressed.

People living in this period also began to witness extensive migration of workers from the family- and community-oriented rural areas to the cities. These workers sought substitutes for the recreation they previously enjoyed as part of their rural lifestyles, and began to look to their employers, commercial organizations and their governments for leisure opportunities (Wetherell & Kmet, 1990). In these early years of Canada's history, the commercial sector was most responsive to the need for recreation services and provided such opportunities as beer gardens, bars, dance halls, amusement parks, and stage shows.

Labour unions during these years were growing and pushing for other rights and benefits that had very direct implications for recreation development in Canada. Standardization and reduction of the work week provided more leisure time in some parts of Eastern Canada, but in the west, the norm of nine hour work days, Monday to Friday and nine to one o'clock in the afternoon on Saturdays was unchanged until the 1920s (Wetherell & Kmet, 1990). Limits to employment demands on children facilitated their natural yearning to play, and increased job security and disposable income supported participation by workers in a variety of commercial recreation activities.

In the mid-to-late 1800s there was also the beginning of a change in the attitudes of men towards women. Previously, women were expected to find their recreation in their domestic activities and with their families. During this period of renewed interest in recreation, certain activities became acceptable forms of 'public' recreation for women. They included croquet, lawn tennis, golf, archery, roller skating, and ice skating.

The development of improved transportation systems in Canada during this period also influenced recreation and leisure. The railroad not only opened up the west and connected British Columbia to the rest of the country, but it opened up opportunities for new forms of recreation. Recreational travel over long distances could now be undertaken with relative comfort and speed. This meant that en route lodging and entertainment had to be developed, and the commercial sector did not miss this opportunity. The railroads also played a key role in the discovery and designation of some of the scenic natural areas that are now our national parks. Improved transportation systems facilitated greater exposure to theatre companies, circuses, and entertainers (Wetherell & Kmet, 1990). They aided in the distribution of leisure goods such as books, specialty foods, and sporting equipment.

The commercial sector was not the only part of our society to respond to the growing demand for recreation services and opportunities in the mid-1800s. In Canada and in the U.S. there were public and not-for-profit organizations, movements and activities that were designed to support people's leisure needs. Several key events and developments are highlighted here:

- In 1763, the Halifax Common was established for recreational purposes. This protected open space, was under the management of the local Horticultural Society, and was developed to accommodate skating, lawn tennis, croquet and archery (Wright, 1983).

- In 1807, Scottish settlers began holding annual festivals in which they would slide specially shaped granite stones across lake ice towards a designated target. These festivals were called 'bonspiels' and the activity came to be known as curling.
- In 1851, the Toronto City Council established the Committee on Public Walks and Gardens (McFarland, 1970). This action is recognized as one of the earliest acknowledgements by a major local government of the importance of public open space.
- Gore Park in Hamilton, Ontario was established in 1852 (McFarland, 1970).
- In 1853, New York City authorized the purchase and development of Central Park (Wright, 1984). This extensive municipal park was designed by F. L. Olmsted who also designed Mount Royal Park in Montreal. The design features of Central Park rapidly became the design standards for most municipal parks in the United States and Canada (Wright, 1984).
- English troops stationed in Kingston, Ontario are credited with introducing ice hockey in 1855.
- Boys' Clubs (now Boys' and Girls' Clubs) were founded in the 1860s in Hartford, Connecticut. This not-for-profit agency was one of the first non-commercial organizations to target a specific segment of the population and adopt recreation as its primary mandate for the client group (Boys' Clubs of America, n.d.).
- In 1867, the year of Confederation, the City of Toronto acquired the property for what became Toronto Island Park (McFarland, 1970).
- In 1872, the Congress of the United States set aside 1.6 million acres of scenic and geologically significant land as a "national pleasuring ground". We now know of this area as Yellowstone National Park (Chubb & Chubb, 1981).
- The Public Parks Act of Ontario was passed in 1883 facilitating the development of municipal public parks throughout Ontario (Wright, 1984).
- In 1885, at the suggestion of the tourism-conscious Canadian Pacific Railroad, Rocky Mountain Park (Banff) was established. Within two years, the Banff Springs Hotel was serving Canadian and international guests with fine accommodations and a variety of recreation opportunities (Wetherell & Kmet, 1990).

Leisure in Young Canada

Recreation development in the years between 1880 and 1900 was characterized by a marked increase in government involvement. This was particularly evident in the establishment of numerous municipal park authorities in cities and towns across North America before the turn of the century. Drawing from the work of Elsie McFarland (1970), the following were trends in evidence during this formative period in the country's history.

In the early 1880s the local government in the Ontario community of Port Arthur (now Thunder Bay) used its legislative authority to enable its administrative officers to provide public park services. It was one of the first smaller communities in Canada to do this.

In 1882, the provincial government of Manitoba passed the *Public Parks Act*. This act authorized cities with a population of 25,000 or more residents to acquire up to 600 acres of land for park development purposes. Through the *Public Parks Act*, smaller communities were permitted to purchase up to 400 acres for parks. Note that the provincial legislation only *allowed* municipalities to acquire park lands. With that permission, the local authorities still had to decide that park development was worthwhile, find the required resources, and amend local legislation (by-laws) to authorize action. The City of Winnipeg saw the new legislation as a welcome opportunity and, in 1883, established the Winnipeg Parks Board. The board was authorized by the city's taxpayers to borrow $74,000 to purchase eight park sites in different parts of the city. In so doing, the Board set a precedent and established a policy of positive intervention in the provision of community recreation and park services.

Many cities in other provinces established parks boards during this time period. With one notable exception, these boards were appointed bodies acting under the authority and resource generosity of the municipal council. The exception to be noted is the Vancouver Board of Parks Commissioners. This locally elected group of individuals has had varying levels of financial management authority and autonomy. It has been an active proponent of parks and recreation in the Vancouver area, and was instrumental in the land dedication and development of Stanley Park. It may seem only natural to establish a large area like Stanley Park in a sprawling urban area like Vancouver, but the foresight of this board is emphasized when we recall that the population of Vancouver at the time of the park's establishment was only 10,000.

Thus far we have described much of the advancement of recreation and leisure during the late 1800s in terms of open space development. It is important to realize that the early parks were not the same as the parks we find in most of our contemporary communities. For example, both Montreal and Toronto had, in these earlier years, city by-laws which strictly prohibited the playing of games in public parks.

McFarland (1970) pointed out that the parks of a hundred years ago were thought to be the 'lungs of the city' but they were not places to exercise the human lungs through vigorous or noisy activity. These parks were to be passive and serene places, focussing on ornateness and floral beauty. "Do not walk on the grass" signs were plentiful, and activities were limited to such things as walking, riding in one's carriage, botanical appreciation, and bird watching. Due mostly to temporal resourcefulness and mobility, it was the upper class that most frequently visited these public 'breathing spaces' and enjoyed their benefits.

In addition to being a time of public park development at the municipal level, the late 1800s was a period of emerging interest in public recreation programming. The most significant event relating to recreation programming around the turn of the century was the formation of the National Council of Women. The organization was formed in 1893 and shortly thereafter began to consider the issue of youth and the potential positive influence that could be exerted on youth through recreation. In Canada, the National Council of Women is considered to be the driving force behind the Playground Movement (McFarland, 1970).

1900-1920

The Playground Movement that was so active after the turn of the century was based on the idea that recreation and play was the only appropriate method of physical development for children and it was necessary for their health, strength and moral character. This social welfare role of play was promoted extensively by the National Council of Women which encouraged communities to sponsor 'vacation schools' and develop play facilities for their constituents. These early playgrounds were called *sand gardens*.

In the United States, the Playground Movement was being championed by Joseph Lee. Lee founded the Playground Association of America which is a forerunner to the National Recreation and Park Association.

There were other significant recreation-related events that took place in the first two decades of this century. They are:

- The growing popularity of public parks boards in the U.S. In 1880 there were only 80 such bodies, but by the early 1900s there were over 800 parks boards operating in the United States. By 1920, most major Canadian urban centres had organized public park and recreation systems (McFarland, 1970).
- Boys' Clubs, Boy Scouts and Girl Guides were growing in popularity. They were providing more recreation opportunities for the youth than were previously available.
- Work patterns were changing and blocks of leisure time were becoming available to many people. In the early 1900s the protection of Sabbath (Sunday) was introduced through the Federal Government's enactment of the *Lord Day's Act* (1907) and, in some ways, the concept of the 'weekend' was born (Wetherell & Kmet, 1990). By this time the, one-week annual vacation was beginning to be a standard employment benefit and some people were beginning to be offered two-week leaves. However, as Wetherell and Kmet (1990) pointed out, this benefit of vacations was not always extended to construction workers, railroad workers and other casual labourers. It was not until 1922 that there were seven statutory holidays in most parts of Canada (Christmas, Dominion Day, Labour Day, Victoria Day, Thanksgiving, Good Friday, and New Year's Day).
- The invention and mass production of the Ford Model-T automobile in 1908 greatly enhanced individual mobility and introduced new forms of mechanized recreation. Pleasure travel became more popular and people were no longer limited to recreation opportunities that were available only within the immediate area (Wetherell & Kmet, 1990; Chubb & Chubb, 1981). Indeed, between 1924 and 1929, the number of automobiles that entered Banff National Park tripled (Wetherell & Kmet, 1990).

- Physical education and athletics became an acceptable activity for public school systems to promote. Recreation and physical education were closely aligned during this period. It was Joseph Lee's Playground Association of America that created the National Physical Education Service which promoted mandatory physical education in American schools. It wasn't until the Canadian Physical Education Association (CPEA) was formed in the 1930s that advocacy for physical activity in the school setting gained a national voice in Canada (Gurney, 1983).

1920-1940

Many important social and technological changes happened in the years between the world wars. Those with the greatest impact on recreation development in Canada are highlighted here:

- Canada's voting population expanded to include women. As the "mothers of the nation" now had a political voice with which to demand recreation opportunities for their children, governments took a greater interest in their expanding role with respect to public leisure services. Women also demanded more equitable treatment for themselves as consumers of public recreation services. More opportunities were made available, but progress in this area of social reform was slow and much discrimination continued (Wetherell & Kmet, 1990). Women's participation in high profile athletics was looked upon with disdain, as evidenced by a particular fiasco associated with the 1928 Olympic Games. When several women from the United States entered the Olympic Games as competitors in the track and field event there was a storm of protest. Even the Women's Athletic Section of the forerunner to the American Alliance of Health, Physical Education, Recreation and Dance objected to the entry (Chubb & Chubb, 1981)!
- Commercial radio broadcasting began in the 1920s. Its popularity spread rapidly and the number of people in the U.S. who purchased radios grew from 5,000 in 1920 to 5,000,000 just four years later (Chubb & Chubb, 1981). In Canada it became the vehicle through which that great Canadian institution "Hockey Night in Canada" was launched (Wetherell & Kmet, 1990).
- Attendance at major sporting events increased during this period of time. Annual competitions such as the Stanley Cup, the World Series, and the Grey Cup became well established and provided an apex for the broad-based pyramid of sport development (Wetherell & Kmet, 1990).
- The 1920s gave rise to the formation of the Canadian National Parks Association. It was formed to fight the development of hydroelectric power in the Spray River Basin in Alberta (Bella & Markham, 1984). This was the forerunner of the National and Provincial Parks Association.

- Nineteen-twenty eight saw the introduction of talking movies. Going to the picture show became a popular pastime and was a special recreational treat for rural communities where entertainment opportunities were somewhat limited.

- Any description of life in the 1930s must be related to the state of the economy. The Great Depression had its grip on Canada and the unemployment rate climbed to nearly 20 percent. In an attempt to create employment and stimulate economic recovery, the Government of Canada spent great sums of money in several areas including parks and recreation. Job creation programs were (and, to a much lesser degree, still are) instrumental in the development of recreation and park facilities and programs. One such training program was called the Youth Training Programme (Wetherell & Kmet, 1990). In a sense, the recreation movement was a benefactor of our nation's economic woes (McFarland, 1970).

- As the stage was being set for a second global war, a small but significant event occurred in 1938 that set the stage for our present practice of balancing work and non-work time. In that year, the *U.S. Fair Labor Standards Act* established 40 hours of work over 5 days per week as the desirable industrial standard. This ultimately served to influence the direction of labour codes in Canada.

- Community and provincial government involvement in recreation increased dramatically between 1920 and 1940. In Edmonton, the community league concept, which began with the establishment of the Jasper Place Community League in 1917, had expanded to include 10 leagues in the city's various suburban districts. In the early 1920s, many service clubs became involved in the Playground Movement through fund raising and development projects that resulted in the construction of many neighbourhood playgrounds (Bowler & Wanchuk, 1986). The first major involvement in the area of recreation by a provincial government occurred during this time period. In 1934, the British Columbia Ministry of Education established classes for recreational and physical education. Other provinces followed the British Columbian lead in later years (McFarland, 1970).

Leisure in Post-War Canada

As we entered the fifth decade of this century, Canada was at war. Great Britain went to battle against Hitler's Germany on September 3, 1939, and Canadian forces joined the fray one week later. The United States was drawn into the war after the Japanese attack on Pearl Harbor on December 7, 1941. Many thought that leisure would be put on hold, but the stress of combat actually served to reinforce the need for recreation and diversion as a means of maintaining morale and psychological health.

The war gave millions of men an exposure to 'camping'. It certainly wasn't for pleasure that the soldiers pitched their tents in foreign lands, but when they returned to Canada many continued to 'rough it' with their families as a form of recreation.

Post-war camping and outdoor recreation was engaged in with the advantage of greatly improved equipment (thanks to the lessons of war), and renewed apprecia- tion of Canada's peaceful environment.

War also provided opportunities for travel and facilitated the development of reliable international transportation systems. In peacetime, the interest in travel was maintained and overseas pleasure travel (particularly to Europe) increased signifi- cantly.

During the Second World War, an important event took place in the House of Commons. On October 1, 1943, the federal government proclaimed the *National Physical Fitness Act* to be in force. This pioneering legislation had as its main purpose the promotion of physical fitness, but was motivated by the need to ensure improved levels of fitness among recruits for the armed forces. However, the Act was interpreted broadly and thereby served to facilitate the promotion of amateur sport and healthy leisure pursuits. The *National Physical Fitness Act* enabled the federal government to train instructors, develop school curricula in physical educa- tion, provide direct fitness programs, and enter into agreements with the provinces for the financial support of provincial fitness initiatives. During the decade following the introduction of the Act, numerous initiatives were undertaken and, more importantly, a public expectation was created concerning government in- volvement in leisure service provision. In spite of the positive results of these federal and provincial fitness initiatives, the *National Physical Fitness Act* became a pawn in a political entanglement and was repealed without protest in 1954 (Westland, 1979).

Other important developments immediately following the war included the formation of The Parks and Recreation Association of Canada in 1945 (the forerunner of the Canadian Parks/Recreation Association) and the incorporation of the Canadian Association for Health, Physical Education, and Recreation in 1951, which had previously been known as the Canadian Physical Education Association (Gurney, 1983). Both of these national associations continue to be strong advocates for leisure services in national, regional and provincial settings.

Today's number one leisure activity (watching television) became a possibility in the early 1950s (Burton, 1976) as the first programs were broadcast and the North American industrial machine turned its attention to mass produced consumer goods. It has been suggested that no single event has changed the face of leisure and recreation more than the invention and production of the television (Godbey, 1990).

In the mid-1950s, TV was just one of the many recreation goods that were being produced at an alarming rate to feed society's appetite for material items. Perhaps this excessive materialism was a result of latent demand built up during the war years of restraint, or perhaps society was now inclined to flaunt its leisure opportunities with tangible evidences such as boats, cars, sports equipment and labour-saving (leisure providing) devices. Whatever the cause, leisure and materialism were closely aligned.

Professional and government attention turned to social issues after the war, and in 1956 the International Recreation Association (now called the World Leisure and Recreation Association) was formed (Westland, 1987). Two years later, the U.S. Congress established the Outdoor Recreation Resources Review Commission

(ORRRC). ORRRC was a bipartisan commission charged with studying outdoor recreation in America. The 28-volume report of the commission's findings was published in 1962. It contained many important recommendations, some of which also provided direction for recreation development in Canada (Burton, 1976).

In the 1950s, the military machine had not been totally dismantled and the cold war was looming. The abundance of manpower controlled by the military forces was used to re-establish the enthusiastic program of park and recreation program development that had begun just prior to the war.

In this period of time there was an increase in the use of mechanized vehicles as a part of the recreation experience. Cars were abundant, motorboats became popular, motorcycles were used extensively, and the snowmobile had just been invented in Canada.

The concepts of community centres and community schools were introduced in the 1950s and began to gain wide acceptance. Community centre facilities were usually joint ventures of the municipality and an organized community organization. Often the town council would build the facility and then turn its management and operation over to a community group. Community schools were public educational facilities that, by night, served as recreation centres for the entire community. Both concepts have endured to this day and have been refined in light of today's conditions.

Leadership development became an issue in the late 1950s and several provinces undertook ambitious programs of training for people who were employed or volunteered in public recreation settings. Some attention had been given to the matter of professional training earlier in the decade (a diploma program in recreation leadership was instituted in British Columbia), but financial resource limitations made it impossible for this pioneering effort to be sustained. The University of Toronto offered a Bachelor of Social Work in Community Recreation during the 1951-52 academic year, but nobody enrolled in the program and the courses were suspended. An attempt to offer a Bachelor of Physical Education degree with a recreation emphasis was made at the University of Western Ontario but was ended in 1955 when registration for the program option was too low to justify its continuation (McFarland, 1970). Such programs would have to wait until the 1960s for their next chance at success.

1960-1970

As we entered the tumultuous sixties, renewed concern for the physical fitness of Canadians was emerging. Frequently, politicians lamented the generally low levels of fitness in the population, and complained about the poor performance by Canadian athletes in international competition. To help allay these concerns, the Government of Canada passed the *Fitness and Amateur Sport Act* in 1961. This act redefined the role of the senior government in sport, recreation and leisure, and established principles for federal and provincial cooperation. Since the repeal of the *National Physical Fitness Act* in 1954, some of the provinces had continued with whatever fitness and recreation initiatives they could support alone, and the re-entry of the federal government required the development of a new working relationship (Westland, 1979). Some provinces, such as Manitoba, repealed their provincial legislation with the termination of federal funding.

The 1960s was a decade of tremendous growth and development in the recreation community in Canada and the United States. The ORRRC Report in the U.S. prompted the establishment of high-level government agencies to facilitate recreation research, planning and development. The ORRRC Report presented many recommendations with respect to outdoor recreation in America, and they formed the foundation for policy and action in the 1960s. In 1967, Canada initiated the Canada Outdoor Recreation Demand Study (CORDS) (Burton, 1976). This study was aimed at measuring outdoor recreation demand, developing alternatives from which policy could be determined for the federal government, preparing predictions for future use, and guiding the management of the outdoor recreation system in Canada. Unfortunately, as Burton noted, the goals of this study have never been realized. It has, however, served as a catalyst for other studies such as the Ontario Tourism and Outdoor Recreation Plan Study (TORPS) and the first national study on leisure by Statistics Canada called *A Leisure Study Canada 1972*.

In Canada during the 1960s, governments at all levels became involved in financial assistance programs to promote the development of recreation. Unfortunately, most of the funding was provided for facility construction and very little was available for facility operation or activity programming.

Also, during the 1960s, most provincial governments established some kind of organizational unit or department with responsibility for recreation. This usually required the passage of specific enabling legislation and the public commitment of resources to recreation. Some provinces adopted a facilitator role, while others became very directly involved in the provision of public leisure services.

Professional organizations continued their evolution through this decade of change. The National Recreation and Parks Association (the U.S. equivalent to the Canadian Parks/Recreation Association) was formed in 1965 (McFarland, 1970) when several recreation and park related organizations operating at the national level merged. International attention was focused on the recreation and parks movement when, in 1962, Seattle hosted the first World Congress on National Parks. The Congress was held the following year in Japan with 32 nations being represented (Westland, 1987).

Professional training programs were again introduced, but this time were successful in attracting students and resources. The University of British Columbia offered a four-year degree in Physical Education with a specialization in Recreation, and the University of Alberta began its four-year Bachelor of Arts in Recreation Leadership program in 1962. Many other recreation education programs were introduced during the 1960s including those at the University of Waterloo, the University of Ottawa, Mount Royal College, Centennial College, and Lethbridge College (McFarland, 1970).

1970-PRESENT

The rapid development of recreation resources and opportunities that characterized the 1960s continued in the first few years of the 1970s. This pace of development was sustained by the relative prosperity of the nation and our access to industrial energy. The Arab oil embargo of 1973 changed all this in a most dramatic fashion. While most have seen television images of motorists lined up at gas pumps as a reminder to us of the difficulties faced by consumers, few witnessed the empty arenas and poorly maintained parks that were forced into this state by intolerably high energy costs. Until this point in time, money had been available for building, but not for operation. The meager resources that were devoted to the operation of many recreation areas and facilities were no longer sufficient.

The energy crisis also had an impact on pleasure travel, as gasoline was rationed and increases in jet fuel costs made airline tickets very expensive.

A tax revolt began in the United States in 1978 with California's Proposition 13. While it had some effect on public spending on recreation throughout much of the United States, it never really seemed to take hold in Canada. Proposition 13 was a referendum about property taxes and public spending. The citizens of California voted to cut taxes and severely limit spending in all areas of public expenditure. This sent shock waves through the recreation community as many proponents of recreation believed that, as a perceived "frill" service, recreation would suffer major budget reductions. As it turned out, recreation fared well and received a welcome vote of public confidence. Recreation services were recognized as being important, but that didn't change the fact that the financial resources were limited (Klar & Rodman, 1984). In Canada, it has only been in the last two years that taxpayers have become increasingly militant in their refusal to bear further costs associated with government services. The contradiction, however, is that few of these same taxpayers are prepared to tolerate reductions in services to match the reductions or freezing of tax levels. This will be a major challenge for governments at all levels for the foreseeable future.

The problem of limited resources for recreation and other social services hit close to home in the latter part of the 1970s. Except in oil-rich Alberta, provincial and municipal governments were forced to limit the growth of recreation services and to adopt a new style of recreation leadership. Partly because of financial need and partly because of the community development potential of such an approach, municipal recreation agencies became more facilitative and less involved in direct service provision. It was in these circumstances that leisure education (a concept that is heavily oriented to facilitation—see Chapter Twelve) became a popular focus of public recreation agencies.

Perhaps among the most positive events to influence leisure in Canada in the 1970s was the creation of the national, not-for-profit, agency called PARTICIPaction (Ferris, Kisby, Craig, & Landry, 1987). The sole purpose of PARTICIPaction was and is "to encourage Canadians to become more physically active" (p. 26). The organization started by launching a massive national advertising campaign telling us that the average 30-year-old Canadian was not as fit as the average 60-year-old Swede. In 1972, Canadians believed this message and it became an effective vehicle to grab our attention and initiate a program of communications, networking with other organizations and sponsored promotions to encourage higher levels of physical activity. Ferris, et al., (1987) reported that studies done by PARTICIPaction between 1972 and 1982 showed that the percentage of Canadians committed to a physically active lifestyle increased from 5 percent to 37 percent.

Arising from this increased interest in physical activity, the Canadian Government, through Fitness and Amateur Sport Canada, conducted one of the largest and most comprehensive surveys ever done to assess the fitness of the nation. In 1981, the Canada Fitness Survey (1983) was completed with a national sample of 23,500 subjects in 11,800 households. Each person in the household who was 10 years of age or older completed a survey while those who were between the ages of 7 and 69 (who passed a screening questionnaire), were given a fitness test. This study became an invaluable benchmark for assessing the future fitness levels of Canadians and comparing Canadians fitness to persons from other nations.

In 1985, the need for more research concerning the lifestyles of Canadians and the need for a central organization to facilitate its conduct and dissemination resulted in the creation of the Canadian Fitness and Lifestyle Research Institute. In 1988, the Institute was able to secure the sponsorship of Campbell Soup Company to conduct another national survey and a portion of those studied in the 1981 Canada Fitness Survey were studied again in 1988. This has now formed the basis for longitudinal data on the fitness levels of Canadians and many of their physical activity patterns. Over time, this will have important historical significance as the trends emerge and help us to understand the target groups within the country who may need greater attention in order to enhance their health through physical activity.

The financial woes of the late 1970s forced recreation and park agencies to consider new approaches to the delivery of their services. In the 1980s we saw a renewed interest in community schools (sharing resources with the school system), tourism (tapping the potential economic benefits of non-resident participants), public sector entrepreneurship (enterprise management), and marketing (consumerism). The recreation community has matured. Postsecondary educational institutions are preparing trained, dedicated leaders with a good foundation in leisure studies and a variety of sophisticated and timely practical skills that enhance their professional activities.

The recent past has also seen more provincial governments enunciate their policy concerning recreation. In previous years, the provincial governments have largely engaged in services, but have not publicly asserted a position on the relative goodness of recreation or its importance to societal development. This emergence of public policy in recreation during an era of economic decline is important as it suggests that recreation services will not be singled out for undue reductions, but rather, are seen as central to sustaining the quality of life we enjoy. Indeed, the right to leisure was to be part of the proposed social charter in the recently defeated national referendum on the constitution. Although defeated, the fact that the right to leisure was being considered for inclusion in such a document is significant.

The Future

Our society and the role of recreation in society have changed a great deal during the past 150 years. It would be unwise to suggest that change will not continue, since Canada is a dynamic nation and we revere progress. The future of recreation and leisure in Canada depends on many things, not the least of which are (1) the evolving role and nature of the family, (2) economic prosperity, (3) cultural diversification, (4) government policy, (5) technological advancement, and (6) our aging population. Having discussed in this chapter the impact of many other influences on recreation development since the mid-1800s, it should be clear that making an educated guess concerning the future of leisure and recreation in Canada is possible. As you study Figure 2.1, (p. 26) consider the significant historical events and social trends that have affected recreation development in Canada and make your own crystal ball prediction of tomorrow's leisure and recreation environment.

FIGURE 2.1
SOCIAL TRENDS FROM 1840 TO THE PRESENT

Development of Halifax Common (1763)	1840	The "Recreation Renaissance"
Toronto Committee on Public Walks and Gardens	1850	Diminishing influence of Church
		Christian reform recognizes physical fitness
		Ice hockey
Gore Park in Hamilton, Ontario Central Park in New York City	1860	Non-family social networks in urban settings
Boys' Clubs		Commercial amusements
Canadian Confederation Toronto Island Park	1870	Employers and governments looked to for services
Yellowstone National Park Arbor Day	1880	Liberalization of attitudes towards women
		Railroad system provides travel opportunity
Public Parks Act (Ontario) Rocky Mountain Park (Banff)	1890	Increased government involvement in municipal park development
National Council of Women formed	1900	Limited physical activity allowed in parks
Playground Association of America Production of Model-T Ford		The Playground Movement
	1910	Municipal sand gardens developed
Jasper Place Community League		More recreation opportunities for women
Women win right to vote	1920	Community leagues established
Commercial radio broadcasting		High attendance at major sporting events
Women in Olympic Games		Service clubs adopt playgrounds as a cause
Talking movies	1930	Make-work projects benefit public parks
The Great Depression		20% unemployment
Recreation classes in BC schools		
Fair Labour Standards Act	1940	Health value of recreation recognized
World War II		Extensive exposure to camping
National Physical Fitness Act		Increased international travel
Parks and Rec. Assoc. of Canada	1950	'Limitless materialism'
		Military used in promoting recreation programs
Television		Increased use of mechanized recreation
International Recreation Assoc.	1960	Community schools and community centres
Fitness and Amateur Sport Act		Leadership training for recreation professionals
CORDS		
National Recreation and Parks Assoc.	1970	Provincial grants for facility development
World Congress on National Parks		Concern over ability to operate facilities
Arab oil embargo	1980	Spirit of entrepreneurship
Proposition 13		Tourism connections
Interprovincial Rec. Statement		Marketing orientation to public services
National Recreation Statement	1990	High tech recreation
		Limited financial resources
?	2000	?

STUDY QUESTIONS

1. Describe the contribution of Ancient Greek civilization to the development of leisure.

2. How did the Catholic Church and the Protestant reformation influence leisure in Europe?

3. Describe the importance of developing a sound understanding of other North American cultures to the development of leisure.

4. In what way are the leisure interests of aboriginal persons in Canada different from those of other Canadians?

5. What was the first formal federal government initiative in leisure services? What was the incentive for this action?

6. Why was Banff National Park created?

7. Describe several major municipal park developments in the history of Canada.

8. What is the significance of PARTICIPaction?

9. What was CORDS and what, if anything, is its relationship to ORRRC?

10. Describe the Canadian playground movement at the turn of century.

11. What were some of the major technological changes that have influenced leisure in the 20th century?

12. Would you describe the roots of leisure services in Canada to be based primarily on its economic contribution? Explain.

References

Blanchard, K. & Cheska, A. (1985). *The anthropology of sport: An introduction.* South Hadley, MA: Bergin and Garvey.

Bella, L. & Markham, S. (1984). Parks first. *Recreation Canada, 42*(5), pp. 5-16.

Boys' Clubs of America. (n.d.). *Manual for administration and management of a Boys' Club.* New York, NY: Author.

Bowler, V. & Wanchuk, M. (1986). *Volunteers.* Edmonton, AB: Lone Pine Publishing.

Burton, T. L. (1976). *Making man's environment.* Toronto, ON: Van Nostrand Reinhold Ltd.

Canada Fitness Survey. (1983). *Fitness and lifestyle in Canada.* Ottawa, ON: Canada Fitness Survey.

Chubb, M. & Chubb, H. R. (1981). *One-third of our time? An introduction to recreation behavior and resources.* New York, NY: John Wiley & Sons.

Cross, G. (1990). *A social history of leisure since 1600.* State College, PA: Venture Publishing, Inc.

Ferris, B. F., Kisby, R., Craig, C. L. & Landry, F. (1987). Fitness promotion and research in Canada. *Journal of Physical Education, Recreation and Dance, 58*(7), pp. 26-30.

Godbey, G. (1990). *Leisure in your life: An exploration (3rd ed.).* State College, PA: Venture Publishing, Inc.

Gurney, H. (1983). *The CAHPER Story.* Ottawa, ON: CAHPER.

Ibrahim, H. (1991). *Leisure and society: A comparative approach.* Dubuque, IA: Wm C. Brown Publishers.

Klar, L. R. & Rodman, C. (1984). Budgetary and administrative impacts of tax-limiting legislation on municipal recreation and park departments. *Journal of Park and Recreation Administration, 2*(4), pp. 31-44.

Malloy, D. C. (1991). Cross-cultural awareness in administration: An interview with Harold Cardinal. *Recreation Canada 49*(3), pp. 40-44.

McFarland, E. M. (1970). *The development of public recreation in Canada.* Ottawa, ON: Canadian Parks/Recreation Association.

McInnis, E. (1969). *Canada: A political and social history.* Toronto, ON: Holt Rinehart & Winston.

Plato. *The republic* (translated by Paul Shorey, 1930). Cambridge, MA: Harvard University Press.

Roberts, V. M. (1962). *On stage: A history of theater*. New York, NY: Harper and Row.

Ulich, R. (1950). *History of educational thought*. New York, NY: American Book.

Westland, C. (1979). *Fitness and amateur sport in Canada—The federal government's programme: An historical perspective*. Ottawa, ON: Canadian Parks/Recreation Association.

Westland, C. (1987). I.R.A.-W.L.R.A. 1956-1986. Thirty years of service. An historical perspective. *World Leisure and Recreation, 24*(1), pp. 9-13.

Wetherell, D. G. & Kmet, I. (1990). *Useful pleasures: The shaping of leisure in Alberta 1896-1945*. Regina, SK: Canadian Plains Research Centre.

Wright, J. R. (1983). *Urban parks in Ontario, Part I: Origins to 1860*. Toronto, ON: Ministry of Tourism and Recreation.

Wright, J. R. (1984). *Urban parks in Ontario, Part II: 1860-1914*. Toronto, ON: Ministry of Tourism and Recreation.

Chapter Three 3

Concepts and Philosophical Underpinnings

Overview

PURPOSE

The purpose of this chapter is to describe the basic concepts that underlie leisure services in Canada. Those concepts include leisure, play, recreation, sport, and work. The chapter will present several definitions of these concepts and include a discussion of the basic philosophical positions adopted by the professional practice at different times. How those philosophies have influenced the development of these conceptual perspectives will also be discussed. The dominant philosophies have been drawn from existentialism, pragmatism, idealism, and realism. Finally, this chapter will explain why an understanding of these concepts and philosophical foundations is important for leisure service professionals, and how the adoption of different conceptualizations and philosophical positions ultimately influences the leisure services provided.

LEARNING OBJECTIVES

At the completion of this chapter, you should be able to:

1. define the terms leisure, recreation, play, sport, and work, and describe how they differ from each other,

2. identify the philosophical basis for the different definitions of these terms,

3. recognize the contributions of several philosophical perspectives which have influenced the development of the field of leisure services, and

4. explain how different philosophical positions result in different approaches to service delivery.

Concepts and Philosophical Underpinnings

In Search of Meaning

Understanding the meaning of certain words can be difficult when their context is changed or they are used both as verbs and nouns. Moreover, words take on different meanings in different professional settings. In some cases, such as the language of law or medicine, words which might be used somewhat indiscriminately in common language take on very specific meanings to those who practice in these professions. Or conversely, words to which we may ascribe specific meanings might not enjoy universal definition. The word health, for example, means different things to different people and may be defined by some health service professionals in a way that is not acceptable to others. Consider these questions which arise when attempting to define health: Does health refer to the absence of biological illness? Does it refer to some state of being involving physical, social and psychological states? Does health mean simply "feeling good"? It is easy to see how quickly it becomes a problem to define health terms in a manner with which everyone can agree. This is also true of terms used by researchers and practitioners in the field of leisure services. There are words which may be thought of as having a common definition yet, when tested among a diverse population, may prove to carry many different meanings. There are also words used within the field that may be more appropriately described as jargon (defined as "a mode of speech familiar only to a group or profession," from *The Concise Oxford Dictionary*, 1982). Herein lies the challenge of searching for a clear and widely accepted definition and conceptualization of leisure.

In trying to understand terms such as leisure, recreation and play it is important to recognize that various traditional disciplines can help us in the search for meaning. For example, when we talk about leisure we often refer to the notion of leisure behaviour. Thus, psychology has some importance to understanding this term. Similarly, leisure has been described with respect to one's social or economic status. As a result, sociology has a useful contribution to our understanding of leisure. This is also true for human physiology and biology which help us to understand the limits of human performance, and for geography which helps us to understand spatial aspects of leisure behaviour. Indeed, as we examine the concepts in this chapter, we will see that leisure is not explained in only one way nor should it be viewed from a singular disciplinary perspective.

One of the challenges in developing meanings for words in the social sciences generally, and with respect to leisure studies and services in particular, is the lack of preciseness inherent in the use of many words. Physical scientists like chemists do not struggle so much with their terms because formulae can be used to express chemical relationships, reactions and observations. For example, water may be defined as a transparent, inert liquid, a combination of certain elements at a standard temperature and pressure, or simply as H_2O. This last definition is clear. Water is a combination of hydrogen and oxygen. There is no vagueness in this description.

Arnold (1991) has pointed out that words are symbols and if we fail to understand our symbols then we jeopardize the chances of comprehending the conceptual reality or actions that surround us.

In recent years the literature has described the increasing number of attempts to determine what exactly leisure, recreation and play mean as well as define such related concepts as sport. As we examine each of these concepts, this growing body of literature will be introduced.

Looking for Leisure (in all the right places!)

As was explained in Chapter Two, the concept of leisure has been with us since the time of the Ancient Greek civilization. The individual to whom most of the early conceptualization of leisure has been attributed is Aristotle. Aristotle was a citizen of Greece which meant he had certain privileges not available to women, children or other males in Greece. The free men of Ancient Greece ruled the country and were able to spend their days in pursuit of knowledge and personal development. They were characterized as philosopher-kings. The labour necessary for the operation of the country was performed by slaves acquired by Ancient Greece's conquering armies.

Arising from this civilization was a conception of leisure. In the language of Greece, it was called *schole*. *Schole*, as Plato described it, referred to the opportunity to participate in activities of one's choosing when obligatory tasks were completed (Hunnicutt, 1990). Aristotle introduced the notion that work was an activity to be disdained. It was Aristotle who described work as being important not because of the contribution arising from one's work or the provision of necessities from work, but rather because it led to leisure. From Aristotle's notion came the view that leisure was freedom *from* the necessity to labour (de Grazia, 1964). Thus, emerged the first conceptualization of leisure as a state of being.

The concept of state of being was brought to the attention of leisure scholars through the work of de Grazia in his 1964 book titled *Of Time, Work and Leisure*. In this book de Grazia (1964) described leisure as a state of being free from the requirements of work. For many students of leisure, the notion of a state of being was not easy to comprehend. "State of being what?" was an often asked question. In developing a response to that question, it is important to remember that leisure was a contemplative activity to the ancient Greeks. It was a time for learning, for debate, for enjoyment. The state of being referred to the opportunity to be free from work in order to engage in such pursuits. In the classical Greek culture such opportunities were available to only a few individuals and were not for women or those who were bound by slavery.

Regardless of its practical acceptability in contemporary society, this view of leisure has some attractive properties that many people interested in leisure studies and services have sought to promote. First, this view of leisure pointed to the centrality of freedom as a factor in determining a leisure state. Second, it presented leisure as an objective in itself, rather than a means to an end. Third, leisure was viewed as more than activity and not bound by time. The idea that leisure was a state of being gave rise to the adoption by leisure service agencies of mission statements which included the mandate to help society deal with expanding leisure and shrinking requirements for work. This was particularly evident in the 1960s and early 1970s when predictions abounded about the imminent evolution of a leisure society. In such a milieu, leisure as a state of being was consistent with the trend that appeared to be emerging in society. Fourth, the Ancient Greek view of leisure provided an inspiring goal: A life of leisure or, at very least, a life where leisure was the focus.

From State of Being to State of Mind

Leisure as a state of being was limited by its male, slave-driven economic perspective and is, therefore, unlikely to be available to many in our society. Most importantly, the state of being perspective on leisure suggested that leisure was a subjective experience and that the perception of freedom was central to that experience. As such, leisure was not an experience that could easily be defined in objective terms. This conceptualization, with its focus on subjectivity, gave rise to an examination of leisure from a social-psychological perspective. The result of that examination was the development of another conceptual perspective on leisure which viewed the interaction of the individual and the environment as the critical process which determined the perception of leisure in any experience.

The early work in this area was done by Neulinger (1974) with important contributions coming from researchers such as Iso-Ahola (1980) and Mannell (1979), among others. Their research showed that leisure as a state of mind (as opposed to state of being) was determined by several factors: (1) freedom of choice, (2) source of motivation (intrinsic or extrinsic), (3) relationship to work, and (4) goal orientation. In other words, the more one had the ability and opportunity to choose, was motivated from within rather than having someone else impose the activity, was enjoyed in an activity that had little relationship to their work, and had a goal, the more likely it is that the experience would be defined as leisure.

It is clear from the socio-psychological research that leisure, as determined by these four variables (of which freedom to choose is most important), would be a subjective experience. As a result, professionals working within this conceptual perspective must consider how they can contribute to creating choices of which individuals can take advantage in accordance with their own motives. Those studying leisure from the subjective perspective have found this to be a useful model because it focuses on the individual and allows for different and more detailed information concerning the individual's behaviour and concerning the decisions that regulate that behaviour.

One issue related to this state of mind conceptualization of leisure is the question of whether there exists an optimum leisure experience. Mihalyi Csikszentmihalyi (1975, 1982, 1990) has written extensively on this subject and asserts that optimal experiences do exist and are characterized by certain qualities. Michaelis (1991) has summarized these six qualities: First, they are characterized by a loss of self and time consciousness. Second, the individual focuses their energy and awareness on a relatively small stimulus or set of stimuli. Third, individuals feel they are in control of themselves and their environment. Fourth, the pursuit in which the individuals were involved was chosen by them. Fifth, the participation was intrinsically motivated. Sixth, individuals received clear and immediate feedback concerning their actions. Experiences meeting these qualities are described as "flow" experiences. Flow is a match between an individual's ability or skill level and the challenge demanded by the activity. Leisure often provides the best opportunities for individuals to experience "flow" and thus have an optimal experience.

The subjective view of leisure as described in the works of Neulinger, Iso-Ahola, Mannell, Csikszentmihalyi, and others, provides a different perspective than that derived from the Ancient Greek philosophers. Rather than being class-based, leisure is based on the individual and his or her interaction with the environment. Moreover, recent research by Samdahl (1991) has suggested that the subjective view of leisure as characterized in the research reported above, is consistent with the meanings given to leisure in common language. Since professionals can provide services which mitigate the environment in which we live, this perspective has considerable potential to influence the services provided and ultimately the target of those services—the individual. Nonetheless, it would be a grievous error for us to not point out that, despite the positive attributes associated with this conceptual perspective on leisure, we need to be aware that most of the research in this subject has been on North Americans or Europeans with little being done in other cultural milieu. Furthermore, little has been done to examine gender differences associated with leisure until recently (Bella, 1989). There is a need for further socio-psychological research to ascertain the application of the earlier findings to women and to people in other cultures.

A Good Time or an Activity?

Among the more common conceptualizations of leisure has been the temporal one. That is, leisure is viewed as simply a function of time. In this context, it is defined as time left over from work, family and other necessary activities (Farina, 1991). One sage stated that "when a man retires and time is no longer a matter of urgent importance, his colleagues generally present him with a watch" (R. C. Sherriff). Time is an important concept, especially in western culture where attention to the clock seems paramount. So much so that it starts at an early age. Ask young children if they are hungry and they will probably ask you what time it is. They use the clock to confirm whether or not they should be hungry.

Similarly, a temporal definition of leisure has been widely used. It refers to an individual's discretionary time. Frequently this view is among the first stated when persons are asked what is leisure. However, to accept such a view is to accept a rather objective definition that lacks substantial validity. There are many circumstances in which an individual may have discretionary time, but because of a lack of resources, choices, or abilities is unable to engage in a leisure experience. One only needs to think of the individual who is unemployed and, while possessing many hours of discretionary time, lacks leisure. Or think of the mentally handicapped person restricted by the supervisors in the group home from engaging in the leisure of their choice. Think also of the executive who works 60 hours a week and is too exhausted to utilize discretionary time for anything other than recovery for work. Thus, while a seemingly useful measure because of the common measuring unit, time fails to capture the essence of leisure definition.

Beyond time, leisure is also characterized by a certain contentment with life or, as some put it, being "alive". Citing the work of Stuart Chase, Goodale (1991) asks whether we are alive. By this, Goodale was questioning whether individuals were involved with life and absorbed in their activities. He went on to assert that he felt alive when creating something, enjoying art, being in the mountains or by the sea, being at play, engaging in good conversation, having feelings of sorrow, laughing, loving, sleeping, and satisfying hunger or thirst. He lamented that he was probably alive only about 25 percent of the time. Certainly this suggests that time for leisure is important but we also need to focus more on the experiences of life and less on the time being consumed as leisure. As Goodale (1991, p. 45) stated, it would appear that:

> Since there is more time than life, we could easily give some away and we could become so absorbed in living that time simply fades away. There can be no harm in that. On the contrary, it appears that your life and mine depend upon it.

Another popular conceptualization of leisure has it defined as activity. Often this activity definition includes a temporal dimension in that leisure could be further described as activity which is engaged in during leisure time. Once again, the problem in such an objective description lies in determining what activities constitute leisure. Is gardening a chore or a leisure activity? Is building a playhouse for your children a leisure activity or a family obligation? The objective definition which establishes leisure as activity engaged in during leisure time or simply as activity is fraught with problems.

Perhaps the most cogent perspective on the notion of leisure as activity is derived from the work the French sociologist Dumazdier (1967, 1974) who stated that:

> Leisure is activity—apart from obligations of work, family and society—to which the individual turns at will, for either relaxation, diversion or broadening his knowledge and his spontaneous social participation, the free exercise of his creative capacity (1967, p. 16-17).

In this definition, Dumazdier has suggested that leisure is purposeful. In order to help us to determine what activities might be classified as leisure, he created four categories. These are: (1) paid work, (2) family commitments, (3) obligations of a social or spiritual nature, and (4) activities which are designed to facilitate self-fulfillment or self-expression. Dumazdier suggests that leisure only exists in the fourth category. He argues that the element of obligation in family and social situations makes these activities "semi-leisure".

While the definitions of leisure as activity or as time have many problems associated with them, they nonetheless present integral elements of leisure. After all, activity is ultimately involved and, in order participate, one must have some discretionary time. It may be, however, that these are precursors to leisure but not necessarily characteristics of the experience.

So, What is Leisure?

This discussion has suggested that leisure may be viewed as time, activity or a condition of the individual. There are roles for all three in understanding leisure. So you may now be asking yourself, "what is leisure?" To provide a simple answer to a complex question is not particularly useful. However, if one first accepts the premise that leisure is essentially a subjective experience, then the range of answers is much smaller. Furthermore, based on the knowledge we have today we might argue that leisure among western industrialized countries is characterized by freedom to choose, intrinsic motivation, and the enjoyment derived from the experience which is, in turn, derived from a successful match between skill and challenge.

Throughout all of this, we must be cognizant of the fact that this discussion does not apply to all cultures nor necessarily does it apply to women. Recent research by Bella (1989), Frisby and Brown (1991), Bialeschki and Henderson (1986), and Bolla, Dawson, and Harrington (1991) has clearly shown that leisure among women has more and different connotations than those discussed earlier. Women's perceptions of leisure include more than activity. Many women perceive personal development to be an important part of their leisure and, as Bolla et al. reported, some women perceive leisure in a more negative light due to the constraints they experience.

If That's Leisure, What is Recreation?

Is there a difference between recreation and leisure? This question has often been raised and some would assert that leisure and recreation are equivalent (Kelly, 1990). However, for most persons (including most leisure service professionals and researchers), recreation has a different connotation to that of leisure. The root of the difference in connotation can be found in the Latin word from which recreation is derived. Recreation is from the Latin *recreatio* which means recovery or restoration from something (Arnold, 1991). Over the course of the 16th and 17th centuries, the word recreation evolved to represent activities that provided opportunities for physical and psychological refreshment from the day's labour. Clearly this was a concept that acquired much of its meaning from the circumstances and demands of the industrial revolution.

Moreover, recreation became more widely accepted as time passed and, in the 19th century, the YMCAs were created, Scouting began and other forms of organized recreational activity took root in society. Recreation maintained a certain moral meaning in that it was perceived to have a contribution to make in improving the quality of life for the indigent, immigrants, workers, and others outside the elites. As a result, at the turn of the century the National Council of Women (McFarland, 1970) initiated the play movement to promote positive recreational experiences for children who would otherwise be involved with the criminal justice system or who were in need of opportunities for healthy developmental activities. Indeed, as we will see in the next section concerning play, play has been defined similarly to recreation as relaxation and restoration. Thus recreation has come to be associated with activity which is beneficial to the individual.

Some scholars who have studied meanings in more depth have pointed to the fact that recreation has become an integral element in the social organization of society (Cheek & Burch, 1976). Recreation is part of the western cultural system and is, in the words of Cheek and Burch (p. 224), "the routinization of enjoyment". They argue that leisure is a human phenomenon but recreation is a social one. That is, recreation is characteristic of a particular culture but not all cultures. Moreover, recreation has been organized and programmed in order to achieve certain purposes. In this way one might consider recreation to be an instrument of social public policy. Governments may use recreation services to achieve certain ends such as reducing crime, increasing political profile (e.g., through the creation of new parks or facilities), changing attitudes (e.g., through the development of integrated recreation facilities where persons with physical or mental handicaps may participate with the "normal" population). Recreation not only connotes activity but may also be used to achieve certain ends.

One definition that has been offered which integrates this view of recreation as activity and the social purpose element has been developed by Kelly (1990). He suggests that recreation be defined as "voluntary non-work activity that is organized for the attainment of personal and social benefits including restoration and social cohesion" (p. 27).

Sessoms (1984) has argued that recreation has eight characteristics. These are:
1. Recreation involves activity.
2. Recreation has no single form.
3. Participation in recreation is entirely voluntary.
4. Recreation occurs during leisure.
5. Recreation is motivated by the satisfaction derived from the experience. (This may refer to the motives of both participants and leaders or sponsors).
6. Recreation is like play: It is serious, purposeful, and uncertain.
7. The outcomes of the recreation experience cannot be predetermined.
8. Recreation has by-products such as learning, better health, prevention of delinquency, etc.

These characteristics summarize many of the points raised by a wide array of scholars in the field. It also shows the linkage to social organizations but respects the individual nature of the experience.

A much more psychological view of recreation, as opposed to the mainly sociological views represented above, was offered by Gray and Greben (1974, p. 49). They stated that recreation is:

the emotional condition which flows from a feeling of well-being and satisfaction. It is characterized by feelings of mastery, achievement, exhilaration, acceptance, success, personal worth and pleasure. It reinforces positive self image...it is independent of activity, leisure or social acceptance.

This view of recreation differs in its focus from the role of recreation within society to its role within the individual. Gray and Greben's definition is similar to others suggested earlier in that it maintains the focus on relaxation, re-creation and recovery which are consistent with other views of recreation.

Recreation is different from leisure. It is closely associated with the industrial revolution, it is somewhat culture-bound, it exists in part to achieve broader social purposes (and, perhaps, political purposes), it generates enjoyment, and it occurs as one form of expression during leisure.

The Play's the Thing!

The most thorough examination of play theories and the meanings that have been associated with play over time is found in Ellis' (1973) book *"Why People Play"*. Ellis notes that there have been fourteen different meanings associated with play over the course of the past several hundred years. These are summarized in Table 3.1 (p. 40).

Sport: Where Does It Fit?

Many of us have participated in sport activities at either school, community centre clubs, or other venues. You may still be an active sport participant. While it is relatively easy to list sports, it is much more difficult to define sport. A problem in defining the term is determining whether it should be inclusive—meaning all conceivable sports would be included, or exclusive—meaning some sports will be excluded. For example, are hockey, basketball, darts, billiards, baton twirling, and rowing all sports? Some definitions are motivated by public policy while others are the result of some process to categorize certain activities with certain attributes as sport.

In Canada, different provinces have different sport definitions. In Alberta (Alberta Recreation and Parks, 1983, p. 1), sport is defined as having four essential elements: (1) sport requires that participants execute physical and mental skills which require practice or preparation to improve or perfect, (2) sport involves competition against other participants, oneself, or nature. Levels of competition range from those for the beginning participant to those for the international competitor, (3) sport occurs in a structured and organized environment and is governed by standard rules, and (4) sport is considered as a component of recreation. In Manitoba, sport is defined as "a human activity in which people compete at varying levels of physical exertion, using their strength, will, spirit, co-ordination and intellect to obtain measurable results" (Province of Manitoba Sport Policy, 1991). The federal government of Canada is focused on supporting elite athlete development but recognizes that sport exists on a continuum from beginner and recreational participant to the elite level (Minister's Task Force of Federal Sport Policy, 1992). Each of these definitions is driven by questions of public policy. Who should receive funding from government or its agents? Activities that qualify as sport receive funding, those that do not receive nothing. Thus, the definition chosen has great implications for the potential development of numerous activities.

TABLE 3.1*

CLASSICAL THEORIES OF PLAY

NAME	PLAY IS CAUSED	THIS EXPLANATION ASSUMES THAT	IT CAN BE CRITICIZED BECAUSE
1a. Surplus Energy: I	by the existence of energy surplus to the needs of survival.	1. energy is produced at a constant rate. 2. if stored, storage is limited. 3. excess must be expended. 4. its expenditure is made on overt behaviour which is by definition play.	1. children play when fatigued or to the point of fatigue, so a surplus is not necessary for play. 2. the process of evolution should have tailored the energy available to the energy required.
1b. Surplus Energy: II	by increased tendency to respond after a period of response deprivation.	1. all response systems of the body have a tendency to respond. 2. the response threshold is lowered by a period of disuse. 3. after periods of disuse, eventually all available responses should reach a low enough threshold to be discharged either by some stimulus events or spontaneously.	1. some responses available to the persons are never used.
2. Instinct	by the inheritance of unlearned capacities to emit playful acts.	1. the determinants of our behaviour are inherited in the same way that we inherit the genetic code which determines our structure. 2. some of those determinants cause play.	1. it ignored the obvious capacity of the person to learn new responses that we classify as play. 2. the facile naming of an instinct for each class of observed behaviour is to do no more than to say, "Because there is play, there must be a cause which we will call an Instinct."
3. Preparation	by the efforts of the player to prepare for later life.	1. play is emitted only by persons preparing for new ways of responding. 2. the player is instinctively prepared for responses that will be critical later. 3. the instincts governing this are inherited imperfectly and youth is the period during which these imperfectly inherited mechanisms are perfected.	1. play occurs most frequently in animals that live in rapidly changing circumstances. 2. it requires that the player inherit the capacity to predict which responses will be critical later. This requires the inheritance of information about the future. 3. people do not stop playing as adults, when presumably they are acceptably prepared.

TABLE 3.1 (CONTINUED)
CLASSICAL THEORIES OF PLAY

NAME	PLAY IS CAUSED	THIS EXPLANATION ASSUMES THAT	IT CAN BE CRITICIZED BECAUSE
4. Recapitulation	by the player re-capitulating the history of the development of the species during its development.	1. the critical behaviours occurring during the evolution of man are encoded for inheritance. 2. a person emits some approximation to all these behaviours during his development. 3. since these behaviours are currently irrelevant they are play. 4. the stages in our evolution will be followed in the individual's develop-ment.	1. there is no linear progression in our play development that seems to mirror the development of a species. At one point, late boyhood and adolescence, there may be similarity between sports and games and the compo-nents of hunting, chasing, fighting, etc., but before and after there seems little relation. 2. it does not explain play activities dependent on our advanced technology.
5. Relaxation	by the need for an individual to emit responses other than those used in work to allow recupera-tion.	1. players work. 2. play involves the emission of responses different from those of work. 3. the emission of different responses eliminates the noxious by-products of work.	1. it does not explain the use in play of activities also used in work. 2. it does not explain the play of children—unless they are clearly working some part of their day.

TABLE 3.1A*

RECENT THEORIES OF PLAY

NAME	PLAY IS CAUSED	THIS EXPLANATION ASSUMES THAT	IT CAN BE CRITICIZED BECAUSE
6. Generalization	by the players using in their play experiences that have been rewarding at work.	1. there are at least two separable categories of behaviour. 2. the players transfer to play or leisure, behaviours that are rewarded in another setting. 3. to be useful we understand what rewards individuals at work.	1. it seems to exclude play of preschool children. 2. it assumes that at least some aspects of work are rewarding.
7. Compensation	by players using their play to satisfy psychic needs not satisfied in or generated by the working behaviours.	1. there are at least two separable categories of behaviour. 2. the player avoids play or leisure behaviours that are unsatisfying in the work setting experiences that meet his psychic needs. 3. to be useful we understand the mismatch of needs and satisfactions in the work setting (or vice versa).	1. it seems to exclude play of preschool children. 2. it assumes that work is damaging or does not satisfy some needs.
8. Catharsis	in part by the need to express disorganizing emotions in a harmless way by transferring them to socially sanctioned activity. This concept has been limited almost entirely to questions of aggression, and will be so here.	1. frustration of an intention engenders hostility towards the frustrator. 2. this frustration or hostility can be redirected to another activity. 3. this hostility must be expressed to reduce psychic and physiological stress.	1. it is a partial explanation for only the compensatory behaviour engendered by hostility. 2. the data show conclusively that sanctioning aggression increases it. 3. the planning of activities to provide outlets for aggression constitutes its sanctioning.
9a. Psychoanalytic: I	in part by the players repeating in a playful form strongly unpleasant experiences, thereby reducing their seriousness and allowing their assimilation.	1. stimulating unpleasant experiences in another setting reduces the unpleasantness of their residual effects.	

TABLE 3.1A (CONTINUED)
RECENT THEORIES OF PLAY

NAME	PLAY IS CAUSED	THIS EXPLANATION ASSUMES THAT	IT CAN BE CRITICIZED BECAUSE
9b. Psychoanalytic: II	in part by the player during play reversing his role as the passive recipient of strong unpleasant experience, and actively mastering another recipient in a similar way, thus purging the unpleasant effects.	1. achieving mastery, even in a simulated experience, allows the elimination of the products of unpleasant experience by passing similar experiences on to other beings or objects.	Both I and II ignore play that is not presumed to be motivated by the need to eliminate the products of strongly unpleasant experiences.
10. Developmental	by the way in which a child's mind develops. Thus play is caused by the growth of the child's intellect and is conditioned by it. Play occurs when the child can impose on reality his own conceptions and constraints.	1. play involves the intellect. 2. as a result of play, the intellect increases in complexity. 3. this process in the human can be separated into stages. 4. children pass through these stages in order.	1. it doesn't account for play when and if the intellect ceases to develop.
11. Learning	by the normal processes that produce learning.	1. the child acts to increase the probability of pleasant events. 2. the child acts to decrease the probability of unpleasant events. 3. the environment is a complex of pleasant and unpleasant effects. 4. the environment selects and energizes the play behaviours of its tenants.	1. it doesn't account for behaviour in situations where there are no apparent consequences (However, this theory would maintain that there are no such settings). 2. it doesn't account for the original contributions to behaviours made by an individual's genetic inheritance.

TABLE 3.1b*
MODERN THEORIES

NAME	PLAY IS CAUSED	THIS EXPLANATION ASSUMES THAT	IT CAN BE CRITICIZED BECAUSE
12. Play as Arousal-Seeking	by the need to generate interactions with the environment or self that elevate arousal (level of interest or stimulation) towards the optimal for the individual.	1. there is a need for optimal arousal. 2. change in arousal towards optimal is pleasant. 3. the organism learns the behaviours that result in that feeling and vice versa. 4. stimuli vary in their capacity to arouse. 5. stimuli that arouse are those involving novelty, complexity, and/or dissonance (i.e., information). 6. the organism will be forced to emit changing behaviour and maintain engagement with arousing stimuli.	1. it is very general, but it handles questions of work and play equally well. In fact, it questions the validity of separating work from play.
13. Competence/ Effectance	by a need to produce effects in the environ- ment. Such effects demonstrate competence and result in feelings of effectance.	1. demonstration of competence leads to feelings of effectance. 2. effectance is pleasant 3. effectance increases the probability of tests of competence.	1. for the organism to constantly test whether it can still competently produce an effect seems to require uncertainty as to the outcome. Uncertainty or information seem to be the very attributes of stimuli that are arousing. 2. it can be argued that competence/ effectance behaviour is a kind of arousal- seeking.

*   Tables 3.1, 3.1a, and 3.1b reproduced with permission from M. J. Ellis, *Why People Play*, Prentice Hall, 1973, (Table 3.1 from pp. 46-47, 3.1a from pp. 78-79, and 3.1b from p. 111).

Other definitions, developed by sport scholars also vary. Harry Edwards (1973, p. 52), a famous sport sociologist defines sport as:

Activities having formally recorded histories and traditions, stressing physical exertion through competition within limits set in explicit and formal rules governing role and position relationships, and carried out by actors who represent or who are part of formally organized associations having the goal of achieving valued tangibles or intangibles through defeating opposing groups.

Kelly (1990, p. 196) defines sport as "organized activity in which physical effort is related to that of others in some relative measurement of outcomes with accepted regularities and forms". The key difference between Kelly and Edwards is that Edwards regards sport as only those activities which are institutionalized and formally organized. Kelly includes relatively informal and spontaneous activities.

Beyond the question of what is sport, lies the question of when, if ever, is sport leisure? Certainly we could think of many individuals who choose to participate in sport for intrinsic reasons, to enjoy the goal of achievement or participation derived from the sport experience and accept its low relationship to work. Does that make all sport leisure? For the professional athlete one can argue that sport is not their leisure by virtue of the requirements associated with their performance. That is, no play no pay. Is the individual golfing with a client in order to sell him or her a life insurance policy engaged in leisure? Likely not. While the game itself may have the potential of leisure, the motivation is extrinsic and the work relation is high. That is, the individual is golfing in order to increase his income, sustain his job security, and is participating with an individual with whom he or she does not necessarily wish to socialize. Sport may not be leisure for the student in physical education classes. The mandatory nature of the experience coupled with potential disinterest of the student creates a likely distinction between leisure and sport.

Is sport leisure for the amateur athlete seeking an Olympic medal? This is more difficult to assess. In this circumstance there is clearly an element of choice, a blend of intrinsic and extrinsic motivation, and a definite goal orientation. Yet the relation to work may be perceived to be high. Stebbins (1982) characterized amateurs as individuals who pursue an activity because of its strong appeal but are not prepared to accept the status of player, dabbler or novice. Rather they seek to be excellent in their pursuit of the activity. This activity becomes an avocation according to Stebbins and is motivated by seriousness and commitment and is " . . . expressed both in regimentation (such as practice or rehearsals) and in systematization (such as schedules or organization)" (p. 258). Thus, these amateurs in sport might be engaged in what Stebbins has characterized as "serious leisure".

Work, Work, Work: Can It Be Leisure?

Work has changed dramatically over the centuries and through the industrial revolution and events such as the Protestant Reformation. From the time when we were hunters and gatherers whose work was integrated into other aspects life and leisure to now, when unionized labour, official holidays and predetermined terms of employment characterize our work activities, the whole concept of work has changed. Work, in Ancient Greece was considered by the elite to be a burden. The Greek word for work was _ponos_ which is similar to the Latin word _poena_ which means sorrow. Judeo-Christian views of work generally characterize it as necessary to receive salvation or suggest that work results from a life of sin (Kelly, 1990).

While predictions of increased leisure opportunities through the steady reduction in size of work weeks are common, the evidence suggests that the opposite is taking place. In Canada, the average work week for full-time workers was 45 hours in 1988 according to Statistics Canada. This compares to an average of 50 hours per week for full-time workers in 1926. Today, one in eight workers spends more than 50 hours per week working (Shaw, 1990). It is only when all workers are included (meaning part-time as well as full-time) that average work week for Canadians drops to 37 hours. Shaw has suggested than in examining the work patterns of all members of families rather than just the "head of household", the average family work time per week has grown from 37.5 hours in 1951 to 53.5 hours in 1986.

It is clear that, while unemployment problems in Canada come in cycles, we have yet to experience the notion of structural unemployment that is predicted with each cycle of high unemployment. That is, we do not have 10-12 percent of Canadians who are chronically unemployed as a permanent feature of our society. We do have segments of our society with chronically higher levels of unemployment such as aboriginal persons, young adults (16-24 years of age), and individuals employed in certain industries (e.g., the east coast fishery) but, among these groups, there is no evidence of diminished desire to work.

As a result of the cultural evolution of work and the importance placed on it in our society, there is a need to understand work and its relationship to leisure. Earlier we referred to the work of Csikszentmihalyi (1975, 1982, 1990) in developing the notion of "flow". Among his findings was that experiences of flow could be found in work or leisure. However, as Stormann (1989) has pointed out, work in today's society has become so automated and piecemeal that the creativity, imagination, thoughtfulness, craftsmanship and other positive attributes have been lost for many. At one time work was an important outlet for self-expression and achievement but, increasingly, this is a role played only by leisure.

In attempting to describe the current relationship between work and leisure, Wilensky (1960) developed the "compensation" hypothesis which suggests that individuals may seek opportunities for leisure activity to compensate for the lack of the same or similar activities in the workplace. Wilensky also described the "spillover hypothesis" which suggests that the individual may carry over their interests and skills from work into their leisure. Thus, the accountant may enjoy being the volunteer treasurer for the local youth hockey league. There is also a negative dimension to the spillover hypothesis. If the individual is alienated from his work it could spillover into his leisure behaviour with the result being a rather bored and listless lifestyle.

We do not intend to suggest that work is better than leisure or that leisure is better than work. Rather, we acknowledge that people generally want to work, and that they seek certain material and intangible benefits from the experience. We also recognize that people want to experience leisure and enjoy all its benefits. The demand is for balance in one's life. The challenge, for most, is in obtaining it.

A Philosophy of Leisure?

The philosophical approach one adopts influences how he or she sees the world and, as a result, it influences how he or she conceptualizes leisure, recreation, play, etc. Philosophy, the word, is derived from the Greek "*philosophos*" and means love of wisdom (Ziegler, 1964). More popularly, we think of philosophy as denoting a set of basic values and attitudes toward life, the environment and society. It is the set of beliefs which guides our behaviour. Over time different philosophers have generated statements of belief which have come to be adopted by various professionals in leisure services as part of the basis for their actions.

The major bodies of philosophical thought which have influenced conceptualizations of leisure and leisure services are: (1) pragmatism, (2) idealism, (3) realism, (4) humanism, and (5) existentialism.

PRAGMATISM

Pragmatists may best be described through the use of an illustration. Suppose you came across a camping party in the mountains. Among the group there was an intense philosophical argument underway. The argument centres on the squirrel. It was noted that if you stand on one side of the tree as the squirrel clings to the other, and you move around the tree, the squirrel will always move in the opposite direction and keep the tree between you and itself. The question which started the argument is "Does the man go around the squirrel?" He goes around the tree sure enough. But does he go around the squirrel (James, 1963)?

The pragmatist's solution will depend upon what you mean by "go around" the squirrel. If you mean do you pass to the north, south, east, and west of the squirrel, then the answer is yes. If you mean that you were in front of the squirrel, then on the right, left and back, then the answer is no. The pragmatist philosophy is really a method for settling metaphysical disputes. The pragmatist seeks to resolve questions by tracing the practical consequences. In other words, what difference would it practically make to anyone if concept called "a" were true compared to concept "b"? If there is no practical difference then all alternatives mean the same thing and all disputes surrounding these concepts are without a basis.

For leisure services professionals and those studying leisure, the pragmatic philosophy raises the question why adopt any particular view of leisure? What practical difference does it make to measure leisure, understand leisure behaviour or provide leisure services by adopting one conceptual position as opposed to another? For example, if one adopts the view that leisure is best defined as discretionary time then it limits the measurement of leisure to time budgets, it eliminates the need for psychological study of leisure since it is no longer important what happens to the individual during their discretionary time—only that one has it, and it means that leisure service providers need to focus on non-work and non-school hours for the basis of their efforts and not concern themselves with education activities designed to improve leisure understanding since it is incongruent with the concept that leisure is a form of linear time. Needless to say, other perspectives could be drawn from the pragmatist's consideration of other leisure conceptualizations.

In the relatively brief modern era of leisure services (essentially from 1890 to the present), there have been a number of professionals who subscribed to the pragmatic philosophy and who were inspired by the work of American educator John Dewey (1916). Dewey argued that leisure was necessary because it made a difference in the development of young people and as a result the learning process and abilities that resulted were, in part, a function of the opportunity to engage in leisure pursuits. Thus, many early parks and recreation leaders were influenced by this philosophy and guided their leisure service systems based on it.

IDEALISM

Idealism holds that there is an eternal set of goals or ideals governing human behaviour and that one should seek to understand these truths and work for perfection. Idealists believe the individual should be goal-directed and that the means are as important as the ends. The idealist does not, however, subscribe to the belief that the ends justify the means.

McFarland (1970) suggests that some of the early leaders in the leisure movement at the turn of the century such as those employed by the City of Toronto were idealists. These Toronto leaders made it clear that the playground supervisor was to protect the children from evil (a temporary but destructive force within the idealist's spiritual reality), inculcate high ideals, and to use a process which respected each child's desires on the playground. Such idealism was commonplace among the organizations at the turn of the century. This philosophy was the foundation for the work of early leisure theorist Jay Nash (1953) who developed a hierarchy of values associated with leisure participation. He argued that there was an order to the quality of leisure experiences and that leisure service providers had an obligation to provide a range of leisure experiences but encourage individuals to move their participation to the highest levels (see Figure 3.1).

The following describes the four positive levels of leisure participation that Nash developed within the philosophical framework of idealism:

1. *Passive participation* (the least valued form of recreation participation), according to Nash, represents entertainment, amusements and other activities which limit participation to watching or listening. According to Nash, these may reduce or eliminate boredom but they do not have a profound effect on the individual bettering himself or herself in any appreciable way. Typical passive participation activities are watching television, listening to the radio, etc. Nash coined the phrase "spectatoritis" to describe the condition of people who are stuck at this level of participation.

2. *Emotional participation* is still watching or listening but the individual is moved to greater levels of appreciation, to higher ideals, to a resolution to make some positive change in his or her life. Emotional participation is based on a rich background of experience which gives the activity meaning and purpose. For example, the individual may participate in a music appreciation group through which he or she may learn about the influences on music, be motivated to learn an instrument, or better understand other cultures.

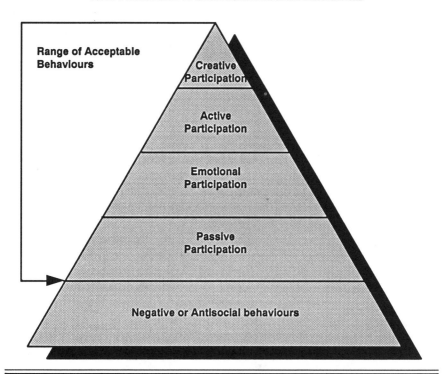

FIGURE 3.1
NASH'S HIERARCHY OF RECREATION PROGRAM EXPERIENCES

3. *Active participation* is the category of the "doers". These are the people who seek to participate as athletes, artisans, musicians, actors, craftsmen, dancers, campers, stamp collectors, public speakers, club presidents, etc.

4. Finally, there are those who participate at the *creative level*. This participant is searching for new methods, new devices, and new solutions to a problem. Others may ultimately participate in these new creations or use them, but those who create them participate on a higher level. Nash might have likened this to Maslow's (1970) need for self-actualization.

This hierarchical view of leisure services is still popular among many leisure service professionals. As with any philosophical approach, the issue that is debated is the value system upon which it is based. Idealists subscribe to the belief in a soul or spiritual reality which lives beyond the human form. Naturally, those who do not believe as idealists do criticize the service systems that are developed on the basis of idealism.

REALISM

Realism is a more contemporary alternative to idealism and reflects the emergence of the scientific method. Realists are largely determinists (i.e., they have a healthy respect for science and the exactness it suggests). The realistic approach suggests that things do not just happen but, rather, they happen because a set of interrelated forces create the observed result (Ziegler, 1964). A realist lives in a world of cause and effect and relies on science to confirm his or her beliefs about what causes what. In his excellent discussion of the nature and history of time, Hawking (1988, p. 1) wrote of a learned scientist giving a public lecture on astronomy. After he had described the nature of the universe to the attentive crowd, an elderly lady rose and stated " 'What you have told us is rubbish. The world is really a flat plate supported on the back of giant tortoise.' The scientist gave a superior smile before replying, 'What is the tortoise standing on?' 'You're very clever young man, very clever,' said the old lady. 'But it's turtles all the way down!'" Such descriptions seem ludicrous to the realist. In the world of the realist relationships are either substantiated by observed phenomena or they simply do not exist.

In leisure services, realists have been interested in the role of leisure relative to work. They do not see work as less important than leisure but see leisure as a complementary event to work. Realists support the need for high levels of education to improve the leisure skills of individuals. They would argue that specific education for leisure is unnecessary because all knowledge contributes to the improvement of leisure opportunities. There is some merit in adopting this position as recent research on constraints on leisure frequently identifies items such as "I don't have the skills," "I don't know where to learn it," and "I don't know where to participate" as principal limiting factors (Searle and Jackson, 1985).

In application, one place realists have had a demonstrated effect has been in the development of standards for planning of parks and recreation areas and facilities. For example, the standard of 10 acres of open space per 1,000 population has been widely used in North America when community plans have been established (Wilkinson, 1985). The establishment of standards is founded in the realist's belief in the scientific method and its application to the orderly development of leisure services.

HUMANISM

Humanists believe that the human being is supreme and that we should, therefore, be primarily concerned with what happens to individuals and their humanity rather than being overly concerned with the interest of a deity. The humanist advocates for the elimination of the referential barriers that hinder growth and development among human beings. Humanism is an attractive philosophy in that it stresses purposeful living, higher functioning, and a sense of social consciousness. Humanism recognizes the interaction between the individual and the environment and the forces that the latter imposes on the former. Humanists believe that oppressive environments must be altered and that the failure of individuals to grow is a function of the environment rather than the individual.

Among the leisure service professionals and scholars, humanism has had a significant attraction. Murphy (1975) captured the ideal/philosophy of humanism quite well in his "Action Plan for the Recreation and Park Movement". Humanists believe in the potential of all individuals and seek to structure the delivery of leisure services in a manner that would lead to realization of that potential. In Canada, humanism was manifested in many programs and services during the late 1960s and 1970s which aimed at individuals who have been typically forgotten or excluded or did not have resources (financial, education, etc.) to be involved in leisure pursuits. There was a great emphasis on outreach. Recreation professionals were placed in local community centres and some were given the task of working on the street to attract young people into more positive life experiences available through the parks and recreation department, YMCA, Boys' and Girls' Club or other like organizations. A growing number of professionals believe that this focus is not only correct but that it has been lost over that past 15 years and that there is a need for a return to this philosophical position (see *Recreation Canada 12*(4) for a special issue on the "Forgotten Client").

EXISTENTIALISM

The final philosophical position that has been adopted by some in leisure services and studies is existentialism. Existentialists regard a person's freedom as all important. As a result, an individual's task is to be responsible to himself or herself, and create his or her own values and ideals. In essence, each person must do what they need to in order to fulfill their own life. The key root of the word existentialism is existence. In this philosophy, human beings are said to exist and then develop an essence. This contrasts strongly with humanism and idealism.

How has existentialism developed in leisure services? It would be the belief of existentialists that leisure can only be determined subjectively with variation from individual to individual and from moment to moment. There have been several examples of its application. Some have noted the *ad hoc* processes employed by many administrators who subscribe to the belief that everything is subject to change and only individuals, not organizations, exist. Existentialists have also found a home among those providing leisure services in clinical settings (Mobily, 1985). In that context it has been argued that the focus is on each day, improving existence, and helping individuals to develop or reclaim their existence. Existentialist programmers would argue that if they make a difference in a particular day for an individual then they have achieved success. Little attention is given to the question of sustaining impact. This is one of the biggest problems with existentialists. They tend to underestimate the future and the consequences of their decision making by forgetting that the "now" does have a way of becoming the past and affecting decisions for today and the future.

The philosophical position adopted by any particular leisure service professional or scholar will influence their conceptualization of leisure and leisure services. There have been a number of views expressed over time and, more recently, there has been growing interest in studying philosophy and leisure contextually. It is important for leisure service professionals and scholars to consider their philosophy because it contributes to the perspective they adopt and guides much of their behaviour. For professionals, it is essential that they articulate their philosophy so employees and employers may better understand the goals they seek to achieve.

Summary

This chapter has served to introduce the various conceptualizations of leisure, recreation, play, sport, and work. In addition, we have reviewed five major philosophical positions that have been prevalent over the course of the modern era of leisure services and provided some indication as to how those varying philosophies influence leisure conceptualizations and leisure services.

STUDY QUESTIONS

1. Describe the difference between a subjective definition of leisure and an objective definition.

2. What is the most critical component of leisure when defined as a state of mind?

3. What are the problems with using time and activity as definitions of leisure?

4. Why is leisure, as the Ancient Greeks described it, an unlikely prospect for most of us living today?

5. What is "flow" and what does it have to do with the experience of leisure?

6. Describe the difference between recreation and leisure.

7. There were many play theories described by Ellis. Explain the modern definitions of arousal seeking and competence/effectance.

8. What are the difficulties in defining sport?

9. What does "serious leisure" mean and how might this apply to our understanding of sport as leisure?

10. What do the "spillover" and "compensation" hypotheses mean?

11. What is the difference between idealists and existentialists?

12. How does a humanistic philosophy influence the provision of leisure services?

13. What would pragmatists want to know about the question: What does leisure mean?

14. How have realists influenced leisure services?

15. Why is a philosophy important and why should professionals and researchers alike clarify their philosophy?

References

Alberta Recreation and Parks. (1983). *Sport development policy* (executive summary). Edmonton, AB: Author.

Arnold, S. (1991). The dilemma of meaning. In Goodale, T. & Witt, P. (Eds.) *Recreation and leisure: Issues in an era of change*. (pp. 5-20). State College, PA: Venture Publishing, Inc.

Bella, L. (1989). Women and leisure: Beyond androcentrism. In Jackson, E. L. & Burton, T. L. (Eds.) *Understanding leisure and recreation: Mapping the past, charting the future*. (pp. 151-180). State College, PA: Venture Publishing, Inc.

Bialeschki, D. & Henderson, K. (1986). Leisure in the common world of women. *Leisure Studies*, *5*, pp. 299-308.

Bolla. P., Dawson, D. & Harrington, P. (1991). The leisure experience of women in Ontario. *Journal of Applied Recreation Research*, *16*, pp. 322-348.

Cheek, N., & Burch, W. (1976). *The social organization of leisure in human society*. New York, NY: Harper and Row.

Csikszentmihalyi, M. (1975). *Beyond boredom and anxiety*. San Francisco, CA: Jossey-Boss.

Csikszentmihalyi, M. (1982). Toward a psychology of optimal experience. *Review of Personality and Social Psychology*, *3*, pp. 13-36.

Csikszentmihalyi, M. (1990). *Flow: The psychology of optimal experience*. New York, NY: Harper and Row.

de Grazia, S. (1964). *Of time, work and leisure*. Garden City, NY: Doubleday and Company.

Dewey, J. (1916). *Democracy and education*. New York, NY: Macmillan, Inc.

Dumazdier, J. (1967). *Toward a society of leisure*. New York, NY: Free Press.

Dumazdier, J. (1974). *Sociology of leisure*. New York, NY: Elsevier North-Holland.

Edwards, H. (1973). *Sociology of sport*. Homewood, IL: Dorsey.

Ellis, M. (1973). *Why people play*. Englewood Cliffs, NJ: Prentice-Hall.

Farina, J. (1991). Perceptions of time. In Goodale, T. & Witt, P. (Eds.) *Recreation and leisure: Issues in an era of change* (pp. 21-32). State College, PA: Venture Publishing, Inc.

Frisby, W. & Brown, B. (1991). The balancing act: Women leisure service managers. *Journal of Applied Recreation Research*, *16*, pp. 297-321.

Goodale, T. L. (1991). Is there enough time. In Goodale, T. & Witt, P. (Eds.) *Recreation and leisure: Issues in an era of change* (pp. 33-46). State College, PA: Venture Publishing, Inc.

Gray, D., & Greben, S. (1974). Future perspectives. *Parks and Recreation, 9*(7), pp. 9.

Hawking, S. W. (1988). *A brief history of time.* New York, NY: Bantam Books.

Hunnicutt, B. K. (1990). Leisure and play in Plato's teaching and philosophy of learning. *Leisure Sciences, 12*, pp. 211-227.

Iso-Ahola, S. E. (1980). *The social psychology of leisure and recreation.* Dubuque, IA: Wm. C. Brown and Company.

James, W. (1963). *Pragmatism and other essays.* New York, NY: Simon and Schuster.

Kelly, J. R. (1990). *Leisure.* Englewood Cliffs, NJ: Prentice-Hall.

Mannell, R. C. (1979). A conceptual and experimental basis for research in the psychology of leisure. *Society and Leisure/Loisir et Société, 2*, pp. 179-196.

Maslow, A. (1970). *Motivation and personality.* New York, NY: Harper and Row.

McFarland, E. M. (1970). *The history of public recreation in Canada.* Ottawa, ON: Canadian Parks/Recreation Association.

Michaelis, B. (1991). Fantasy, play, creativity and mental health. In Goodale, T. & Witt, P. (Eds.) *Recreation and leisure: Issues in an era of change* (pp. 55-72). State College, PA: Venture Publishing, Inc.

Minister's Task Force of Federal Sport Policy. (1992). *Sport: The way ahead.* Ottawa, ON: Minister of Supply and Services.

Mobily, K. E. (1985). A philosophical analysis of therapeutic recreation: What does it mean to say "we can be therapeutic?" Part I. *Therapeutic Recreation Journal, 28*(1), pp. 14-26.

Murphy, J. (1975). *Recreation and leisure service.* Dubuque, IA: Wm. C. Brown and Company.

Nash, J. (1953). *Philosophy of recreation and leisure.* Dubuque, IA: Brown and Co.

Neulinger, J. (1974). *The psychology of leisure.* Springfield, MA: Charles C. Thomas Publishers.

Province of Manitoba Sport Policy. (1991). Winnipeg, MB: Manitoba Sport Directorate.

Samdahl, D. (1991). Issues in the measurement of leisure: A comparison of theoretical and connotative meanings. *Leisure Sciences, 13*, pp. 33-49.

Searle, M. S. & Jackson, E. L. (1985). Socio-economic variations in perceived barriers to recreation participation among would-be participants. *Leisure Sciences, 2*, pp. 227-249.

Sessoms, H. D. (1984). *Leisure services.* Englewood Cliffs, NJ: Prentice-Hall.

Shaw, S. (1990). Where has all the leisure gone? The distribution and redistribution of leisure. In B. Smale (Ed.) *Proceedings from the Sixth Canadian Congress on Leisure Research* (pp. 1-5). Waterloo, ON: University of Waterloo Press.

Stormann, W. (1989). Work: True leisure's home? *Leisure Studies*, *8*, pp. 25-33.

Wilensky, H. (1960). Work, careers, and social integration. *International Social Sciences Journal*, *12*, pp. 543-560.

Wilkinson, P. F. (1985). The golden fleece: The search for standards. *Leisure Studies*, *4*, pp. 189-203.

Ziegler, E. (1964). *Philosophical foundations for physical, health, and recreation education.* Englewood Cliffs, NJ: Prentice-Hall.

Chapter Four

Dimensions of Leisure Behaviour

Overview

PURPOSE

This chapter is focused on the explanation and elaboration of the following concepts: leisure participation, leisure repertoire, leisure motives, leisure attitudes and constraints on leisure. The intent is to explain each of the concepts briefly, reflect on some of the principal research conducted in each area, and summarize the main findings to date on these aspects of leisure behaviour.

LEARNING OBJECTIVES

At completion of this chapter, you should be able to:

1. describe the concepts of leisure participation, leisure repertoire, leisure motives, leisure attitudes, and leisure constraints;

2. explain the principal factors which influence each concept;

3. understand the role of these concepts in shaping leisure behaviour; and,

4. understand and apply the information to the leisure services field.

Dimensions of Leisure Behaviour

The study of leisure behaviour has progressed substantially from twenty years ago when participation rates were the primary measure of all aspects of leisure, and the use of sociological and social-psychological measures was in its infancy. The understanding of the nature of various concepts such as attitude, motives, and participation is an important step in developing an appreciation of the nature of leisure. In the previous chapter, we examined the different ways leisure has been conceptualized or defined, and in this chapter, we examine some of the specific concepts that help us understand why and how individuals engage in leisure pursuits.

It is critical that we see leisure behaviour as more than participation in an activity we choose to do or activity done in free time. Rather, we need to understand why we participate in that chosen activity during our free time, why some people like some activities while others seem to favour different ones, what limits our leisure participation, what factors, if any, help us to predict leisure participation, and how the answers to these questions affect the leisure service professional?

Leisure Participation

Among the questions that leisure service professionals and leisure researchers are most interested in are who participates, how much, how intense is that participation, what factors influence leisure preferences and is any of this predictable? The major source of information on leisure participation is survey research (Stockdale, 1990). This includes mail questionnaires, telephone interviews, and in-person interviews. In addition, time-budget studies have been popularly used (Robinson, 1977; Szalai, 1972) as well as qualitative techniques such as observational studies, ethnographies (Glancy, 1986; Howe, 1985) and innovative approaches such as the experience sampling method (Csikszentmihalyi & Larson, 1987; Samdahl, 1992). Many of these studies have focused on the factors associated with leisure participation and more recently some causal models (i.e., models which explain causes of leisure participation) have been suggested (cf. Ewert & Hollenhorst, 1989).

To begin our discussion of leisure participation it is important to distinguish between and among the terms *participation*, *repertoire*, and *favourite*. Generally, measures of *participation* examine what activities individuals engage in and how often. From such data we learn what people do most often, but not necessarily what they prefer to do. *Repertoire* refers to the number of different leisure activities in which individuals engage. Thus, some people report a wide variety of pursuits while others concentrate on a few. *Favourite* leisure activities are those in which people report they prefer to participate. Very often individuals report preferences for activities in which they infrequently participate. For example, an individual may prefer downhill skiing, but live in Saskatchewan where opportunities are limited. Another individual might enjoy sailing, but lack the resources to sail. Yet, another individual might enjoy carpentry, but lack the skills to perform at the level desired. Participation, repertoire, and favourite are key terms with distinct meanings when discussing leisure participation.

What does the data tell us about leisure participation? Table 4.1 shows the ten activities with the highest reported levels of participation from surveys conducted in Alberta, Manitoba, Ontario and nationally. Each of these surveys were conducted with different size samples, different techniques (e.g., Alberta and Manitoba used mail questionnaires, Ontario used in-person interviews and the national survey used a combination of both) and asked their questions in different formats. Moreover, some asked questions not asked by others. For example, the Manitoba questionnaire excluded items about television watching while the national study excluded questions relating to non-physical leisure pursuits. Nonetheless, they provide a snapshot of the broad range of leisure activities and the frequency with which Canadians engage in them.

TABLE 4.1
TOP TEN ACTIVITIES WITH HIGHEST LEVELS OF PARTICIPATION IN
ALBERTA, MANITOBA, ONTARIO, AND CANADA

RANK	ALBERTA[1]	MANITOBA[2]	ONTARIO[3]	NATIONAL[4]
1.	Walking for pleasure	Visiting Friends/Relatives	Reading	Walking
2.	Driving for pleasure	Dining out	Socialize	Gardening
3.	Gardening	Listen to music	Listen to radio	Swimming
4.	Doing a craft or hobby	Shopping	Watch television	Bicycling
5.	Visiting a museum, live theatre, or gallery	Reading	Spend time outdoors	Dancing (social)
6.	Bicycling	Walking	Hobbies	Home Exercise
7.	Attending a sports event as a spectator	Playing cards, or games	Sports & fitness	Skating
8.	Swimming (in pools)	Travelling for pleasure	Rest and relaxation	Skiing (downhill)
9.	Picnicking in the country	Gardening	Shop, browse	Jogging
10.	Overnight camping	Attending a sporting event	Camp, hunt	Golf

1. Alberta mail survey conducted in 1988 with a sample of 4,044 households. These data represent household participation rates.
2. Manitoba mail survey conducted in 1990 and represents Manitobans living outside Winnipeg. Sample consisted of 1,209 individuals age 16 and over.
3. Ontario data were derived from a 1989 study in which 2,024 individuals were interviewed.
4. National data from the 1988 Campbell Survey on Well-being of Canadians. These data were derived from interviews with a sample of 3,068. These data only reflect the physical activities of Canadians.

Even though methods of collecting data influence the outcomes reported, some consistencies do appear in these data. First, Canadians seem to report high levels of participation in physical activities even when asked about the whole range of pursuits available. Second, there are regional variations which should be expected as different trends emerge in different areas based on the influence of media, local culture, traditions, local personalities (e.g., having a world champion figure skater in your community such as Kurt Browning in Caroline, Alberta may shape attitudes toward that sport and influence participation). On a national basis, the effect of the personality has been best demonstrated through the influence of hockey. Virtually every part of Canada has a local person who has made it into the ranks of professional hockey. As a result, there was for many years and continues to be the influence of these "stars on ice" on the aspirations of young boys and sometimes their parents. This is one factor contributing to high levels of participation in hockey. However, local patterns are generally more important to the planning and management of leisure services than national indicators since the bulk of service providers are locally based (Smith, 1991).

A third conclusion to be drawn from Table 4.1 is that many of the activities in which participation is the greatest require little organization, and most do not require the technical assistance of leisure programmers. This does not denigrate the need for such professional leadership. Rather, it points to the fact that people engage in leisure activities which are most easily accessible and require the least amount of reliance on others. This points to the need for distinguishing between what Canadians do most often and what they consider to be their favourite activity. We will discuss that shortly, but first it is important to consider other factors which influence leisure participation.

SOCIO-ECONOMIC FACTORS INFLUENCING LEISURE PARTICIPATION

What other factors influence leisure participation? Data reported by Searle (1987), Peppers (1976), Jacobs and Havens (1985) and others have shown that age is clearly a factor in leisure participation. The older one gets the lower the level of participation. There has been some indication that this may be changing. The 1981 Canada Fitness Survey showed that persons over age 65 increased their participation in physical activities at a greater rate than those younger. Nonetheless, the preponderance of evidence suggests a downward trend in participation with advancing age.

Recent research by Jackson and Dunn (1988) provided a framework for understanding the role of age more effectively. They developed a model for leisure decision making. Their data showed that some individuals expanded their leisure participation, some quit an activity but then replaced it with another, others simply quit an activity without replacing it, and a fourth group did not change their leisure participation. In a replication and extension of this study (Searle, Mactavish, & Brayley, in press), the data showed that quitters and continuers tended to be among the older respondents while persons adding to their participation and replacing old activities with new ones tended to be younger. These results show that age is a powerful force influencing leisure participation, but it is not the only force. Furthermore, it is not known why some persons increase their leisure participation as they grow older.

Among the other factors that influence leisure participation are education, income, marital status (and number of children and their age), sex, leisure attitude, leisure motivation (intrinsic versus extrinsic), and leisure satisfaction. The influences of each of these variables on leisure participation is not simply a linear one. That is, more education does not directly relate to more participation. It does influence certain forms of participation such as outdoor recreation pursuits (Stankey, 1980). Income often correlates positively with education since higher incomes are often associated with higher levels of education.

Marital status often effects leisure participation through the obligations that individuals assume in a relationship. Marital status also influences participation where individuals who have been married now find themselves alone either through widowhood or through divorce. Searle and Jackson (1985) reported that lack of a partner with whom to participate was the most often reported constraint on the leisure of older adults. There is also limited evidence that shows widowed males have a more restricted leisure lifestyle than females (McPherson, 1983). This is a result of females often assuming the role of "social convenor" in married relationships. The male partner, when left alone, is often lacking in the confidence or skills to effect social relations.

GENDER

The effect of gender on leisure participation is complex (Chambers, 1986; Deem, 1982, 1986; Shaw, 1985; Wearing & Wearing, 1988). In some cases there are different patterns between males and females based on preferences. In many cases differences are due to opportunities available (or not available), societal sanctions or approval (e.g., in Canada we have not generally encouraged women to participate in hockey nor have we encouraged men to participate in synchronized swimming), and household duties and child-rearing responsibilities (the greater part of the burden of which is borne by women). Moreover, differences in male and female participation are also attributable to the experiences they have had as children through the education, recreation, and sport systems. Many of these systems have had systemic bias which have limited the opportunities of women. Only recently have these begun to change but restrictions still persist in some quarters.

SOCIAL PSYCHOLOGICAL FACTORS AFFECTING LEISURE PARTICIPATION

While many of these factors will be explored in more detail in a subsequent section of this chapter, it is important to highlight these relationships while focusing on leisure participation. Leisure attitude has been shown in numerous studies to be linked to leisure participation (Ajzen & Driver, 1992; Ragheb, 1980; Ragheb & Griffith, 1982; Searle & Iso-Ahola, 1988; Young & Kent, 1985). There is evidence which substantiates the hypothesized attitude-behaviour linkage which is proposed in the theory of planned behaviour (Ajzen, 1985). In this theory, attitude toward the activity, subjective norms, and perceived behavioural control with respect to the activity are all said to lead to an intent to participate or not participate. Intention to participate is a reliable predictor of actual behaviour. This theory was confirmed in the recent research reported by Ajzen and Driver (1992). Attitude did have direct effects on shaping the intention of an individual to engage in a leisure activity.

Leisure motivation does influence leisure participation. It has been argued (Iso-Ahola, 1989) that intrinsic motives result in more stable leisure participation than extrinsic motives. More specifically, it is the satisfaction that one derives from intrinsic motives which seem to be more effective in influencing participation decisions. Iso-Ahola (1980) has stated that a positive leisure attitude is a manifestation of intrinsically motivated behaviour. Thus, there is an important link between leisure attitude, leisure motivation, and leisure participation.

Generally, leisure satisfaction is an outcome of leisure participation and, as such, will be discussed later in this chapter. However, there is limited evidence (Jackson & Searle, 1983; Searle, Mactavish, & Brayley, in press) that suggests that higher levels of leisure satisfaction result in the desire for more leisure experiences. In other words, among the likely sources of desire for participating in new leisure activities is the level of satisfaction derived from current participation.

Leisure Repertoire

Leisure repertoire has received considerably less attention in the leisure research literature than its associated concept "participation". Mobily, et al. (1984) reported several predictors of leisure repertoire among older adults, and Searle and Iso-Ahola (1988) used leisure repertoire as a dependent variable to assess the effects of health, leisure attitude and the choice one had in retiring. Some practitioners and researchers have speculated that leisure repertoire among older adults might decrease but the intensity of involvements among the remaining activities increases. Leisure repertoire refers to the number of different activities individuals engage in during their leisure. It is an important concept because it allows us to measure whether the range of leisure activities is expanding or contracting, whether individuals in certain neighbourhoods or in certain socio-economic groups have lower repertoires, and whether the introduction of new leisure opportunities influences the repertoire of individuals.

FACTORS THAT INFLUENCE LEISURE REPERTOIRE

Factors that influence repertoire have largely been focused on older adults. These data have shown that age, self-perceived health, leisure attitude, and life satisfaction have an effect on leisure repertoire. However, the leisure of youth and particularly "youth at risk" needs to be examined as it relates to leisure repertoire. Evidence from Winther's (1989) study of youth in northern Manitoba native communities indicates that, among youth with few alternatives, increased leisure repertoire through the introduction of new opportunities can positively affect behaviour and reduce participation in criminal activity. Repertoire has also been limited by one's gender as suggested in the earlier discussion in this chapter about participation. Finally, recent research by Iso-Ahola and

Weissinger (1987) suggested that one of the reasons individuals experience boredom in their leisure is that they have a small leisure repertoire. Certainly, more investigation is needed about leisure repertoire and how it interacts with the volume of leisure participation and increasing levels of satisfaction. Nonetheless, it is clear that leisure repertoire is an important consideration in the planning and delivery of leisure services.

Leisure Motivation

Leisure motivation is, as noted above, an important element in leisure participation. Iso-Ahola (1989, p. 268) stated "Intrinsic motivation is the heart of leisure behaviour". Motives are internal forces which arouse individuals and direct them to act. Motives, while not observable, come from either internal forces or external ones. Internal forces are those such as the recollection of a past experience which was positive while external forces are such things as weather or encouragement from a family member. Research indicates that individuals seek neither excessive stimulation or too little stimulation. Rather, they seek an optimum level of stimulation and this is what their motives regulate. Through his review of the literature, Iso-Ahola (1989) has demonstrated that it is intrinsic motivation that is preferred for self-determined behaviour. This is due to two factors (Iso-Ahola, 1989, p. 252):

1. Intrinsically motivated behaviours facilitate people's attempts to pursue and achieve optimum levels of sensory stimulation and arousal and therefore also their efforts to maintain motivational normalcy; and,

2. Intrinsically motivated behaviours are inherently pleasure- and satisfaction-producing.

Intrinsic motivation is comprised of two dimensions: seeking and escaping. No behaviour is entirely motivated by seeking tendencies or escaping tendencies. However, Iso-Ahola (1989) argues that both play a role in the motives of individuals engaged in leisure behaviour. In each case it is possible and indeed likely that one motivational dimension will be more dominant than the other. For example, Canadians who escape our harsh winter to enjoy the Florida sunshine may be dominated by the escape motive but also seek certain outcomes from this escape such as relaxation, better health, entertainment, etc. Similarly, the individual who plays old-timers hockey may do so in order to seek affirmation of his competence, sustain his health, and socialize. However, at the same time, he may be escaping the pressures of the job or home. Thus, all leisure behaviours can be accounted for in this two-dimensional model created by Iso-Ahola. It eliminates the need for long lists of motives to understand behaviour, although such lists are still required by professionals to understand the range of experiences they are seeking to satisfy. The leisure service provider must be aware that individuals want health benefits or socialization opportunities if she or he is to adequately provide leisure opportunities for them. It is important to reiterate that all leisure behaviour can be explained through this model and that both dimensions are present in all leisure behaviours.

LEISURE AS BOREDOM

What happens when intrinsic leisure motivation is lacking? Iso-Ahola and Weissinger (1987) have suggested that this is a state of boredom. If the opposite of intrinsic leisure motivation is boredom, then those factors that create boredom effectively undermine leisure motivation. Those factors which contribute to boredom, in addition to having a small leisure repertoire as noted earlier in the chapter, are:

1. a more negative leisure attitude;
2. a stronger work ethic;
3. low levels of leisure awareness;
4. high levels of perceived constraint on leisure; and,
5. low levels of self-motivation.

Among these six variables (including repertoire), the effect of leisure awareness on boredom was greatest. Second, among these factors influencing the perception of leisure as boredom is leisure attitude, third is leisure repertoire, and fourth is self-motivation. It should be made clear that it was not the lack of leisure opportunities that generated these results, but rather, the lack of awareness of the psychological values of leisure. Thus, these findings, as suggested by Iso-Ahola and Weissinger, indicate that leisure service organizations should put some energy into the development and implementation of leisure education programs. These programs would serve to enhance understanding of leisure's value and increase knowledge and skills for leisure. This would address the factors of leisure awareness, leisure attitude, work ethic, and leisure repertoire.

The research suggests that leisure as boredom is an important discovery in the understanding of leisure motivation. Thus, there is an imperative to address this issue by leisure service organizations if they are to take the steps necessary to create more and better leisure for the individuals they serve.

Leisure Attitudes

Leisure attitudes, as indicated in the preceding sections of this chapter, are strongly linked to leisure motivation and ultimately to leisure participation. But what is an attitude? An attitude is the feeling you have toward something. More specifically, attitude has been defined as "a learned predisposition to respond in a consistently favourable or unfavourable manner with respect to a given object" (Fishbein and Ajzen, 1975, p. 6). Iso-Ahola (1980, p. 251) defined leisure attitude "as the expressed amount of affect toward a given leisure-related object". You possess both an overall leisure attitude as well as attitudes toward individual activities. This feeling or attitude is influential in determining your leisure behaviour.

Why do we need to understand leisure attitudes? What role does the information play in leisure services? Crandall (1979) suggested three purposes to acquiring knowledge and understanding of leisure attitudes:

1. to measure important trends in society, such as the relative importance of work and leisure;
2. to improve service delivery; and,
3. as a basis for leisure education and counseling, to help people clarify and improve their attitudes about leisure.

As noted earlier in this chapter, the theory of planned behaviour (Ajzen, 1985) has become a widely accepted premise for understanding the role of leisure attitudes in influencing leisure participation.

Leisure Satisfaction

In the discussion of leisure participation, leisure satisfaction was described as an outcome of a leisure experience which subsequently serves to influence future leisure behaviour. Leisure satisfaction may be rooted in one's motives, that is, the satisfaction is dependent upon the activity's satiation of important needs or it may be independent of such needs and simply be an appraisal of an activity or circumstance relative to your expectations (Mannell, 1989). Moreover, leisure satisfaction may be thought of in terms of a narrow, specific context (the specific appraisal of an activity) or as it relates to, what Mannell (1989) describes as a larger "global" level (the satisfaction one derives from their leisure in general).

A needs-driven approach to leisure satisfaction could be derived from the work of Abraham Maslow (1970). Maslow developed a hierarchy of needs model. This five-part hierarchy depicted in Figure 4.1, (p. 66) shows that once people satisfy lower level needs, they seek to satisfy higher order needs. Leisure and recreation service providers have a definite role in the top three need levels and arguably can influence security needs as well.

Having satisfied physiological needs, individuals seek to make sure that they are secure with regard to their personal safety and feelings that they are safe from threats to their security. Their participation in recreation programs can lead to enhanced feelings of physical competence which in turn lead to feelings of greater safety. One must remember that threats to personal safety can be perceived in harsh weather as much as they can be perceived in another individual. Keeping this in mind, recreation participation which leads to improved physical health can have benefits which relate directly to the need to feel safe.

The next level of need is called belongingness and refers to individual's needs to be accepted and be part of a group. This group can be family or friends, social organizations or employee groups. Indeed, it can be all of these things. Clearly, recreation programs can facilitate such involvement and thus contribute to the satisfaction of this need.

The next level need is called esteem needs and goes to the desire for individual's to feel good about themselves. In this regard individual's want to have positive self-esteem, internal locus of control, and high levels of competence (not just physical competence). Locus of control refers to the degree to which individuals feel they are in control of their lives or victims of circumstances and powers beyond their influence (Rotter, 1966). Those in control of their lives are said to have internal locus of control while those not feeling in control are said to have external locus of control. The issue of competence is important as it involves physical, social, intellectual and general competence (Harter, 1978). Individuals who feel competent are more self-assured and more able to manage their lives and tend to report higher levels of leisure and life satisfaction (Sneegas, 1986). These psychological variables may all be influenced through participation in recreation programs. Recreation programs,

FIGURE 4.1
MASLOW'S HIERARCHY OF NEEDS

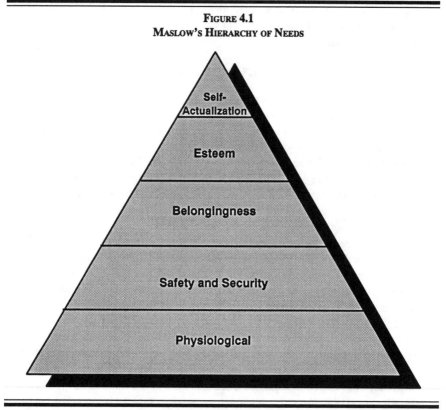

through improving skills, facilitating social interaction, and promoting positive feedback and achievement can enhance the opportunities for individuals to satisfy their esteem needs.

This leads directly to the highest level of need satisfaction posited by Maslow (1970). That is, self-actualization. Although this state of being has rarely been defined in satisfactory terms and has not been measured, there seems to be reasonable agreement that such a higher order need exists. It may best be defined as the desire for self-fulfillment, namely the tendency for individuals to become actualized in what they consider to be their potential. It is the desire to become more and more of what one is. The forms it takes varies with each individual and is highly disparate depending upon what each person seeks to be. Recreation programs offer the opportunity for greater and greater levels of performance and thus greater opportunity for satisfying the need for self-actualization.

The conceptualization of leisure satisfaction as an appraisal process involves the assessment of both specific aspects of leisure experiences and more global aspects of the leisure experience. Mannell (1989) points out that examples of leisure satisfaction in an appraisal context was measured in studies of provincial campgrounds and tourist destinations. Global assessments have been asked in studies attempting to determine the overall evaluation of the individual's leisure lifestyle. In addition, global leisure satisfaction measures have been used to assess the role of leisure in the overall quality of life.

The leisure services professional is concerned with leisure satisfaction because if consumers of the service are dissatisfied, then the future portends poorly for the service organization. If on the other hand, satisfaction with the opportunities and amenities provided is high, then the outlook will be considerably brighter. The obvious question to follow, is, what if anything can a leisure service organization do to influence the leisure satisfaction of its customers? The answer is complex. There are known factors which influence the leisure satisfaction of individuals but these are largely individualized. Moreover, there is doubt according to Iso-Ahola (1980) about whether expressed needs are accurate indicators of what individuals seek to satisfy. Perhaps expressed needs are just a function of societal expectations. Regardless, steps need to be taken to develop a thorough understanding of the user group or, in the case of more therapeutic or special circumstances, the individual, and through that enhanced understanding develop services which are consistent with user expectations or needs.

Constraints on Leisure

The fastest growing area of interest among leisure researchers has been the area of leisure constraints and reasons for ceasing leisure participation. Strangely, this has long been an interest of professionals charged with the responsibility of encouraging as many individuals as possible to be involved in leisure activities. In Canada, we have had Participation since 1972 and more recently the Active Living Campaign as means to encourage active lifestyles. There have been provincial initiatives such as Get Up Alberta in 1980 and initiatives from provincial and local recreation organizations to encourage greater participation. However, until recently there has been little research which has addressed the issue of encouraging participation by reducing constraints.

We now understand that in order to address the issue of constraints on leisure we need to consider two types of constraints (Crawford & Godbey, 1987). First, there are constraints which intervene between our desire to participate and our actual participation. This type of constraint does not permit us to participate in an activity in which we have identified an interest. This might be something like a lack of money, lack of transportation, or lack of a partner with whom to participate. The second form of constraint is labeled antecedent. This simply means that the constraint came before and acts to limit an individual's overall choice set. For example, you may have experienced a childhood where few leisure activities were taught in school and none were available to you outside of school due to your socio-economic status. These circumstances act to constrain your leisure participation through limiting the choices you have had.

Besides understanding that constraints are both intervening and antecedent, we have learned that constraints affect different socio-economic groups (Searle & Jackson, 1985) and males and females differently (Henderson, Stalnaker, & Taylor,

1988). Those in lower socio-economic groups, single parents, and the elderly seem to be most affected by constraints. Women are constrained by some factors that do not affect men to the same degree, or at all, such as body image and household duties. More recently, evidence from Shaw, Bonen, and McCabe (1991) and Kay and Jackson (1991) suggests that those who report the most constraints are also those who are most active. This raises a question about when a constraint is a constraint. Substantially more research is needed in this area to follow individuals and assess how transient constraints are, how they interact with other factors in the individual's environment, who is most affected by constraints and which type are more potent than others, along with a whole host of related questions.

The related question of why individuals cease participation in leisure activities has also been receiving more attention in recent years. However, our understanding of this phenomenon is less thoroughly understood. Jackson and Dunn (1988) reported on the discontinuation rates among Albertans for specific activities. They found that exercise-oriented activities experienced the highest rate of discontinuance but also had the highest rate of new participants. Other research by Snow (1980) has suggested that those activities with highest rates of new participants were the ones with the lowest rates of discontinuance. Evidence from Backman (1991) has suggested that discontinuation may likely be driven by some change in attitude that the individual has experienced relative to the specific activity. This provides a linkage between the theory of planned behaviour (Ajzen, 1985) and discontinuation decisions. That is, if environmental factors or some experience with the activity give rise to a change in attitude (i.e., the development of a more negative attitude toward the activity), then this will likely change the intention of the individual to participate and thus result in ceasing participation. The question of ceasing leisure participation is a complex one in need of considerably more study. The information derived from such investigations has direct application in the field of leisure services. Results from this research will possibly influence promotional strategies, pricing, social climate, customer relations, and other central factors in the operation of leisure services.

Summary

Leisure behaviour is a complex phenomenon. Issues involved are the rates at which people engage in different activities, the size of the leisure repertoire, the distinction between favourite activities and those with the highest rates of participation, the attitudes individuals bring to their leisure, the motivations, the satisfactions derived, and the constraints that influence most of the above. Leisure researchers are continuing to explore this area with great intensity. Leisure service professionals need to use the information generated to determine the best ways they can fulfill their mandate.

Among the conclusions professionals can draw from the existing research are:

1. Leisure participation includes activities across a great range of pursuits from painting portraits to broomball. Furthermore, participation varies across ages, regions, socio-economic groups, sexes, and social groups.

2. Leisure participation does not necessarily reflect leisure preference.

3. Participation may be influenced by availability, skills, knowledge, and a wide range of other factors which leisure service organizations should assess to determine the extent of management control and market potential.

4. Repertoire influences the degree to which leisure represents a varied set of activities or a narrow range of pursuits. In the case of the latter, evidence now suggests that limited repertoires result in a greater likelihood of leisure being viewed as a boring experience. Boredom, can lead to other social problems such as substance abuse (Iso-Ahola & Crowley, 1991).

5. Motivation which is intrinsic is the most stable and results in sustained leisure participation. This suggests that incentives and rewards would have only limited value in encouraging participation and that other efforts are needed to help develop intrinsic motives.

6. Leisure attitudes are key regulators of what is considered to be a leisure experience. They influence the decisions to cease or continue leisure participation. Leisure education programs may directly effect leisure attitudes and leisure motivation.

7. Leisure satisfaction has several dimensions associated with it that need to be understood by professionals in order to understand the kinds of satisfactions sought and the effect that dissatisfaction has on participation.

8. Constraints on leisure are principally of two types—antecedent and intervening. Leisure service professionals need to consider strategies to help individuals overcome both.

9. Decisions to cease leisure participation may be a result of attitude shifts, or extrinsic motives, or it may be associated with the lack of anticipated rewards (intrinsic or extrinsic) (Searle, 1991).

10. Leisure participation has many dimensions. Understanding of this major aspect of human behaviour requires constant attention through research and professional leadership.

1. Describe the difference between leisure participation and repertoire.

2. Does the term favourite leisure activity imply the activity in which participation is greatest? Explain.

3. What factors are known to influence leisure behaviour and what are their effects?

4. Why is knowledge of leisure repertoire important to researchers and professionals?

5. Explain the difference between extrinsic and intrinsic leisure motivation.

6. Why is intrinsic leisure motivation more stable?

7. What is the opposite of intrinsic leisure motivation?

8. What are the six suggested causes of boredom in leisure? Which is the most important factor?

9. Explain the role of leisure attitude in influencing leisure participation.

10. What are the different ways one can think of leisure satisfaction and why does this matter?

11. Describe the two types of leisure constraints?

12. What might professionals do with the information concerning constraints?

References

Ajzen, I. (1985). From intentions to actions: A theory of planned behaviour. In Kuhl, J. & Beckmann, J. (Eds.), *Action-control: From cognition to behaviour* (pp. 11-39). Heidelberg, Germany: Springer-Verlag, New York, Inc.

Ajzen, I. & Driver, B. L. (1992). Application of the theory of planned behaviour to leisure choice. *Journal of Leisure Research, 24*, pp. 207-224.

Backman, S. (1991). An investigation of the relationship between activity loyalty and perceived constraints. *Journal of Leisure Research, 23*, pp. 332-344.

Chambers, D. A. (1986). The constraints of work and domestic schedules on women's leisure. *Leisure Studies, 5*, pp. 299-325.

Crandall, R. (1979). Social interaction, affect and leisure. *Journal of Leisure Research, 11*, pp. 165-181.

Crawford, D. W. & Godbey, G. (1987). Reconceptualizing barriers to family leisure. *Leisure Sciences, 9*, pp. 119-128.

Csikszentmihalyi, M. & Larson, R. (1987). Validity and reliability of the experience sampling method. *Journal of Nervous and Mental Disease, 175*, pp. 526-536.

Deem, R. (1982). Women, leisure and inequality. *Leisure Studies, 1*, pp. 29-46.

Deem, R. (1986). *All work and no play: The sociology of women and leisure*. Milton Keynes, UK: Open University Press.

Ewert, A., & Hollenhorst, S. (1989). Testing the adventure model: Empirical support for a model of risk recreation participation. *Journal of Leisure Research, 21*, pp. 124-139.

Fishbein, M., & Ajzen, I. (1975). *Belief, attitude, intention and behavior: An introduction to theory and research*. Reading, MA: Addison-Wesley Publishing Co.

Glancy, M. (1986). Participant observation in the recreation setting. *Journal of Leisure Research, 18*, pp. 59-80.

Harter, S. (1978). Effectance motivation reconsidered: Toward a developmental model. *Human Development, 21*, pp. 34-36.

Henderson, K. A., Stalnaker, D., & Taylor, G. (1988). The relationship between barriers to recreation and gender-role personality traits for women. *Journal of Leisure Research, 20*, pp. 69-80.

Howe, C. (1985). Possibilities for using a qualitative research approach in the sociological study of leisure. *Journal of Leisure Research, 17*, pp. 212-224.

Iso-Ahola, S. E. (1980). *The social psychology of leisure and recreation*. Dubuque, IA: Wm. C. Brown.

Iso-Ahola, S. E. (1989). Motivation for leisure. In Jackson, E. L. & Burton, T. L. *Understanding leisure and recreation: Mapping the past, charting the future,* (pp. 247-279). State College, PA: Venture Publishing, Inc.

Iso-Ahola, S. E. & Crowley, E. D. (1991). Adolescent substance abuse and leisure boredom. *Journal of Leisure Research, 23,* pp. 260-271.

Iso-Ahola, S. E. & Weissinger, E. (1987). Leisure and Boredom. *Journal of Social and Clinical Psychology, 5,* pp. 356-364.

Jackson, E. L. & Dunn, E. (1988). Integrating ceasing participation with other aspects of leisure behavior. *Journal of Leisure Research, 20,* pp. 31-45.

Jackson, E. L. & Searle, M. S. (1983). Recreation non-participation: Variables related to the desire for new recreation activities. *Recreation Research Review, 10*(2), pp. 5-12

Jacobs, B. & Havens, B. (October 1985). *Leisure activities as related to age, sex, health, economic circumstances and location.* Hamilton, ON: A paper presented at the Canadian Association on Gerontology Conference.

Kay, T. & Jackson, G. (1991). Leisure despite constraint: The impact of leisure constraints on leisure participation. *Journal of Leisure Research, 23,* pp. 301-313.

Mannell, R. C. (1989). Leisure satisfaction. In Jackson, E. L. & Burton, T. L. (Eds.) *Understanding leisure and recreation: Mapping the past, charting the future,* (pp. 281-301). State College, PA: Venture Publishing, Inc.

Maslow, A. (1970). *Motivation and personality.* New York, NY: Harper and Row.

McPherson, B. D. (1983). *Aging as a social process.* Toronto, ON: Butterworths.

Mobily, K., Leslie, D. K., Wallace, R. B., Lemke, J. H., Kohout, F. J. & Morris, M. C. (1984). Factors associated with the aging leisure repertoire: The Iowas 65+ rural health study. *Journal of Leisure Research, 16,* pp. 338-343.

Peppers, L. G. (1976). Patterns of leisure and adjustment to retirement. *The Gerontologist, 16,* (in press).

Ragheb, M. G. (1980). Interrelationships among leisure participation, leisure satisfaction, and leisure attitudes. *Journal of Leisure Research, 12,* pp. 138-149.

Ragheb, M. G. & Griffith, C. (1982). The contribution of leisure participation and leisure satisfaction to life satisfaction of older persons. *Journal of Leisure Research, 14,* pp. 295-306.

Robinson, J. P. (1977). *How Americans use time: A social psychological analysis of everyday behavior.* New York, NY: Praeger.

Rotter, J. B. (1966). Generalized expectancies for internal versus external locus of control of reinforcement. *Psychological Monographs, 80,* (1, Whole No. 609).

Samdahl, D. M. (1992). Leisure in our lives: Exploring the common leisure occasion. *Journal of Leisure Research, 24,* pp. 19-32.

Searle, M. S. (1987). *Leisure and aging in Manitoba.* Winnipeg, MB: Manitoba Culture, Heritage and Recreation.

Searle, M. S. (1991). Propositions for testing social exchange theory in the context of ceasing leisure participation. *Leisure Sciences, 13,* pp. 279-294.

Searle, M. S. & Iso-Ahola, S. E. (1988). Determinants of leisure behaviour among retired adults. *Therapeutic Recreation Journal, 22*(2), pp. 38-46.

Searle, M. S. & Jackson, E. L. (1985). Socio-economic variations in perceived barriers to recreation participation among would-be participants. *Leisure Sciences, 2,* pp. 227-249.

Searle, M. S., Mactavish, J. & Brayley, R. E. (in press). Integrating ceasing participation with other aspects of leisure behavior: A replication and extension. *Journal of Leisure Research.*

Shaw, S. M. (1985). Gender and leisure: Inequality in the distribution of leisure time. *Journal of Leisure Research, 17,* pp. 266-282.

Shaw, S. M., Bonen, A., & McCabe, J. F. (1991). Do more constraints mean less leisure? Examining the relationship between constraints and participation. *Journal of Leisure Research, 23,* pp. 286-300.

Smith, S. L. J. (1991). The age of outdoor recreation in Canada: A few cautionary comments. *Journal of Applied Recreation Research, 16,* pp. 165-168.

Sneegas, J. J. (1986). Components of life satisfaction in middle and later life adults: perceived social competence, leisure participation and leisure satisfaction. *Journal of Leisure Research, 18,* pp. 259-265.

Snow, R. (1980). A structural analysis of recreation activity substitution. Unpublished doctoral dissertation, Texas A & M University, College Station, Texas.

Stankey, G. H. (1980). *A comparison of carrying capacity perceptions among visitors to two wildernesses.* Washington, DC: USDA Forest Service Research Paper INT-242.

Stockdale, J. E. (1989). Concepts and measures of leisure participation and preference. In Jackson, E. L. & Burton, T. L. (Eds.) *Understanding leisure and recreation: Mapping the past, charting the future,* (pp. 113-150). State College, PA: Venture Publishing, Inc.

Szalai, A. (1972). *The use of time: Daily activities of urban and sub-urban populations in twelve countries.* The Hague, the Netherlands: Mouton.

Wearing, B. & Wearing, S. (1988). All in a day's leisure: Gender and the concept of leisure. *Leisure Studies, 7,* pp. 111-123.

Winther, N. R. (1989). Recreation: An agent of social change. *Recreation Canada, 47*(5), pp. 19-23.

Chapter Five  5

The Public Sector

Overview

PURPOSE

The purpose of this chapter is to describe the public recreation system in Canada. It will explore the roles of the federal, provincial, and municipal governments in providing and facilitating the provision of publicly funded leisure services. Through this exploration we can develop an appreciation for the extent of public sector involvement in the leisure service industry, and begin to understand the nature of public agency involvement in the development of our individual leisure lifestyles.

LEARNING OBJECTIVES

At the completion of this chapter, you should be able to:

1. describe the evolution of public agency involvement in leisure services in Canada,

2. identify the different roles assumed by the federal, provincial, and municipal governments with respect to leisure service delivery,

3. describe alternative approaches to the delivery of public leisure services at the municipal level, and

4. recognize the contribution that public recreation organizations make to your leisure lifestyle.

The Public Sector

In their book on the delivery of community recreation services, Murphy and Howard (1977) explain that the community recreation system is made up of three overlapping sub-systems. One sub-system is referred to as the commercial sub-system and is described as the collection of leisure services providers that operates in an environment where financial profit is the main motive for service provision. Examples of commercial recreation enterprises include amusement parks, movie theatres, bowling alleys, private campgrounds, and resorts. A second sub-system is represented by recreation agencies which are neither sponsored by government nor owned by profit-motivated corporate entities. This is the private not-for-profit sub-system and it includes such organizations as the YM-YWCA, Boys' and Girls' Clubs, Scouts Canada, church auxiliaries, service clubs, sports leagues, arts councils, and others. The third sub-system is the public recreation sub-system, and it is the focus of discussion in this chapter.

Since the public recreation sub-system functions under a broad mandate to enrich life and promote the well-being of the entire community, it would not be unusual to find public agency spokespersons refer to their agencies' activities and resources as programs and services which are designed to deliver benefits to all segments of the population. The 'public' nature of the agency (i.e., the non-discriminatory way in which operating funds are expropriated) requires that services and programs be available to all.

The administrative organizations one could expect to find operating in the public sub-system are typically government agencies which are funded primarily through taxes and revenues generated through tax-supported enterprises. Some of the public sector revenues also come as gifts and grants from private sources.

Areas and facilities maintained by the public recreation sub-system include parks, fields, zoos, beaches, community halls, arenas, and libraries. The public recreation sub-system provides a wide range of programs and services, and most often does so through the work of civil servants who are trained recreation professionals and through the support of volunteers.

In many respects, the public sector is the pivotal force in the community for recreation, as it not only provides recreation services directly to citizens but also exercises control over the ability of other sectors to offer such services within its jurisdictional confines. The public sector (government) is, in a sense, both a player and a referee in the game of leisure service delivery (Burton, 1982). In Canada, this dual role is played by governments at the federal, provincial, and municipal levels. Each level of government in almost every part of Canada is engaged in a variety of recreation and leisure development activities. For some government agencies the involvement is very direct, and in other agencies the recreation development activities are of secondary or *ancilliary* concern.

Federal Government Activities

The authority of the federal government to act on behalf of the citizens of Canada is defined by the Constitution. This primary legal document outlines the responsibilities and jurisdiction of government. In theory, the federal government can do nothing that is not provided for in the Constitution.

Does the Constitution mention parks, recreation or leisure services as a legitimate concern of our national government? No, it doesn't (*Constitution Act*, 1982). Yet we know that the federal government is heavily involved in these areas (e.g., National Parks, museums, sport development, fitness promotion).

This involvement is justified less on legal mandate and more on the principle of convention. That is, the conventional or customary practice of the government has been to support fitness, sport, recreation and parks, so the continuation of this practice is thereby legally justified, although not required. The federal government remains involved in these areas because of the demands of the electorate, not because of legal obligation.

With the exception of a few specific areas of activity, the federal government has passed the responsibility for public recreation to the provinces. Remaining federal activities in recreation are, nonetheless, conducted under the auspices of numerous departments and agencies. In the early 1980s there were sixty-four federal government departments and agencies that were significantly involved in the provision of park, recreation and leisure services. Forty-five of them were involved in arts and culture activities, forty were associated with tourism and travel, forty had mandated activities in the area of outdoor recreation, thirty-nine were sports and physical recreation related, and thirty-nine were involved in the social activity aspect of Canadians' leisure. Those federal government departments with primary mandates for the various forms of public recreation include Fitness and Amateur Sport, Environment Canada (National Parks and Historic Sites), Industry, Science and Technology (Tourism), and Secretary of State (Arts and Culture). Corrections Canada, Health and Welfare, the department of External Affairs, and the department of Consumer and Corporate Affairs also have some areas of responsibility that relate directly to public leisure services.

FITNESS AND AMATEUR SPORT

There are eight principal functions of the federal Fitness and Amateur Sport Branch. The *first* is to support national and international sporting activities. By getting involved in events such as the Olympics, Universiade, the Pan American Games, the Commonwealth Games and other international competitions, the federal government has demonstrated a willingness to promote Canada's international stature through sport and athlete development and through the support of special events. The *second* function of the Fitness and Amateur Sport Branch is to conduct, sponsor and promote applied research which can help to explain human performance and identify more effective ways to enhance that performance. The *third* function is the collection and dissemination of information about leisure lifestyle development, recreation activity and sport. This federal agency acts as a clearinghouse for consumable information generated through research. The *fourth* function is national planning and coordination. The federal government has a national agenda for sport and recreation, and this agenda is promoted through meetings of national organizations made up of provincial representatives with specific interests relating to public recreation. The *fifth* area of activity for Fitness and Amateur Sport is the development of standards. Many safety standards and guidelines for appropriate levels of service or performance in public recreation are developed by this branch. The *sixth* function is to support projects which are innovative and could contribute to a better understanding and appreciation of fitness, recreation and sport. The branch also supports demonstration projects which show the value or need for a particular recreation service (e.g., employee fitness programs). The *seventh* function is to develop leadership in the recreation and sport community. Coaching development and volunteer training are leadership development areas that are supported by the federal government in its effort to promote high performance athletes, increase levels of fitness, and create an awareness of the importance of recreation and leisure. The *eighth* function is to provide assistance for the disadvantaged. Over the years, Fitness and Amateur Sport has targeted groups with special needs and implemented programs to provide equal opportunities for recreation. The support of the Active Living Alliance: For Persons with a Disability is one example of the federal role in this area.

In order to accomplish these functions, Fitness and Amateur Sport is divided into two units: Fitness Canada, and Sport Canada. Fitness Canada offers services such as funding to national recreation and fitness associations such as CP/RA, Scouts Canada, and Canadian Fitness and Lifestyle and Research Institute. In addition, it supports the Alliance structures, develops national plans (most recently referred to as Blueprints for Action), liaises, with and provides support to, PARTICIPaction. Sport Canada supports the elite athlete system which includes funding to Canada's athletes who are competing internationally in sports recognized by Sport Canada, support to national sport governing bodies, support to hosting of international and national multisport events, among other activities. The budget for Fitness and Amateur sport is primarily invested in Sport Canada's activities.

ENVIRONMENT

The unit within Environment Canada with the most direct responsibility for recreation and leisure is the Canadian Parks Service (CPS). This unit is responsible for the development, maintenance and operation of all national parks and national historic sites in Canada. These parks and sites facilitate self-directed recreational activity as well as act as a setting for the direct delivery of recreation services provided by the CPS. By preserving and enhancing our unique natural resources and expanding outdoor recreation opportunities in the national parks, the federal government is contributing to another important leisure activity tourism.

Industry, Science, and Technology

Direct responsibility for recreational travel and tourism at the federal government level is given to Tourism Canada, a division of the Department of Industry Science and Technology. This unit promotes Canada as a travel destination, supports research concerning international pleasure travel and vacation behaviour, and encourages development of the national tourism system. Tourism was one of the areas of responsibility that the federal government had hoped to pass on to the provinces through the constitutional reform package debated in 1992. Although the reform package was rejected in a national referendum, it is likely that the provinces will again be given the opportunity to take on greater roles in regional and national tourism development.

Other Federal Government Units

Corrections Canada is involved in providing recreational opportunities for its wards, Health and Welfare Canada promotes healthy lifestyles through its health promotion unit and through its support of programs for seniors such as New Horizons. External Affairs gets involved with facilitating recreation and culture whenever international exchanges are a part of the program or event, and Consumer and Corporate Affairs watches over and regulates the business aspects of the leisure service industry. Though public recreation is not their primary concern, these federal government units have important roles to play in the development and delivery of leisure services in Canada.

Provincial Government Activities

Writing on behalf of the Government of Canada, Prime Minister Trudeau (1978) stated that he believes "recreation services to be the domain of no single government jurisdiction. Recreation is a very personal activity which demands the same recognition, respect and encouragement as is afforded to all other basic social concerns. No one jurisdiction can fully provide for all the recreational services required by the citizen and no jurisdiction can operate effectively without some impact on recreation." Clearly, the federal government, at that time, saw the need for sharing responsibility for publicly-supported recreation with the provincial partners of confederation. By and large, that attitude is still dominant among the current government.

Provincial governments in Canada have only recently played an extensive role in the provision or support of public recreation. They became active in this field of endeavour in response to public demand and financial incentives first offered by the federal government under the *National Physical Fitness Act* of 1943 and subsequently reintroduced in *Fitness and Amateur Sport Act* of 1961. Prior to that time, many provinces had established enabling legislation which provided for municipal involvement in recreation service delivery, but the provincial governments themselves did not offer programs of public recreation services (McFarland, 1970; Westland, 1979).

With increased provincial government activity after 1961, a broader range of services and opportunities became available to the public either directly (provincial parks, provincially sponsored arts and recreation events, etc.) or indirectly through financially assisted municipal programs. The public developed an expectation of provincial government involvement in leisure services.

In the late 1960s and early 1970s, changing priorities and redefinition of the scope of recreation by the federal government led to a significant reduction in federal support for provincial programs. While retrenchment was possible for the federal government, the expectations of the public made it impossible or politically unwise for the provinces to reduce their activity in this area. By convention, the provinces now have the major responsibility for recreation development.

All provincial and territorial governments in Canada have ministries or departments with a mandate to support public leisure services. A typical provincial government department having responsibility for recreation might also have a mandate with respect to parks, culture, heritage, tourism, sport, or health. A quick survey of department titles used during the past few years demonstrates the varied placement of leisure service responsibility in provincial government structures.

TABLE 5.1

A SAMPLING OF TITLES FORMERLY AND CURRENTLY USED FOR PROVINCIAL GOVERNMENT DEPARTMENTS OR MINISTRIES WITH PRIMARY CONCERN FOR PUBLIC LEISURE SERVICES

DEPARTMENT OR MINISTRY OF		
RECREATION, PARKS, AND WILDLIFE	SPORT AND RECREATION	HEALTH AND SPORT
Culture, Youth and Recreation	Recreation and Tourism	Culture and Recreation
Community Development	Tourism, Parks and Recreation	Fitness Recreation and Sport
Culture, Heritage and Citizenship	Education	

Through departments like those listed in Table 5.1, most provincial governments offer some direct sport, recreation, or cultural programs, but their contribution to public leisure services is mostly in the form of financial aid, planning assistance, regulation, leadership and other technical support to municipal or special interest organizations in the community recreation system.

Provincial leisure service departments are usually staffed by people who administer grants, provide consultation in a variety of areas (e.g., planning, programming, leadership, facility operation, etc.), conduct research, distribute information, conduct leadership training, monitor and regulate practices, and coordinate the activities of non-public agencies operating in the provincial recreation environment. The primary clients of provincial leisure service departments are most often identified as municipalities (local government), provincial sport and recreation associations, and the general public.

There are also provincial government departments that have indirect but important roles to play in the delivery and support of public leisure services. They include Labour and Employment (safety and workplace standards), Consumer and Corporate Affairs (regulation of the leisure service industry and protection for consumers of public, private and commercial recreation services), and Lotteries (distribution of publicly controlled lottery revenues that are earmarked for recreation, sport or cultural applications).

Municipal Government Activities

Most individual citizens receive public leisure services through their local government. It is a common (almost universal) practice of Canadian municipalities to establish commissions, boards and civic departments that have as their major function the promotion and facilitation of recreation, parks, sport, and culture.

The authority to establish these units of local government rests in 'enabling legislation' enacted by the provincial government. Enabling legislation is that which allows, but does not necessarily require, something to happen. Municipalities can exist only if the province has legislation to enable or allow it to do so, and departments within the municipal government structure must also be based on appropriate legislative authority.

Where they exist, municipal recreation departments in Canada are typically involved in providing community facilities (parks, playgrounds, halls, arenas, rinks, swimming pools, trails, etc.), offering programs (craft classes, learn-to-swim lessons, day camps, sports leagues, etc.), providing leadership and administrative support to local clubs and organizations, and regulating leisure opportunities through local by-laws. Their primary clients are the general public, local sport and recreation associations, and local special interest groups. In smaller centres, the recreation agency may be made up entirely of volunteers while larger communities may have trained, professional recreation staff to manage recreation services and coordinate volunteer activities. Regardless of the size of the municipal recreation organization, it will have a corps of volunteers as an important dimension of its human resource inventory. A particularly important volunteer body in the municipal setting is the recreation board or commission. The nature and impact of recreation boards is discussed later in this chapter.

Table 5.2 on the following page summarizes some of the important differences between public recreation providers at each of the three levels of government.

The Roles of Government in Public Leisure Service Delivery

Regardless of the level of government at which it operates, a public leisure service organization will play one or more of five distinct roles in discharging its duty to the recreation community and consuming public. It should be noted that the roles may differ according to the client group or the type of service being offered. In addition, they may differ in time according to the philosophical orientation of the policy making body. Perhaps the best description of these varying roles was developed by Burton (1982). The following is a summary of his work.

The first role that might be played is that of direct provider of services. As a direct provider, the government develops and maintains leisure facilities, operates programs and delivers services using public funds. The public agency applies financial, human and political resources to the offering of services to a general clientele. Examples of direct service provision in the public sector include national, provincial and municipal parks, city-operated swimming pools, playground programs, adult education courses, galleries, museums, and historic sites.

TABLE 5.2

A COMPARISON OF PUBLIC RECREATION INVOLVEMENT OF THE THREE LEVELS OF GOVERNMENT

LEVEL OF GOVERNMENT	AUTHORITY	MANDATE	PRIMARY CLIENTS
Federal	Convention	To promote health and well-being through recreation and sport	• National sport and recreation associations
Provincial	Convention	Varies, but may include the following: • To promote health and well-being through recreation. • To promote preservation, protection and enjoyment of natural resources. • To preserve cultural heritage. • To promote citizenship. • To stimulate economic development through the leisure industry.	• Municipalities • Provincial sport and recreation associations
Municipal	Enabling Legislation	Usually akin to the following: • To encourage the development of recreation programs and facilities • To act as a catalyst for recreation development in the community	• The general public • Local sport and recreation associations • Local special interest groups

The second role is that of an arm's length provider of services. To act in this role the government may create a special-purpose organization that is publicly supported, but operates outside the normal apparatus of government. The arm's length organization is funded by the government and receives direction from a government appointed board of directors. Crown corporations (e.g., CBC, Alberta Sport Council) and regulatory commissions are examples of arm's length agencies through which the government provides services.

Enabling or coordinating services is the third role that a government recreation agency might play. In this role the government identifies agencies that could provide the needed leisure services and then encourages them and helps to coordinate their efforts, resources and activities. This is often achieved through leadership training programs and government supported consultation services. More recently, the federal government has done this through the creation of *alliances* which are organizations of organizations to promote greater coordination.

The fourth role involves supporting and acting as a patron of leisure service organizations. The government may recognize that an existing organization already provides a valuable service and can be encouraged to continue doing so through specialized support (usually financial). Recipient organizations could be from the public, private not-for-profit, or commercial sectors. Many cultural organizations receive this kind of support from public agents.

Finally, the government may act as a legislator and regulator of activities and organizations. Using its authority to create laws and establish regulations, the government can exercise protective control over agencies and individuals engaged in the provision of leisure services. In addition, it can be used to regulate personal behaviour in leisure environments such as national or local parks.

As illustrated in Figure 5.1, the roles are distinguished primarily by the degree to which the government provides financial support and program/operational direction in the delivery of specific leisure services.

In discussing the roles played by government in the delivery of recreation and leisure services, the question comes to mind: What is the 'best' role or the 'right' role for government now and in the future? The first part of the question can only be answered on the basis of what we believe about government and about the way it should influence our lives. Some believe that government should not play any role in our leisure while others see extensive and direct government involvement as being both essential and desirable. Some also recognize that one role could be appropriate in a particular situation but not be suitable in another.

The second part of the question about future roles can be answered only if we are willing to speculate. If the present is a good indicator of the future, we could take note of the way that government is currently withdrawing direct services and

FIGURE 5.1
MAJOR ROLES OF PUBLIC RECREATION AGENCIES

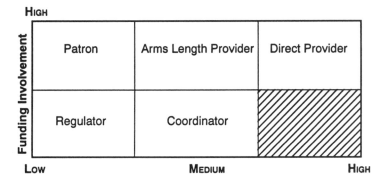

resources and predict that there will be more emphasis placed on governments acting in the enabler and coordinator role and less evidence of direct service provision. In the 1990s, the Canadian public seems to want less intrusive government and less taxation, and this will limit the ability of the public recreation sub-system to provide direct services or to sponsor arm's length or autonomous recreation agencies.

Whatever the future holds for public recreation, there is little doubt that governments and their agencies will continue to respond to the demands of their constituents for recreation and leisure services that promote the common good and the health of the community. There is no legal requirement for public sector involvement in recreation, but the conventional wisdom and practice establishes public recreation as a fundamental aspect of our community lives.

Developing a National Policy on Recreation

In 1974, the provincial government ministers responsible for recreation met in Edmonton to establish a definition of recreation and to articulate their shared beliefs about the essential nature of public recreation services. At the conclusion of this conference, they passed the following resolution (National Recreation Statement, 1987, pp. 5-6):

> *Whereas* recreation includes all of those activities in which an individual chooses to participate in his leisure time, and is not confined solely to sports and physical recreation programs, but includes artistic, creative, cultural, social, and intellectual activities;
>
> *and whereas* recreation is a fundamental human need for citizens of all ages and interests and for both sexes and is essential to the psychological, social, and physical well-being of man; and whereas society is rapidly changing and leisure time is increasing:
>
> *be it therefore resolved* that this Conference recognize the fact that recreation is a social service in the same way that health and education are considered as social services and that recreation's purpose should be (a) to assist individual and community development; (b) to improve the quality of life; and (c) to enhance social functioning. Such recognition will indicate the constitutional responsibility of the Provinces and Territories in recreation services.

In adopting this resolution, the provincial ministers emphasized that the primary role for recreation development belonged to the provinces and territories. This was supported by the federal government at the 1978 Recreation Ministers Conference in Montreal when the Minister of State for Fitness and Amateur Sport declared "I do indeed recognize the primacy of the Provinces in the field of recreation" (*National Recreation Statement*, 1987, p. 6). The Provinces added that "primacy does not mean exclusivity" and "the resources and the cooperation of all jurisdictions and a wide variety of private and community agencies are required to meet the recreation needs of all citizens" (*National Recreation Statement*, 1987, p. 6).

Work on detailing the implications of this resolution and the federal minister's declaration continued and, during a 1983 meeting in New Brunswick, the Provincial Ministers Responsible for Recreation and Sport (1983) issued An *Inter-Provincial Recreation Statement*. This 19-page statement defines provincial and municipal roles and establishes mechanisms for inter-governmental and intra-governmental cooperation. The *Inter-Provincial Recreation Statement* is the keystone in the complex structure of public sector involvement in the delivery of recreation services. This subsequently led to the signing of the *National Recreation Statement* in 1987. The major impact of this document was that it signalled the federal government's agreement to the arrangement of federal and provincial responsibilities with respect to recreation development in Canada. The *Inter-Provincial Recreation Statement* was an agreement among the provinces but did not include the federal government as a signatory. It should be noted that both of these documents also assert the roles of municipalities in the provision of recreation services. This is a result of the municipal level of government not being recognized as an independent form of government but rather is, as the Constitution asserts, a function of provincial government control.

As noted in Chapter Two in our discussion of history, the most significant aspect of the recent years, has been the pronouncement of public policy in recreation by various provincial governments (Ontario Ministry of Tourism and Recreation, 1987; Alberta Recreation and Parks, 1988). This arose as a direct consequence of the Inter-Provincial Recreation Statement and the National Recreation Statement. In these documents, the respective governments agreed to develop a policy concerning recreation. This is important because it becomes a statement of the beliefs of a government concerning recreation's value and is used to base decisions on funding of programs and services. It is also important because once stated, it becomes a benchmark for subsequent governing parties to base their decisions concerning recreation. Moreover, they are then obligated to explain departures from past policy (even if it is likely to result in increased financial support). Thus, this move by the provincial governments has been positive for the development of recreation in Canada.

Sport, Recreation, and the Public Sector

In describing recreation and leisure, most Canadians would probably include in their list of illustrative activities some type of organized sport. Most recreation practitioners would also identify sport as an area for which they have some professional responsibility, but would be quick to explain that recreation is more than just sport.

The delivery of sport services in Canada is dependent on all sectors, but relies heavily on the public sector for introductory and basic skill development programs, as well as for facilities. Sport is an important part of the community recreation program and, through sport, other personal and lifelong recreational skills and attitudes can be developed. This is why public sector recreation agencies at the community level assist in the delivery of sport programs that are essentially governed at the provincial or national level by organizations who are extremely focused on achievement and performance in one specialized activity.

The fact that community recreation leaders are interested in the recreational, mass-participation aspects of sport, and sport governing bodies at provincial and national levels direct much of their attention to high performance and elite athlete development often causes conflict between the two groups. The conflict is fuelled by what is perceived to be inequality in the allocation and distribution of resources. Whether justified or not, sport organizations are frequently cast as having bundles of money to support a very small number of people, while community recreation agencies feel that they must serve a large, diverse population with limited resources. This strained relationship is often manifested in duplication of structures and programs, and less-than-efficient correlation and coordination of activities. Balancing sport development objectives and mass recreation needs is one of the major challenges faced by public recreation organizations.

Financing Public Recreation

Public recreation is financed primarily through tax revenues. Federal and provincial revenue is largely dependent upon income tax. Property taxes form the largest source of revenue for municipal governments. In addition, local school taxes are also used to support the provision of recreation services. The amount of tax money required to develop and operate recreation facilities, programs and services can be reduced by the amount of money generated through charges and user fees, license and permit sales, gift giving, and access to lottery funds. In recent years, government controlled lotteries have had a major impact on the availability of financial resources to the public recreation sector.

A 1983 report prepared for the Ontario government referred to recreation as: Recreation...a changing society's economic giant (Ontario Ministry of Tourism and Recreation, 1983).

The report emphasized the significant financial commitment of that province's government to recreation and detailed the extent to which personal and family recreation was subsidized by the public purse. A more recent study by Harper and Johnston (1992) focused on municipal financing of recreation and identified the variation in municipal taxation to support recreation in the four western provinces. Figure 5.2 facilitates a comparison of key results.

It should be noted that some of the variation in municipal taxes required to support recreation can be explained by different provincial government support programs as well as by variable success in recovering costs through more direct means such as user fees and charges. In the Harper and Johnston (1992) study, a common characteristic of the Western Canadian municipalities where average per capita local tax support for recreation was lowest was the absence of long-term debt charges and current capital costs. The one exception was in Manitoba where the Rural Municipality of Springfield (population 9,836) had the lowest local tax cost for a municipality in that province even though it had a relatively major capital project underway. Springfield kept local tax costs down by achieving a remarkably low operational deficit (under $51,000). The other municipalities with the lowest per capita costs in their respective provinces were Creston, British Columbia (population 15,000), the County of Stettler, Alberta (population 5,959), and Delisle,

Saskatchewan (population 986). Delisle's costs were all operational, and it managed to generate program and user fee revenues in excess of those operational costs.

The communities where residents paid the highest average amount of local taxes to sustain public recreation were Tumbler Ridge, British Columbia (population 5,000), Swan Hills, Alberta (population 2,510), Creighton, Saskatchewan (population 1,624), and Leaf Rapids, Manitoba (population 1,526). In all of these communities, long-term debt charges combined with current capital project costs to

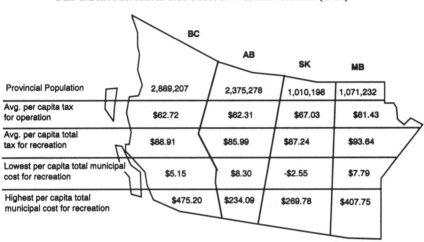

FIGURE 5.2
PER CAPITA MUNICIPAL TAX COSTS IN WESTERN CANADA (1989)

	BC	AB	SK	MB
Provincial Population	2,889,207	2,375,278	1,010,198	1,071,232
Avg. per capita tax for operation	$62.72	$62.31	$67.03	$81.43
Avg. per capita total tax for recreation	$88.91	$85.99	$87.24	$93.64
Lowest per capita total municipal cost for recreation	$5.15	$8.30	-$2.55	$7.79
Highest per capita total municipal cost for recreation	$475.20	$234.09	$269.78	$407.75

keep the local tax bill for recreation high. The per capita local tax support for recreation in the major western cities (Vancouver, Victoria, Edmonton, Calgary, Regina, Saskatoon, and Winnipeg) ranged from $70.92 to $102.50.

Approaches to Municipal Leisure Service Delivery

Typical public recreation agencies in Canadian municipalities are departments of civic government that receive advice and/or direction from a recreation board or commission. As permitted by provincial legislation and local by-laws, a town, city or municipal district establishes a department with responsibility for recreation programs, facilities and services, and then seeks volunteers to be appointed to serve on a board that gives counsel to policy-makers and administrators regarding the principles and practices that will govern the delivery of public leisure services. Sometimes, the board has authority to hire or release department staff and to administer the department's budget. It may also have delegated to it the authority to set civic policy on matters within its mandated area. Such boards are referred to as policy or operational boards. Where the board only has authority to advise, it is referred to as an advisory board. Most recreation boards in Canada are advisory and, unlike in the United States, only one is elected by the public (Vancouver Parks Board is the exception).

Recent research by Searle (1989) suggested that municipal recreation and park boards may not be operating as effectively as might be hoped. In his study, Searle noted that there was a significant gap between board members and recreation directors concerning the power each has in the decision-making process. The board members reported less power than the directors and the directors sought to maintain that differential. Unfortunately, this situation gives rise to questions about the viability of recreation boards. If the directors do not give board members an equal role in decision-making and board members continue to perceive this, it is likely that the board will wither and fade away. The advantage of the recreation board is in the role it can play as an advocate for recreation in the community and with the elected council, as a sounding board for new ideas, as a "sixth sense" for the recreation director gaining insightful feedback from the community, and for promoting volunteer development in the town. The future of the recreation board in municipal recreation hinges, at least in part, on it regaining its role and having stature in the community.

An issue which must be addressed when establishing or reviewing the municipal leisure service delivery system is the cultural appropriateness of advisory or policy boards for recreation. In certain cultural or political contexts they may be extremely valued and, therefore, extremely valuable. In a study of the impacts of a formal recreation structure in remote northern communities, the appropriateness of the structure (which included a recreation advisory board) was questioned (Searle, Mactavish, Adam-Sdrolias, Brayley & Winther, 1992). These researchers suggested that traditional leadership beliefs and styles that are unique to such communities may not be entirely consistent with the consultancy form of leadership being imposed. It is important that the structure of the public recreation delivery system reflect the values and cultural demands of the society whose needs it is established to meet.

Public leisure service agencies may have broad or narrow mandates. Some are charged with responding only to physical recreation issues. Others are responsible for a wide range of leisure opportunities and resources including visual and performing arts, sports, fitness, outdoor recreation, leisure education, family recreation, parks (including boulevards and cemeteries), and local tourism. Similarly, recreation boards may have a limited range of responsibilities or be expected to oversee recreation development in its broadest sense. In some situations the recreation board has taken on the role of the local arts council, but this aspect of recreation has more often been served by a separate delivery mechanism and governing structure.

Whatever form it takes, the public recreation delivery system can function both as a catalyst for positive social change as well as a culturally neutral provider of marketable services. Godbey (1991) concluded that "the basis for operating public recreation, park and leisure services has been transformed from a series of reform agendas for society to, essentially, public demand. That is, the notion that government provides such services simply because people want them rather than because they produce certain benefits." That transformation has not been complete and most public recreation agencies in Canada have found a level of comfort in proactively championing certain causes (e.g., active living, health and fitness, family unity, community pride, etc.) while, at the same time, responding to public demand for programs and services that are justified purely by the willingness of the community to pay for them.

Summary

This chapter has provided an overview of the different roles and responsibilities associated with different levels of government involving respect to leisure services. There are clearly delineated roles for each level of government as a result of the recent adoption of the *National Recreation Statement*. However, despite the role clarification, there remains disputes in interpretation of these roles and the exact responsibilities that accompany them. Nonetheless, there continues an active national dialogue on the development of leisure services in Canada. The content of the chapter has also provided you with some background on the different roles government may play in the provision of leisure services and the means of financial support for public leisure services.

1. Describe the role of Canada's constitution in determining what government's role is in leisure services?

2. What are the principal activities of the Federal Fitness and Amateur Sport Branch?

3. What motivated provincial action in the area of leisure services?

4. What are some the typical services provincial government departments provide?

5. Distinguish the municipal role from the provincial and federal role in leisure services. How are they similar?

6. What are some of the issues facing municipal recreation boards?

7. Describe the five roles government can play in the provision of leisure services according to Burton?

8. Describe the significance of the *Inter-Provincial Recreation Statement* and the *National Recreation Statement*.

9. What is the difference in revenue sources between municipal and provincial governments?

10. What trends are apparent from the Harper and Johnson study?

References

Alberta Recreation and Parks. (1988). *Foundations for Action Corporate Aims for the Ministry of Recreation and Parks*. Edmonton, AB: Author.

Burton, T. L. (1982). *The roles of government in the leisure services delivery system*. A paper presented at the VII Commonwealth and International Conference on Sport, Physical Education, Recreation and Dance.

Godbey, G. (1991). Redefining Public Parks and Recreation. *Parks and Recreation 23*(10), pp. 56-75.

Harper, J. A. & Johnston, B. L. (1992). Balancing the scales in public parks and recreation departments. *Recreation Canada, 50*(4), pp. 18-20.

McFarland, E. M. (1970). *The history of public recreation in Canada*. Ottawa, ON: Canadian Parks/Recreation Association.

Murphy, J. F. & Howard, D. R. (1977). *Delivery of community leisure services: An holistic approach*. Philadelphia, PA: Lea and Febiger.

National Recreation Statement. (1987). Ottawa, ON: Fitness and Amateur Sport.

Ontario Ministry of Tourism and Recreation. (1987). *A community recreation policy statement*. Toronto, ON: Author.

Ontario Ministry of Tourism and Recreation. (1983). *Recreation...A changing society's economic giant*. Toronto, ON: Author.

Provincial Ministers Responsible for Recreation and Sport. (1983). *Inter-provincial recreation statement*. New Brunswick, NB: Author

Searle, M. S. (1989). Testing the reciprocity norm in a recreation management setting. *Leisure Sciences, 11*, pp. 353-365.

Searle, M., Mactavish, J., Adam-Sdrolias, H., Brayley, R. & Winther, N. (1992). *An assessment of the northern recreation director pilot project*. Winnipeg, MB: Manitoba Culture, Heritage and Citizenship.

Trudeau, P. E. (1978). Prime Ministerial correspondence to Mr. Emile J. St. Amand, President of the Canadian Parks/Recreation Association (dated July 12, 1978).

Westland, C. (1979). *Fitness and amateur sport in Canada: The federal government's programme: An historical perspective*. Ottawa, ON: Canadian Parks/Recreation Association.

Chapter Six

Volunteers and The Voluntary Sector

Overview

PURPOSE

The purpose of this chapter is to examine the nature of volunteering, voluntary agencies, and various issues associated with the not-for-profit sector. We will examine where Canadians volunteer their time and energy, the kinds of activities they engage in as volunteers, and the role and importance of volunteers in leisure service organizations.

LEARNING OBJECTIVES

At the completion of this chapter, you should be able to:

1. describe the social and economic importance of volunteering in Canada,

2. describe some of the characteristics of voluntary leisure organizations and what distinguishes them from other sectors of the leisure service delivery system,

3. describe and explain the motives of volunteers, and

4. identify and discuss many of the issues facing the voluntary sector.

Volunteers and The Voluntary Sector

An important subsystem of the community recreation system, as described by
Murphy and Howard (1977) is the private not-for-profit subsystem. Like the public
subsystem and unlike the commercial subsystem, private organizations that offer
recreation services without striving for financial profit rely heavily on volunteers.
This chapter discusses volunteers and the delivery of leisure services through the
voluntary sector (which has, elsewhere in this book, also been referred to as the
private not-for-profit sector).

Volunteering in Canada has a long history and tradition. Volunteers have served
the public good in many ways through their varied and valuable efforts. Examples
of Confederation-era Canadians voluntarily coming together through formal
association to help each other can be found in the formation of the Society of Saint
Vincent de Paul in Quebec City in 1846, the Children's Aid Society of Toronto in
1891, and the St. John Ambulance Society which was organized in 1877
(Lautenschlager, 1992). Recreation-related examples of organizations for volunteers
include the YMCA in Montreal (established in 1851), the YWCA in Saint John, New
Brunswick (founded in 1870), and the National Council of Women which was
organized in 1897 in Vancouver, Winnipeg, Toronto, Montreal, and Halifax. The
National Council of Women played a central role in the development of the
playground movement and the eventual establishment of formal public recreation
services in many Canadian cities. Further momentum for the involvement of
community volunteers in recreation was demonstrated in the rise of community
leagues in Edmonton during the 1920s (McFarland, 1970). The community leagues
were established to help volunteers organize and provide local recreation and sport
services for their neighbourhoods.

Volunteers are advocates, providers of services and programs, fund raisers, and
most of all, helpers. They are helpers without whose help we would be a substantially
poorer nation. Graff (1989) estimated the labour value of volunteering in Ontario to be
worth $4.5 billion. In Nova Scotia, volunteers are estimated to make a labour equivalent
contribution of just under $500 million and, in Quebec, the value of volunteer work is
estimated to be $2.5 billion. In Saskatchewan, the estimate is near $600 million (Ross &
Shillington, 1990). These figures are a product of the total recorded number of hours
volunteered by persons in each province and the average hourly wage of workers in the
province (e.g., $12.85 in Ontario in 1988, $11.07 in Nova Scotia). It is considered to be
better to use average wages in the estimation than minimum wage which tends to
significantly undervalue the contribution (Fisher, 1988).

Consider the value of volunteering in Canada where, in 1986-87, 5.3 million
Canadians gave one billion hours of unpaid labour or, on average, 16 hours per
month! Ross and Shillington (1990) estimated this to be worth $13.2 billion (in 1990
dollars). If you converted the total number of hours volunteered in Canada in one
year to full-time job equivalents, you would realize that 617,000 jobs would have to
be created to do the work of the volunteers. It is extremely unlikely that the
organizations from across all sectors of the economy which rely on volunteers could
find the resources to replace them with full-time paid staff.

Volunteering in Canada

According to the 1987 National Survey on Volunteer Activity which was conducted by Statistics Canada on behalf of the Secretary of State, 27 percent of Canadians volunteer their services through some organization. This landmark study, which is cited extensively in this chapter, involved approximately 70,000 Canadians aged 15 and over and examined formal volunteering over a 12-month period. Formal volunteering was defined as "volunteering through an organization" and included work with which the volunteer may have been assisted by paid staff. Formal volunteer work, according to Ross and Shillington, (1989) is often performed on a regular or planned basis and involves a degree of commitment to the recipient organization.

What do we know about these Canadians who volunteer? Does the rate of voluntary activity vary by where they live? Why do people volunteer? To what organizations do Canadians prefer to give their time? These are just some of the questions this survey addressed. In addition, it provides some insight into the reasons Canadians volunteer for leisure and recreation organizations, and it helps to identify the characteristics of volunteers.

As stated above, over one in four Canadians volunteer each year. Twenty-nine percent of all women over age 15 in Canada volunteer while 25 percent of men 15 years and over volunteer (Catano, 1989). Among married men and women these percentages rise with 32 percent of married women volunteer and 28 percent of married men. Table 6.1 shows the percentage of volunteers in each province and the average number of hours given each year by those volunteers.

TABLE 6.1

PERCENT OF INDIVIDUALS IN EACH PROVINCE VOLUNTEERING AS PERCENT OF PROVINCIAL POPULATION AND AVERAGE NUMBER OF HOURS PER VOLUNTEER PER YEAR[1]

Province	Percent of Population	Average Hours Per Year
British Columbia	29	205
Alberta	40	172
Saskatchewan	38	183
Manitoba	38	161
Ontario	26	189
Quebec	19	206
New Brunswick	30	211
Prince Edward Island	34	148
Nova Scotia	32	188
Newfoundland and Labrador	26	206
CANADA	27	191

1 Data were not available for the Yukon or Northwest Territories.

What Do Volunteers Do?

There were some differences in the activities of Canadian men and women in the organizations for which they volunteered. For comparison, the top ten volunteer activities are listed in Table 6.2 (Catano, 1989).

TABLE 6.2
TOP TEN ACTIVITIES IN WHICH CANADIANS ENGAGED WHILE
VOLUNTEERING FOR AN ORGANIZATION

Activity	Percent of volunteers that do the activity		
	Total	Males	Females
1. Fund raising, canvassing for funds	38	37	39
2. Providing of information	36	40	34
3. Organizing events, supervising or coordinating activities	35	38	32
4. Sitting as a board member	26	33	21
5. Recruiting volunteers	24	26	22
6. Counselling, providing advice, friendly support	23	26	12
7. Promoting ideas, researching, writing, speaking	22	25	19
8. Teaching, educating	22	24	21
9. Preparing or serving	20	11	27
10. Office work, administration, bookkeeping, library work	17	15	19

There are some notable differences between men and women as it concerns their volunteering activities. There are 5 activities among the 25 examined in which the participation of women and men differ by more than ten percent. It was observed that:

- 27 percent of women prepared or served food compared to 11 percent of men,
- 18 percent of women made things compared to 5 percent of men,
- 33 percent of men sat as board members compared to 21 percent of women,
- 20 percent of men did coaching, refereeing, or judging compared to 7 percent of women, and
- 17 percent of men repaired, maintained, or built facilities compared to 4 percent of women.

In response to the question: "Did you help run this organization?," 42 percent of men answered in the affirmative while 32 percent of women answered that they had served in a leadership role.

These responses represent rather stereotypical views of male and female roles. There is, however, no valid justification for the low number of women volunteers involved in boards of directors and in running the organizations.

It was also clear in this important study that women did more informal voluntary compassionate service such as helping someone with their shopping or getting to appointments, baby-sitting for free for friends or neighbours, visiting the sick or elderly, etc. Obviously, the blurred roles of women as caregiver, professional, wife, mother, daughter, friend, and "volunteer" make their lives more complex, and the measures of formal volunteering clearly do not fairly represent their extensive contribution to society. It is because of these multiple roles women play that the national statistic concerning the average number of hours per year volunteered by women must be viewed with some circumspect. According to the 1987 National Survey on Volunteer Activity, women averaged 106 hours per year for the organizations in which they served as volunteers while the average for men was 118 hours (Catano, 1989).

DEMOGRAPHICS OF CANADIAN VOLUNTEERS

Men and women volunteers belong to religious organizations in equal proportion. They are equally satisfied with their standard of living, they are similar in age, educational attainment, and household income. They are equally likely to live in urban or rural settings. In Canada, 23 percent of individuals living in large urban areas volunteer compared to 32 percent of rural citizens (Gagne, 1989). Major Canadian cities with the highest volunteering rate were Edmonton (38 percent), Winnipeg (35 percent), and Halifax (34 percent). Cities where the participation rates in volunteering as a percentage of the population were lower than the national average of 27 percent were Montreal (17 percent), Toronto (21 percent) and Vancouver (23 percent) (MacLeod, 1989).

The major difference that is demonstrated between volunteers and non-volunteers is employment status. Seventy-three percent of male volunteers were employed full-time compared to 38 percent of women. Of the females surveyed, 40 percent were not in the labour force while only 16 percent of the males were in this category. The results of this breakdown of labour force involvement statistics are similar to those of the same kind of analysis of the general population. According to Statistics Canada (1988), 66 percent of males over age 15 are employed full-time compared to 39 percent of women. Twenty-three percent of males are not in the labour force compared to 43 percent of females. Seniors represent 21 percent of all volunteers in Canada.

Seniors who participate in formal volunteer activities rate themselves healthier than other seniors. In fact, 67 percent of seniors who volunteer report that they are in good health compared to 44 percent of seniors who do not volunteer. These senior volunteers tend to be more religious, more involved in their community, and have had more formal education. They volunteer for the same activities as do younger adults, and generally give more time for their volunteer endeavours than their younger counterparts (Brennan, 1989).

With respect to income characteristics, it was observed that one does not have to be rich to be a volunteer. Senior volunteers generally have lower incomes than their younger counterparts. Thirty-four percent reported an annual income of $19,999.00 or less while this is only true for 14 percent of the younger respondents. Nineteen percent of the seniors reported incomes in excess of $40,000.00 per year compared to 27 percent of the non-seniors. Interestingly, 59 percent of seniors reported that they were not at all concerned about the costs of volunteering (Brennan, 1989).

THE MOTIVES OF VOLUNTEERS

Why do Canadians volunteer? What motivates them? In Chapter Four, we discussed the central role of intrinsic motivation in determining whether an activity is perceived as a leisure experience. Keep this in mind as you review the reasons for volunteering. How many are intrinsic motives and how many are extrinsic motives? As can be seen from the data in Table 6.3, the most important reasons for volunteering are intrinsic.

TABLE 6.3

TOP TEN REASONS FOR VOLUNTEERING (THOSE RATED VERY IMPORTANT[1])
FOR ALL RESPONDENTS AND BY SEX

Reason	Total	Males	Females
1. Helping others	63	57	68
2. Helping a cause you believe in	60	57	68
3. Doing something you like to do	55	52	57
4. Feeling that you've accomplished something	54	51	57
5. Doing work that benefits your children, your family or yourself	43	40	45
6. Using your skills and experience	36	35	36
7. Meeting people, companionship	35	32	37
8. Learning new skills	29	27	31
9. Fulfilling religious obligations or beliefs	23	20	26
10. Feeling you owe something to the community	21	2	22

1 The items were measured on a four point scale ranging from not at all important to very important.

Men and women seemed equally committed to their volunteer efforts. Fifty percent of women described their volunteer activities as very important while this was the case for 45 percent of the men surveyed.

How do you get individuals to volunteer? When respondents across all age groups are taken together, 70 percent stated that they were prepared to volunteer more time. Fifty percent of seniors reported that they first volunteered because someone asked them to. Another 25 percent stated that they were prepared to volunteer more hours. It is also important to consider the cultural changes in the country as recruitment of volunteers must be done with sensitivity to the multicultural issues that face the nation.

THE RECIPIENTS OF VOLUNTEER EFFORTS

For whom do men and women volunteer their efforts? Table 6.4 lists twelve agency types and the proportion of males and females that volunteer their services for these types of agencies. The big winners in the game of attracting volunteer efforts are agencies that have a religious and/or recreational mandate. Those of the former type tend to attract women volunteers, while leisure, recreation and sport organizations are well-supported by male volunteers.

TABLE 6.4
COMPARISON OF MALE AND FEMALE VOLUNTEER ACTIVITIES BY ORGANIZATIONAL GROUP

Organizational Group	Total	Males	Females
1. Religion (e.g., church, synagogue, or mosque)	17	14	20
2. Leisure, recreation, and sport	16	23	11
3. Education and Youth Development (e.g., 4-H, Teachers on Wheels, Canadian Parents for French)	14	2	16
4. Health	10	5	14
5. Social service (e.g., Meals on Wheels, day care centres, Association for Community Living, St. Vincent de Paul Society, group homes, Royal Canadian Legion)	9	7	10
6. Multidomain (e.g., Red Cross, YMCA, YWCA, Lions' Club, Elk's Club, Knights of Columbus, Beta Sigma Phi)	9	10	8
7. Society, public benefit (e.g., United Way, Community Chest, United Jewish Appeal)	8	9	8
8. Employment and economic interests (e.g., Junior Achievement)	6	8	4
9. Arts, culture, and humanities (e.g., Toronto Symphony Orchestra, Prairie Theatre Exchange)	4	4	4
9. Other and unknown	3	4	3
10. Environment and wildlife	2	3	1
11. Law and justice (e.g., Elizabeth Fry Society)	1	1	1
12. International/foreign (e.g., OXFAM)	1	1	1

Sectarian and Non-Sectarian Voluntary Organizations

The organizations that comprise the voluntary sector come from sectarian and non-sectarian orientations. Those with religious foundations may be supported by Catholic, Jewish, Mormon, and other faiths. The Catholic Church has long supported youth programs and social gatherings for women. The Jewish Welfare Board works with Jewish community centres and Young Men's Hebrew Associations across North

America which provide a wide array of leisure services from fitness to camping, from seniors programs to day care. The Mormon Church is organized entirely around volunteers, with a lay ministry that oversees compassionate service, scouting, athletics and fitness, and family recreational activities. Many of the services offered by religious organizations are available to the general community, although they are primarily used by the members of the faith that established the service. These organizations sometimes become non-sectarian over time as has essentially happened with the Young Men's Christian Association.

Examples of the non-sectarian organizations include everything from community centres to 4-H Clubs. These organizations do not have a religious foundation nor do they have any elements in their constitution that suggest a belief in some faith. These organizations may seek to redress many of the same social concerns that gave rise to many religious organizations' services, but they are done as a matter of community spirit without any other implication. This variety of religiously based and non-sectarian agencies contributes to the diversity of services available in the community, and it is likely that the hardships or demise of one would be felt by the larger community since their services are important to those who utilize them.

Volunteers in Leisure, Recreation, and Sport Organizations

Volunteering in leisure and sport organizations ranks second among both urban and rural volunteers but a greater percentage of rural volunteers serve with leisure and sport organizations—14 percent in urban areas compared to 18 percent in rural areas (Faid, 1989). In another survey by Decima Research in 1987, respondents identified minor sports, community centre, and guides and scouts as three of the top eight most frequently mentioned organizations for whom they volunteer (Arlett, Bell, & Thompson, 1988). Arlett et al. (1988) also noted that recreation and amateur sports organizations are the sixth most frequently cited areas where big business gives its financial support in Canada while it is the third most frequently cited target for small business giving. Interestingly, both small and big businesses were most interested in contributing to organizations that promoted health and assisted in the prevention or control of illness. Thus, the more the health benefits of recreation activities can be identified and documented, the greater the likelihood of philanthropic support from the private sector.

Kent (1989) reports that almost 1.5 million Canadians volunteered in leisure, recreation, and sport organizations in 1987. These volunteers gave an average of 118 hours. Kent described the average volunteer in leisure, recreation, and sport organizations as "male, employed full-time, has a household income of $40,000 or more per year, has some postsecondary education, and lives in a major metropolitan area" (p. 1). It is interesting that in our field, males are over-represented as a percent of individuals volunteering compared to the national average (60 percent in leisure, recreation, and sport organizations versus 45 percent for the national average). Table 6.5 provides a profile of the volunteer in leisure, recreation, and sport organizations.

Volunteers in leisure, recreation, and sport organizations are involved in a variety of tasks. Many of these are similar to the tasks of volunteers reported in Table 6.2. Volunteers in leisure, recreation, and sport organizations report that they spend 44 percent of their time organizing, supervising, or coordinating activities (35 percent was the national average across all types of volunteering), 40 percent as fund raisers (38 percent was the national average for fund raising), 40 percent coach, referee or judge (compared to the 22 percent national average for those who volunteer in teaching capacities), 37 percent provide information to others (compared to the national average of 36 percent), 29 percent sit on their boards of directors (26 percent was the non-leisure average), and 29 percent recruit volunteers (compared with 24 percent in all voluntary organizations). Kent (1989) has also noted that those in leadership positions in leisure, recreation, and sport organizations tend to reflect more traditional or stereotypical perspectives. She notes that "individuals with higher education levels and higher annual incomes were more involved with managing supervising and coordinating than other volunteers" (p. 2).

TABLE 6.5

A PROFILE OF VOLUNTEERS IN LEISURE, RECREATION, AND SPORT ORGANIZATIONS

Sex	60 percent male 40 percent female
Education	6 percent have less than grade nine education 48 percent some secondary education 11 percent have some postsecondary education 34 percent have completed postsecondary education
Age	7 percent 15-19 years 79 percent 20-65 years 14 percent 65 years and older
Income	42 percent have annual household income less than $30,000 20 percent have annual household income between $30,000-39,999 24 percent have annual household income between $40,000-59,999 14 percent have annual household income greater than $60,000
Residence Location	34 percent live in major metropolitan areas 20 percent in other cities 11 percent in other large metropolitan areas 10 percent in minor metropolitan areas 25 percent in rural and small urban areas
Employment Status	65 percent are employed full-time 10 percent are employed part-time 4 percent are unemployed 21 percent are not in the labour force

Interestingly, many volunteers in our field would be interested in giving more time to the organization with which they are involved. Indeed, according to the 1987 national survey, 31 percent would provide more time on a regular basis, and 39 percent on a special or emergency basis. Most of these individuals volunteered because they were asked by someone. Personal contact was, in fact, the reason for volunteering cited by 65 percent of those surveyed. Obviously, more than the 29 percent of the leisure, recreation, and sport organizations that recruit volunteers need to use personal networks to successfully attract more volunteers.

ARE THERE BENEFITS TO THE VOLUNTEER?

The volunteer experience is also supposed to provide opportunities for individuals to gain something from their experience. In other words, there should be a fair exchange between what the agency gains and what the individual gains from the experience. Yet many people report that they do not gain any skills or knowledge in their volunteer experiences. This will likely create a problem of retention and, ultimately, recruitment. Among those reporting gains in knowledge or skills in the 1987 survey, volunteers in leisure, recreation, and sport reported that they acquired a number of different benefits. These were interpersonal skills (42 percent), organization/managerial skills (36 percent), and communication skills (29 percent). Females reported gaining more skills in fund raising while males gained more coaching skills. Older adults (those age 65 and older) reported less gains in all categories of skill. Also, volunteering in leisure, recreation, and sport organizations does not seem to create opportunities to learn about the environment, health issues, women's issues, political, or legal matters. Only nine percent reported any gains in these areas.

Unfortunately, it appears that little attention is paid to the training of volunteers in leisure, recreation, and sport organizations. Sixty-three percent of those who volunteered in leisure, recreation, and sport organizations reported that they did not receive any training, 21 percent received the right amount of training, while 11 percent stated that they received too little training. This compares with an Alberta Recreation and Parks study in 1988 which found that only 17 percent of volunteers received any kind of formal training prior to taking on the volunteer duties. However, the Alberta study did find that 40 percent of the volunteers in recreation received on-the-job or informal training. This, coupled with the information on benefits derived from the experience, may be indicative of the challenge that lays ahead in the management of volunteers in leisure, recreation, and sport organizations. Despite this lapse in training and only 50 percent reporting benefits from their experience, 86 percent of these volunteers reported either being very satisfied or somewhat satisfied with their involvement.

Voluntary Organizations in Leisure and Recreation

What are the voluntary sector organizations that provide leisure services? Are they just the obvious examples that readily come to mind such as the YM-YWCAs with their children's programs and camps, or are they senior citizen centres with their special programs and services? The range of organizations providing recreation and leisure services is extensive. In this section we will attempt to introduce some of the more familiar voluntary agencies providing leisure services in Canada and in the subsequent section provide a couple of examples of the new ones that have emerged.

In Canada, the Boy Scouts (known officially as Scouts Canada) was started in 1908 just one year after the movement started in England under Lord Baden-Powell (Scouts Canada, n.d.). The aim of Scouts Canada is to "help boys, youth and young adults develop their character as resourceful and responsible members of the community by providing opportunities and guidance for their mental, physical, social, and spiritual development". Scouting is an international organization with more than 150 countries and territories involved. The five programs of Scouts Canada are Beavers (ages 5-7), Cubs (ages 8-10), Scouts (ages 11-14), Venturers (ages 14-17), and Rovers (ages 17-26). In recent years, Rovers became available for girls as well (effective 1974), and Venturers followed ten years later. In 1992, a court ruling and Scouts Canada policy change also made it possible for girls to be included as members of Scout troops. Each of these programs are run on a local level with the national organization providing provincial charters and the provincial organization establishing local programs through new groups or through existing organizations such as churches. Programs focus on outdoor and environmental knowledge and skills as well as games and social activities in order to achieve the aim described above.

The Girl Guides is another youth serving organization with similar interests to the Scouting movement, but with a focus on girls and young women. Perhaps more famous for their cookie sales, the Girl Guides' aim "to help girls and young women become responsible citizens, able to give leadership and service to the community, whether local, national or global". There are five distinct programs available through the organization. These are Sparks (5 year-olds), Brownies (ages 6-9), Guides (ages 9-12), Pathfinders (ages 12-15), and Cadets/Rangers/Junior Leaders (ages 15-17 and over). The Guiding movement was initiated in Great Britain in 1909 by Lady Baden-Powell, (sister to the founder of the Boy Scouts) and began in Canada in 1910. As with the Boy Scouts, Girl Guides is an international organization with members in 112 countries. Similarly, there is a national organization with provincial offices and local or district committees. The district committee is the group which actually provides the programs and services. Many of the guiding activities are concerned with developing leadership through a diverse set of recreational and social activities.

Another volunteer organization known for its work in wartime is also an active and important youth serving agency in many communities throughout the world and certainly in Canada. The Red Cross was formed in 1863 in Geneva, Switzerland (International Committee of the Red Cross, 1987) and, since then, national Red Cross societies have been established worldwide. After World War I, the various National Red Cross societies wanted to put their skills to work in ways to benefit the communities in peace time. As a result, the Red Cross began to expand its services to medical and social activities. This also gave rise to the youth section in most national societies.

The Canadian Red Cross was officially formed in 1909 by an Act of Parliament. However, the organization did exist prior to that as an unincorporated body. The range of services offered by the Canadian Red Cross is substantial. Beyond the blood services, tracing and family reunion activities, emergency services, and sick-room equipment loans and associated services, the Canadian Red Cross offers extensive water safety programs, small craft safety training, and first-aid services. It also offers a variety of services to assist individuals who may be ill, recovering from an injury or displacement through such activities as friendly visiting, Meals-on-Wheels, and transportation assistance. In addition, the Red Cross sponsors and operates fun and fitness programs. Including blood donors, the Canadian Red Cross had 2.5 million volunteers in 1991 (The Canadian Red Cross Society, 1991).

The Young Men's Christian Association (YMCA) is a familiar organization to many Canadians. It has been in existence in Canada since 1851 when the Montreal branch was opened in the St. Helen Street Baptist Church. As with the other organizations highlighted above, the YMCA is an international organization with members in 96 countries. The YMCAs were founded to "save men from the hardship of life in the industrial revolution" (YMCA Fact Sheet, n.d.). The activities of the YMCA expanded over time to become more than religious study and social meetings and now include a wide range of social, recreational, fitness, instructional, community development, and other initiatives. The YMCA Camp Stevens operated by the Winnipeg YMCA is the oldest continuously operating camp in Canada having celebrated its 100th anniversary in 1991. All of the Y's programs are rooted in their commitment to develop individual's mind, body, and spirit. Thus, today, the YMCA operates day care programs, employment counseling and business incubator services, in addition to the other more traditional activities. This voluntary organization serves the entire range of ages and abilities through its branches in all parts of Canada.

The Young Women's Christian Association (YWCA) was founded in Canada in 1870 in Saint John, New Brunswick. This was followed quickly by the establishment of branches in Toronto (1873), Montreal (1874), Quebec City and Halifax (1875). The role of the YWCA has been varied including assistance to returning veterans after the World Wars, Saturday Night Teen Canteen after World War II, the operation of a crisis shelter for women and their children, disaster assistance, camping, fitness, social welfare, and others. Indeed, the first libraries available to the public in Montreal and Quebec City were offered by the YWCA. In many communities, the YMCA and YWCA have merged creating the YM-YWCA organizations. However, the YWCA is rooted in a different focus than the YMCA and even in the merged organizations, attempts are made to sustain the uniqueness. The YWCA has been concerned with the development of girls and women and their needs. In addition, they have served as a powerful advocate for women's rights.

Another prominent voluntary agency in Canada has been the local community centre. These are perhaps best exemplified by the Community Leagues of Edmonton, Alberta. Initiated in 1917, community leagues are neighbourhood associations run by local volunteers (Bowler & Wanchuk, 1986). Unlike the other organizations highlighted in this section, community centres, or leagues as they have been historically called in Edmonton, were established primarily for recreation and leisure activities. These centres exist in communities across Canada with varying organizational formats and responding to varying issues. Nonetheless, they are an important feature of the development and operation of community leisure services in Canada. Typically, community centres or leagues operated a wide variety of sporting leagues (e.g., minor hockey, soccer, baseball) and over time expanded to offer a full range of services to all age groups. To encourage greater levels of leisure participation, many community centres have provided day care and other ancillary services to the communities in which they are situated.

Other youth serving agencies in Canada include the Boys' and Girls' Clubs (approximately 160 across Canada) which are designed to serve children, youth and young adults and, increasingly, has expanded their mandate to include adults. They provide a wide range of social action programs and recreation opportunities primarily targeted to children and their families with reduced financial resources.

4-H (which stands for Head, Heart, Hands, and Health) began in Roland, Manitoba in 1913 and was called Boys' and Girls' Clubs (unrelated to the current national organization of the same name). It was initiated to provide an opportunity for rural youth to get together, make friends, and learn about agriculture through projects. The 4-H program continues to this day as a national organization run by the Canadian 4-H Council with provincial agencies and local clubs. The 4-H organization provides opportunities for travel, exchanges, agricultural education and activities, photography, handicrafts, and the development of many other skills. The Canadian 4-H Council, like so many other youth serving organizations is part of a worldwide network which operates in 80 countries.

CULTURAL ORGANIZATIONS

The leisure service delivery system includes the wide array of cultural organizations that exist in all communities in the country. Whether it be local arts councils, museums, galleries, theatre companies, or poetry reading groups, there is little doubt of the contribution and importance of cultural organizations to the quality of life we enjoy. For many people, their involvement as performers, participants or spectators in the programs of cultural organizations constitutes a key component of their leisure. These organizations are largely volunteer-based, depend on financial support from diverse sources and provide a unique range or set of services. While many cultural organizations do employ professional staff, they depend upon volunteers to actively participate in their governance activities through serving on committees and boards of directors, through participation in programs and services, and through financial support. Without the volunteer such organizations would, for the most part, cease to exist. Examples of large and small cultural organizations include the Toronto Symphony Orchestra, the Saidye Bronfman Centre in Montreal, the Glenbow Museum in Calgary, the Neepawa Arts Council in rural Manitoba, the Gas Station Theatre in Winnipeg, and the Neptune Theatre in Halifax.

OTHER COMPONENTS OF THE VOLUNTARY SECTOR

The voluntary sector also includes organizations as diverse as golf and country clubs, employee fitness organizations, and school-based recreation organizations. Many of these organizations were formed just to provide recreation opportunities, and many offer recreation programs in order to fulfill a broader mandate. Regardless, they are important parts of the voluntary system and should not be excluded from our discussion.

Many businesses such as Dofasco in Ontario, the Canadian Wheat Board, British Columbia Telephone Company, Alcan, and Great West Life Assurance Company provide support for employee recreation and fitness activities. In some cases, there is a high level of subsidy and facilitation provided; in other cases, the support is more rhetorical. For example, British Columbia Telephone Company (B.C. Tel) provides eight fitness centres for its employees for an average fee of

$11.00 per month (Canadian Centre for Active Living in the Workplace, 1991). In addition, where no company recreation facility is located, B.C. Tel. provides partial rebates for the cost of participation in community programs. The company's employee fitness and recreation program involves 90 volunteers from within the company with the support of seven full-time and five part-time professional staff.

For most employee fitness and recreation programs, there is a volunteer group established to assist in running the program or manage it entirely. In some cases, employee fitness and recreation programs are based on support for membership in other agencies such as the YMCA or are provided on a contract basis by an existing recreation agency.

Private golf and country clubs have existed for many years and, while membership is sometimes expensive, they are directed by member volunteers. Similar arrangements exist for a wide variety of private organizations such as tennis clubs, all-purpose sports clubs, social clubs, skydiving clubs, etc. These clubs are different than those discussed earlier in that they do not rely on charitable contributions but increasingly have taken advantage of government grants to improve their infrastructure. These organizations exist to the extent that their members seek to support them. How many there are is difficult to estimate since they are not publicly accountable and most do not seek public notoriety. Indeed, the motivation for belonging is often the exclusivity offered and the privacy enjoyed.

School-based recreation opportunities have faded in some parts of the country as the community school concept (a highly developmental, interventionist perspective designed to recreate the advantages of the one room school house in the schools of today) promoted activities for a wide range of ages being offered by non-school organizations functioning within the school building. The G. H. Dawe Centre in Red Deer Alberta is one example of a successful community school. However, many parent-teacher councils, which formerly encouraged school-based recreation activities, have disappeared or are more concerned with other activities in schools. Additionally, most school boards are increasingly hard-pressed financially and thus cannot provide evening and weekend recreation programs. In many communities, schools, and parks and recreation departments have signed joint use agreements whereby the parks and recreation department provides the evening and weekend program and supervision in the school facility and sometimes contributes to the cost of building new schools. These cooperative agreements result in far greater use of the school building for recreation purposes. However, there is not always a volunteer group established to help with the implementation of such agreements at either the school board level or on an individual school basis. As a result of this lack of community connection and the often noted financial pressures, school-based recreation is frequently reduced in size or eliminated entirely. Among the most important recreation resources proved by the schools are the athletic fields and playgrounds located on school sites. These areas are often shared with community centres or similar organizations and thus sustain themselves far better, and perhaps because of the widespread level of physical activity participation in Canada, are given greater importance to the community. Education in Canada is a provincial matter and, as a result, there are variations in each province concerning the use of schools for recreation purposes. Moreover, when you consider that each province empowers local communities to manage and pay for education, variations in educational administration and school governance are that much greater. For example, in some cities there are a multitude of school boards while in others there is but one. Edmonton has two school boards (public and Catholic) while Winnipeg has 10 (all public). Thus, the role of school boards and schools in the provision of recreation services is different from place to place.

The most important role that the school may play in the provision of leisure services is, of course, that of an educational institution. Leisure education is a process used to enhance the quality of a person's life through the clarification of values, development of positive leisure attitudes, knowledge, and skills for recreation participation (Woodburn & Cherry, 1978). Schools have the opportunity to provide opportunities for leisure education. That is, they can teach many of the skills and enhance knowledge in a way that allows the student to see their value not only for career development but also for leisure. For example, mathematics has applications for the workplace as well as for other aspects of daily living. It is also a valuable skill area that many people use in their recreation activity. The same is true for reading, history, geography and other subjects. It is the challenge of the school system to prepare individuals for life. Life includes leisure and the need for leisure education as part of the elementary and secondary school curricula should be apparent.

Financing the Voluntary Sector

Financing is one of the major challenges of the not-for-profit sector. Increasingly, the costs of operation have outdistanced the revenues of many voluntary agencies. Furthermore, the federal government taxation rules have made charitable giving less of a tax advantage for individuals than it was previously. Finally, the up and down economic cycles we have experienced in Canada since the early 1970s have made it difficult for private sector corporations to make sustained commitments and the same has recently become true for governments at all levels. Federal, provincial, and municipal deficits have made it increasingly difficult for governments to maintain commitments, let alone increase support to respond to inflationary pressures.

So where do these organizations get their financial support? The Boys' and Girls' Clubs receive funding from all three levels of government, the local United Ways in many communities, private donations and grants from foundations. However, in many cases this funding has little long-term reliability attached to it except, perhaps, for the United Way. As a result, it is often difficult to make long-range plans and have the assurance that they can be implemented. The local YMCA receives its funding from a variety of sources, many of which are similar to the Boys' and Girls' Clubs. Other revenue sources are membership fees, program fees, United Way funds, contributions from private citizens and corporations, and grants from all three levels of government. In each community, the funding potential from these sources varies significantly. The 4-H organization is funded differently in some respects. The program was borne out of an initiative of the Manitoba Agricultural College (now the University of Manitoba) to bring agricultural education to the farmer's doorstep. Over time, this responsibility was transferred, for the most part, to the provincial governments' agricultural departments. However, while they provide some of the professional leadership, funding is needed for a wide-range of activities and programs. In 1991 and 1992, the National 4-H Council received contributions from Agriculture Canada, Petro-Canada, Royal Bank of Canada, Air Canada, Sears Canada, Canadian Seed Growers Association and many others representing various sectors of the economy. In recent years, not-for-profit cultural organizations have found the financial pressures to be extreme. In 1992, the Winnipeg Symphony Orchestra was the only symphony in Canada that was operating without a deficit. Theater companies, symphonies, art galleries, and other cultural organizations have had to rely on extensive fund raising efforts as government support has either been reduced or has not kept up with inflation. One recent example of the financial restraint on cultural organizations was the closure of The Royal Ontario Museum for six months in 1992 because it was unable to operate for the whole year within its budget. These financial pressures exist for all agencies in the voluntary sector. Perhaps the most remarkable aspect of voluntary organizations is their ability to survive despite these uncertain sources of income. They somehow do survive, and they continue to be a key component of the leisure service delivery system in virtually every Canadian community.

Challenges Facing Volunteer Agencies

These more traditional volunteer agencies have faced many challenges over the past decades as our economy, education, communication, and other aspects of life became more sophisticated and complex. With changing sex roles and social pressures that were unheard of 90 years ago, the volunteer agency has a whole new set of challenges to address. These include, but are not limited to:

- The advent of satellite communications has meant that the transmission of information has moved from being hours, days, or weeks to minutes. As a result, communities are influenced by changing trends and these agencies are required to respond more rapidly. As an example, consider break dancing (a once popular style of dancing that had its origins in the streets of New York City). In the 1960s a young person in Saskatoon, Windsor or Yellowknife would not have learned about this fad until it was old news. In the 1990s, television broadcasting keeps the youth of Saskatoon, Windsor, Yellowknife and Canadian communities in touch with the latest from all over the world.

- The wave of immigration and the introduction of different cultures coming to Canada has placed additional stress on the volunteer agencies. In earlier days when most of the immigrants came from Europe, the largely European-originated Canadian population knew what they were like and often understood their language. Many immigrants had relatives in Canada and either knew of some of our customs or could easily adapt to them since they were similar to those of Europe. The recent wave of immigration from Central America, Southeast Asia, India, Pakistan, and the countries of the Middle East have provided new challenges for the volunteer agency in meeting the needs of the community while demonstrating cultural sensitivity.

• The opportunities for education in Canada have never been greater than they are today, yet many volunteer agencies are having to assist individuals who do not seem to fit traditional education models. Moreover, the extensive access to education has also created a more sophisticated consumer who demands more from volunteer agencies. Thus, the YMCAs in Toronto, Winnipeg, and Calgary among others, have made extensive renovations, have marketing staff, and seek to attract more and more members by providing more diverse services.

• Voluntary agencies have found that, even with the large number of Canadians that volunteer, there are ever increasing sources of competition for volunteer labour. Volunteers once confined themselves to working within the not-for-profit sector, but we now see recreation agencies in the public sector aggressively seeking volunteers, as are hospitals and other health care institutions, schools, religious organizations, environmental organizations, and others.

• Demographic changes have greatly influenced the direction and focus of services offered by many volunteer agencies in Canada. Where many were instituted to serve youth, most now provide a wide range of services to individuals from infancy to old age. The demands of the baby boom generation have had a dramatic impact as they seek materials and services for themselves, for their children, and for their aging parents. Moreover, the large group of Canadians over 65 years of age continues to grow and make demands on service providers. Agencies have had to respond to this aging membership and shrinking traditional market.

• Finances have also been a major challenge of many volunteer agencies. Increasingly they have turned to use professional staff as a complement to the volunteer base and this has necessitated more money for operations. Also, for those volunteer agencies that are facility based (such as the Y's and Boys' and Girls' Clubs), there is a continual need to sustain the physical plant and this requires extensive capital which is not readily available in an era of declining support from the public sector and increasing competition for the charitable donation.

During the last few of years, we have seen some different kinds of volunteer agencies emerge to deal with some of the gaps and challenges that exist. One such agency is called Creative Retirement Manitoba. Initiated in 1981 as an independent organization, Creative Retirement Manitoba provides "older adults with the opportunity, through a wide-range of experiences, to live creatively, to grow, and to share their knowledge, skills and attitudes with others" (Creative Retirement Manitoba Brochure, n.d.). This organization offers homebound learning programs, training programs for volunteers and community groups, community-based health promotion programs, preretirement education programs, performing groups (e.g., Men's

Chorus, Philharmonic Band), and volunteers to communicate oral history in the schools. Increasingly more new volunteer agencies emerge to fill needs in the community as individuals join together to satisfy their needs.

Another example of a new voluntary organization initiated to address a long-standing social and recreation problem was the Northern Fly-in Sports Camps, Inc. This organization was created to fill the needs of children and youth in remote and northern communities. Since its inception, it has provided services in Quebec, the Northwest Territories, and Manitoba. Simply stated, no one else was providing services in these communities. Through the efforts of one individual, Dr. Neil Winther, the organization was born. Support came from the Royal Canadian Mounted Police, the University of Manitoba, and grants from the federal and provincial governments. Through this initiative has grown a recognition of the need for appropriate training of leaders in northern and remote regions and the initiation of other activities to support community recreation development. This and other new organizations came into being to fulfill needs. Such is the root of all volunteer sector organizations and nothing could be closer to the community or more important to the quality of life we enjoy than the groups that we support with our voluntarily contributed time, efforts and means.

Summary

This chapter has profiled volunteering in Canada, and discussed the issues facing volunteer agencies, and the trends to which they are attempting to adapt as changes in societal structure demand. In addition, several types of voluntary agencies with specific roles in leisure services were highlighted. These clearly show the diversity of voluntary agencies and the roles they play in the leisure service delivery system. Future growth in leisure services is more likely to come from this sector than from the public sector as these organizations exist only as long as the community seeks them out and supports them. Thus, those that successfully respond to their mandate and mission will sustain support and those that cease to be relevant or central to the lives of their constituency will fade away. Furthermore, since such agencies require active participation by their members in their operation and governance, those which sustain their relevance will have the base of support needed to continue to thrive.

STUDY QUESTIONS

1. Why are volunteers so important to the leisure service delivery system?

2. What distinguishes the voluntary sector from the public and commercial sector?

3. What are principal motives of volunteers in Canada?

4. Explain how the lack of training may be a problem in recruiting and retaining volunteers.

5. Where do voluntary agencies get their financial support?

6. What are some of the key trends facing the voluntary sector in the years ahead?

7. Describe an example of a voluntary agency in Canada and its activities.

8. What advantages do voluntary agencies have over the government in terms of responding to consumer demand?

References

Arlett, A., Bell, P., & Thompson, R. W. (1988). *Canada gives.* Toronto, ON: The Canadian Centre for Philanthropy.

Bowler, V., & Wanchuk, M. (1986). *Volunteers.* Edmonton, AB: Lone Pine Publishing.

Brennan, B. (1989). *Seniors as volunteers.* Ottawa, ON: Minister of Supply of Services.

Canadian Centre for Active Living in the Workplace, (1991). Ottawa, ON: Fitness and Amateur Sport.

Catano, J. W. (1989). *Women as volunteers.* Ottawa, ON: Minister of Supply of Services.

Faid, P. T. (1989). *Urban and rural volunteers.* Ottawa, ON: Ministry of Supply and Services.

Fisher, J. (1988, June). Volunteer Time is Money. *Volunteer Montreal* Special Edition, pp. 1-2.

Gagne, J. (1989). *Volunteers in Quebec.* Ottawa, ON: Ministry of Supply and Services.

Graff, L. (1989). *Voluntary activity in Ontario: How much is 4.5 billion dollars worth?* Ottawa, ON: Ministry of Supply and Services.

International Committee of the Red Cross (n.d.). *Red Cross & Red Crescent: Portrait of an international movement.* Geneva, Switzerland: Author.

Kent, J. (1989). *Volunteers in recreation.* Ottawa, ON: Minister of Supply of Services.

Lautenschlager, J. (1992). *Volunteering: A traditional Canadian value.* Ottawa, ON: Ministry of Supply and Services.

MacLeod, F. (1989). *Volunteers in major metropolitan centres.* Ottawa, ON: Ministry of Supply and Services.

McFarland, E. M. (1970). *The history of public recreation in Canada.* Ottawa, ON: Canadian Parks/Recreation Association.

Murphy, J. F. & D. R. Howard. (1977). *Delivery of community leisure services: An holistic approach.* Philadelphia, PA: Lea and Febiger.

Ross, D. P. & Shillington, R. (1990). *Economic dimensions of volunteer work in Canada.* Ottawa, ON: Ministry of Supply and Services.

Ross, D. P. & Shillington, E. R. (1989). *A profile of the Canadian volunteer.* Ottawa, ON: National Voluntary Organizations.

Scouts Canada. (n.d., mimeo). *Life of B.P.*

Statistics Canada. (1988). *Labour Force Annual Averages, 1981-1988.* (Catalogue 71wy7nm88529).

Woodburn, R. & Cherry, C. (1978). *Leisure: A resource for educators.* Toronto, ON: Ministry of Culture and Recreation.

YMCA Fact Sheet (n.d.).

Chapter Seven

The Commercial Sector

Overview

PURPOSE

This chapter provides an overview of commercial sector activities in leisure services. As an important part of the community recreation system, commercial recreation enterprises contribute to the economy and to the quality of life enjoyed by Canadians. The purpose of this chapter is to distinguish commercial leisure services from those provided by public and private not-for-profit recreation agencies, and to offer useful background information to individuals who might pursue careers in the commercial recreation field.

LEARNING OBJECTIVES

At the completion of this chapter, you should be able to:

1. identify key differences between commercial recreation services and those offered by organizations operating in other sectors,

2. appreciate the important contribution of the commercial sector to leisure services in Canada,

3. describe the role of governments in supporting commercial recreation enterprises, and

4. identify attitudes and activities of the commercial sector that could appropriately be incorporated into public and private not-for-profit operations to enhance their effectiveness and efficiency.

The Commercial Sector

In discussing the history of leisure service development in Canada (Chapter Two), it was noted that social and technological changes in the early 1800s facilitated the growth of recreation opportunities provided through the commercial sector. The commercial sector and the private entrepreneurs that operated therein actually established the first true leisure service organizations in Canada. In spite of the subsequent increase in public and private not-for-profit sector involvement in providing leisure services, the commercial recreation industry continues to be an important part of the Canadian leisure service system.

Commercial Recreation Defined

In describing the nature of the commercial recreation subsystem, Murphy and Howard (1977) emphasized that "profit motivation is the paramount difference between commercial operators and other members of the community recreation system". Note that these authors referred to profit 'motivation' rather than profit 'generation'. Of course, the profit-motivated enterprise will eventually disappear if it does not succeed in generating economic gain, but one should not assume that a leisure service provider that generates a profit is, necessarily, operating in the commercial sector with a profit motivation. To find examples of profit-generating programs operated by non-profit agencies, one usually needs to look no further than their public recreation department's directory of services where there may be listed a fitness class, hockey camp, playschool program or sports festival that likely generates revenue in excess of its costs. These are examples of commercialized public recreation, which Crossley and Jamieson (1988) define as "the provision of selected recreation related products or services by a governmental or non-profit organization in a commercial manner, such that much or all of the costs are covered by fees, charges, or other non-tax revenues".

Crossley and Jamieson also recognized that, just as non-profit agencies might sometimes earn profits, profit-motivated recreation enterprises can occasionally lose money on certain aspects of their total service package. They maintain, however, that the ultimate goal of the commercial recreation enterprise will continue to be profit generation, and defined commercial recreation as "the provision of recreation-related products or services by private enterprise for a fee, with the long-term intent of being profitable".

In addition to maintaining a long-term profit motivation, there are several ways identified by Sessoms, Meyer and Brightbill (1975) in which recreation services in the commercial sector differ from those provided through public sector organizations. First, they are administered by corporations, syndicates, partnerships, or private owners who usually have more of a business background than a recreation background. Second, commercial recreation enterprises are financed by the owner(s) or promoters with the expected return on investment coming from user charges, admissions and other private business revenues. Third, commercial recreation programs are designed to tap consumer spending power. Fourth, membership is, within the parameters of the law, limited, and, fifth, smaller commercial enterprises are more likely to operate in leased facilities. Another important difference was revealed in a Canadian study that concluded that recreation services offered through the commercial sector are more attractive to a particular segment of the population (i.e., young adult, single males) than are those offered through public or private not-for-profit agencies (Brayley & Searle, 1991).

Entrepreneurship in Commercial Recreation

A commercial recreation organization is successful if it satisfies consumer needs and wants sufficiently to enable achievement of its corporate objectives. Those corporate objectives are to make significantly more money than has been or will be invested in the enterprise, and one of the quickest ways to generate a positive return on the investment is to be the first to capitalize on a new interest or resource. This sometimes means following leisure fads—a risky business since fads come and go and change so unpredictably. Successful commercial recreation operators recognize that satisfying consumers needs and generating true profits can be very difficult, especially since the leisure product they offer, and the market they aim to satisfy are, in many respects, constantly moving targets.

Responding to the relatively unstable commercial recreation market requires agencies and their operators to be aware of supply opportunities and trends in consumer demand. Not only must they be aware of such trends, but they must respond to these environmental changes in a way that sustains the organization's long-term profitability. Crossley and Jamieson (1988) suggested that, when a recreation organization "searches for trends and changes in its environment then brings together and manages resources to exploit those changes as an opportunity," it is adopting a style of operation that is necessary for success in the commercial recreation arena. That style is the style of the entrepreneur (Drucker, 1985).

Entrepreneurs are often thought of as quick-acting risktakers. They are popularly described as smooth-talking, money-focussed, business-lucky people who are willing to "put it all on the line" for an untried and untested idea that will make them instantly rich. This, however, is not what entrepreneurship is about. Note that the definition for entrepreneurial recreation given in the preceding paragraph refers to a "search" for trends, and the "bringing together" and "managing" of resources to deliberately "exploit" and create opportunity. The true entrepreneur is, in fact, less of a risktaker because of his or her careful attention to staying in tune with market conditions than is the "comfortable" tenured recreation practitioner who flirts with professional redundancy and market irrelevancy by ignoring consumption trends, environmental changes and opportunities to adjust product and service offerings accordingly.

The spirit of entrepreneurship is absolutely essential for the success of recreation organizations that operate in the commercial sector. It also has important benefits for and can make valuable contributions to, public and private not-for-profit recreation. Perhaps the greatest contribution of entrepreneurship in the commercial sector to public and private not-for-profit recreation agencies has been and is product innovation. Most new recreation products and services offered by public agencies had their origins in the commercial sector. Additionally, the entrepreneurial spirit promotes competition and helps to guard against monopolistic inefficiencies that stifle productivity and entrench less-than-optimal levels of service quality. In a sense, the competition that thrives in the entrepreneurial environment keeps leisure service providers honest, and keeps them honestly trying to offer the best and most relevant service possible.

The Scope of Commercial Recreation in Canada

The great number of recreation organizations operating in the commercial sector can be classified in different ways. Bullaro and Edginton (1986) proposed five major groupings: travel and tourism, entertainment services, leisure services in the natural environment, hospitality/food services, and retail activities. Crossley and Jamieson (1988) felt that commercial recreation enterprises might more appropriately be classified as travel and tourism industries, hospitality industries, local commercial recreation industries, or facilitators. We choose to adopt a two-dimensional classification system where commercial recreation organizations are grouped according to the nature of their product (goods or services) and the source of the market (local, non-local or either). Figure 7.1 identifies some of the goods and services that the commercial recreation sector provides to its local and non-local consumers.

When we consider all the organizations in the community that might be involved in providing the leisure goods and services represented in Figure 7.1, it is obvious that the commercial recreation industry is not only pervasive, but extensive. The industry includes movie theatres, sports clubs, amusement parks, archery ranges, bowling lanes, golf facilities, bicycle rentals, fitness facilities, dance halls, gymnasia, sporting goods stores, and a host of other outlets for "pay-as-you-play" services. As shown in Figure 7.2, most of the commercial recreation corporations in Canada are quite small (assets totalling less than $250,000), but there are many of them. Of the corporations that are classified in the Standard Industrial Code as recreational services, only 16 have assets worth more than $25 million (Statistics Canada 1986).

Many leisure-related corporations are not classified as recreation services by Statistics Canada. Restaurants, for example, are classified as food and beverage services even though dining out is a popular recreation activity. In 1986, there were 23,421 restaurants in Canada. Entertainment and amusement businesses are also excluded from the recreation services classification, as are hotels and motels, ticket and travel agencies, and other enterprises which stay in business because they serve the mostly recreational needs of their customers. In 1986, there were 7,801 hotels and motels in Canada, and there were 2,288 ticket and travel agencies. Add to these the number of movie theatres, video stores and other entertainment establishments (totalling 18,453 in 1990) and it becomes clear that commercial recreation is a part of our economy that cannot be overlooked. It also becomes clear that accurately measuring the scope and impact of the commercial recreation sector is very difficult.

Another way to ascertain the scope of commercial recreation in Canada is to examine the expenditure patterns of the public. Statistics Canada reported that, in 1990, average household expenditures on goods and services provided through the major commercial recreation subindustries in 17 selected metropolitan areas exceeded $2,350. Nationally, the total amount spent on commercial sector recreation services was approximately $21 billion.

For comparison purposes, data from a smaller cross-country sample of metropolitan areas are presented in Table 7.1 (page 118). Note that, in each community, household expenditures for commercial recreation were greatest in the area of recreation services (spectator-entertainment performances, use of recreation facilities, single use service

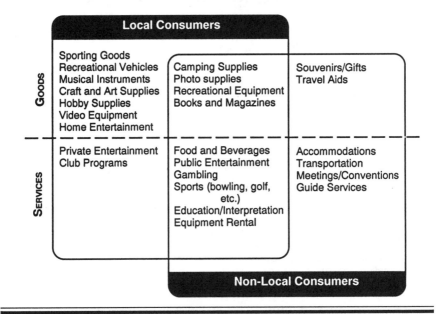

FIGURE 7.1

REPRESENTATIVE GOODS AND SERVICES TYPICALLY AVAILABLE TO LOCAL AND NON-LOCAL
CONSUMERS THROUGH COMMERCIAL RECREATION ORGANIZATIONS.

FIGURE 7.2

NUMBER OF COMMERCIAL RECREATION CORPORATIONS BY SIZE
(AS MEASURED BY ASSETS) SOURCE: STATISTICS CANADA.

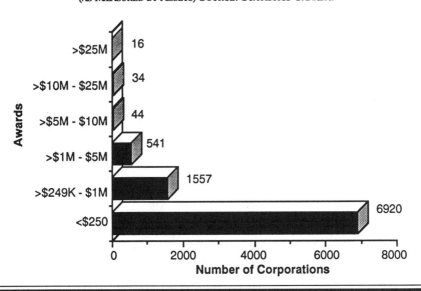

fees, package travel tours, sightseeing tours and excursion packages, and other recreation services). Except in Vancouver, the smallest average amount was spent on recreational vehicles and outboard motors.

TABLE 7.1

CONSUMER SPENDING ON COMMERCIAL RECREATION GOODS AND SERVICES
IN SELECTED METROPOLITAN AREAS (1990).

AREA OF CONSUMER SPENDING	VANCOUVER	EDMONTON	WINNIPEG	TORONTO	ST. JOHN
Recreation equipment and associated services	$ 626	$ 723	$ 513	$ 707	$ 468
Recreation vehicles and outboard motors	$ 754	$ 307	$ 122	$ 76	$ 248
Home entertainment equipment and services	$ 538	$ 543	$ 470	$ 521	$ 467
Recreation services	$ 1,061	$ 1,085	$ 737	$1,088	$ 703
TOTAL	$ 2,979	$ 2,657	$1,842	$2,393	$ 1,923

The statistics presented in Table 7.1 reinforce the earlier assertion that commercial recreation has a major impact on national, provincial and local economies.

Organizational Structures in Commercial Recreation

The organizations that offer commercial recreation services vary in their form as much as they vary in their function. There are, however, some generalizations that can be made about the structure of corporations in specific classes as distinguished by size.

Figure 7.2 illustrates the predominance of small businesses in commercial recreation. Many, if not most, of the nearly 7,000 Canadian commercial recreation corporations with assets valued at less than $250,000 are what the industry refers to as "mom and pop" enterprises. They are usually owned and operated by an individual, family, or small group of partners, and they frequently specialize in only one or two leisure services. Examples are guide services, sporting goods stores, gift/souvenir shops, travel agencies, and craft studios. Unfortunately, the high cost of capitalization, the increasing complexity of operation and management, and the non-objective proximity of the owner/operator to the service often combine to contribute to the high rate of business failure experienced by mom and pop recreation enterprises. Mom and pop ventures do, however, have some unique opportunities to be successful. For example, small businesses are relatively flexible with respect to their responsiveness to rapidly changing market conditions. They do not have major investments to protect nor boards of directors to convince and can quickly change the service according to the owner/operator's perception of consumer demand. In addition, mom and pop operations can be quite profitable with relatively small target markets.

Larger commercial recreation enterprises (assets in excess of $250,000) are usually owned by a local corporation or are franchise operations of a large national corporation. Examples include cinemas, bowling lanes, campgrounds, and fitness clubs. They have the advantage of access to larger markets and to sophisticated management and administrative structures, but their challenge is in responding in a timely manner to changing market conditions. At times, that larger national market and that sophisticated, centralized management structure can be somewhat insensitive to local conditions, challenges and opportunities.

The "Big Ones" like West Edmonton Mall, Canada Wonderland, Canadian Pacific Resorts, and others with assets in excess of $25 million are a unique breed of commercial recreation enterprises. They are managed by boards of directors and complex administrative bodies, whose members might be inclined to think of the recreation resource as just a part of the business rather than part of the community or part of the family. Large scale enterprises have the enviable ability to draw from extensive markets and to diversify their products to meet a wide variety of leisure needs. They also have the financial base to sustain continued operation and, sometimes, growth during times when demand is low. Their financial success helps to underscore the value that Canadians and foreign visitors place on personal and family recreation.

Finally, another structure through which commercial recreation services are delivered is the concession. Examples of concession operations include boat rentals in a national park, a souvenir stand at a major sporting or cultural event, and binocular rentals at the opera. Concessionaires are independent operators whose business depends on access to a resource and market that is managed by some other corporate entity. That other organization concedes, by licensing arrangement with the operator, the right to provide a particular commercial leisure service. Concessionaires have the advantage of someone else's efforts to attract the market but, at the same time, are subject to the variable success of those efforts. Capital investment is usually minimal for concession operations, and many are very successful. Of course, just as many are not successful and therein lies the reality of commerce.

Commercial Recreation and Public Policy

Commercial recreation had its birth and maintains its life in the public sector's inability or unwillingness to meet all the leisure service needs of Canadians. Before public and voluntary agencies began establishing their recreation programs, enterprising individuals capitalized on apparent needs and profited by offering services for a price. At first glance, it may seem that public and commercial recreation organizations compete directly with each other. It would not be difficult, for example, to find a community where there are both commercial and public racquetball facilities that try to attract the same group of players. Many larger urban centres have both commercial and public golf courses and, in some areas, there are public campgrounds right next to privately owned camping facilities. Participants in fitness classes often can choose between a program offered by their local recreation department and one offered by a commercial fitness club. While these examples do support the idea that public/commercial competition is the standard, there are other aspects to the relationship between recreation service providers in these two sectors that suggest support and cooperation is just as common.

As was noted earlier, the commercial sector assists the public sector to meet its broad objectives by responding quickly to changes in consumer demand. Program and product innovation characterize the commercial recreation enterprise, and its efforts to meet the needs of new markets allow the public sector to concentrate efforts and limited resources on serving the larger, slow-to-adopt consumer population. In addition, it was also pointed out that competition from the commercial sector helps to keep the public agencies accountable and vigilant in fulfilling their mandated responsibilities.

Government (representing the public sector) assists the commercial recreation enterprise in many ways. It may assist by regulating the industry, by developing new markets, or by providing resources that facilitate industry development.

Federal, provincial, and municipal governments have authority to enact legislation that regulates and protects commercial recreation enterprises. Laws that regulate commercial activity and business practice (fair-trade laws, anticombines regulations, marketing practice guidelines, land use/zoning by-laws, etc.) not only protect consumers, but also protect the industry from decisions and practices which would, in the long-term, be detrimental to its viability. Such public-sector intrusion into commercial-sector activity is generally viewed as supportive and necessary. Other laws such as those which deal with labour practices and health standards also apply directly to the regulation and protection of the commercial recreation industry.

Where a commercial recreation enterprise relies on business from non-local consumers, it benefits particularly from government efforts to develop new markets for the recreation product. Federal, provincial, and in some situations, municipal governments are actively involved in promotion of their communities and its attractions as tourist destinations. By bringing more customers to the doorstep, the public sector greatly assists the commercial recreation operator to sell his or her product.

A variety of public resources are also made available to support and assist the commercial recreation industry. Most provincial governments, for example, maintain or support small business development libraries where entrepreneurs can research market trends, gather information to improve their business operations, and explore new service opportunities. Another valuable information resource that is available (thanks to the public recreation agency) is the community recreation master plan. This document is a must-read item for any recreation service provider in the community, including those operating in the commercial sector.

An important resource that the public sector extends to the commercial sector is financial aid. Sometimes that aid takes the form of direct grants, start up loans, or low-interest expansion or debt retirement loans. Different levels of government might also provide other special incentives to support the development of commercial recreation services. Murphy and Howard (1977) suggested the offering of nominally priced public lands for private development, reduction of rates for city services, and the provision of attractive lease agreements as examples of other appropriate government assistance.

The existence of competition between public and commercial leisure services is not necessarily negative, nor is it indicative of the working relationship between these two sectors. When viewed in the context of intention rather than highlighted action, public policy and practice is clearly supportive of commercial recreation enterprise.

Pursuing a Career in Commercial Recreation

Individuals who would like to develop a career in some aspect of commercial recreation will find that there are basically two approaches to achieving their goal. One approach requires the investment of creativity, energy, initiative, and learning, and the other approach requires the same plus the investment of financial resources.

The first approach is suitable for an individual who wants to work within an organization that is owned by someone else. Entry level positions in most commercial recreation enterprises require little formal training, but also provide minimal financial remuneration. Employers are most interested in a worker who can learn quickly, be dependable, demonstrate creativity, and work hard. Advanced education through a college or university program may be the key to vertical mobility in the organization and is, therefore, highly recommended. Postsecondary coursework should provide a sound foundation in recreation studies and practical management skills. Since most entry-level positions do not require a person with a diploma or degree, many aspiring commercial recreation professionals take a variety of part-time entry-level positions while advancing their educational standing. They then find that they can move up the corporate ladder fairly rapidly upon completion of their formal educational program.

The second approach to developing a career in commercial recreation requires the individual to become an owner of a recreation business. Successful ownership requires much more than investment resources and a good product. It requires a special set of management skills and market sensitivity. It also requires creativity, diligence, initiative, and, most importantly, patience. Postsecondary training is highly recommended, and coursework should be in the area of recreation studies and business management. A wide range of work experience in commercial recreation organizations similar to the one to be established should also be sought after as an essential part of career preparation.

Postsecondary students who are interested in pursuing careers in commercial recreation can enhance their educational program by seeking summer jobs and fieldwork placements with commercial recreation organizations. They can also take every opportunity to select or orient their class assignments, research activities and term papers to the type of work they would one day like to do. They should develop a network of contacts within the industry by joining and being actively involved in provincial recreation associations and more specialized national or international organizations such as the Resort and Commercial Recreation Association. In addition, students should make sure that they are aware of current local, regional, and national issues that affect commercial recreation.

Summary

The role of commercial leisure services is a longstanding one in Canadian history. The commercial leisure services are those provided by private enterprise for a fee and with the long-term intent of being profitable. The differences between the public and commercial sector were highlighted as we further defined commercial recreation. The entrepreneurial nature of commercial leisure services, sometimes erroneously seen to be exclusively in their domain, was examined along with the scope of commercial recreation activity in Canada. Small "mom and pop" operations were examined in addition to the major corporations that provide leisure services on a commercial basis. The relationship between public policy and commercial recreation was reviewed and prospects for a career in this field were explained at the end of the chapter. The commercial sector is dynamic as it responds to the demands of the marketplace. It will always be an important aspect of the leisure service delivery system.

STUDY QUESTIONS

1. Define what is meant by commercial recreation and distinguish it from public recreation.

2. Is it a fair conclusion that commercial recreation is always a high-risk enterprise? Why?

3. What must a commercial recreation operator do to reduce his or her risk?

4. Describe the two-dimensional classification system of commercial recreation.

5. What facts would you bring to bear to demonstrate the economic impact of commercial recreation in Canada?

6. What often distinguish small "mom and pop" commercial enterprises from larger ones?

7. How does the public sector assist the commercial sector?

8. Should public and commercial enterprises compete in a single marketplace? What are the advantages or disadvantages?

9. What are some of the considerations one should keep in mind when considering a career in commercial recreation?

References

Brayley, R. & Searle, M. (1991). Determinants of Leisure Service Sector Bias. In C. Sylvester and L. Caldwell (Eds.), *Proceedings of the 1991 NRPA Leisure Research Symposium*. Alexandria, VA: National Recreation Parks Association.

Bullaro, J. & Edginton, C. (1986). *Commercial leisure services*. New York, NY: MacMillan Publishing Company.

Crossley, J. & Jamieson, L. (1988). *Introduction to commercial and entrepreneurial recreation*. Champaign, IL: Sagamore Publishing.

Drucker, P. (1985). *Innovation and entrepreneurship*. New York, NY: Harper and Row Publishers.

Munson, K. (1978). Commercial and member-owned recreation forms. In Godbey, G. (Ed.) *Recreation, Park and leisure services: Foundations, organization, administration*, (pp. 133-175). Philadelphia, PA: Saunders.

Murphy, J. & Howard, D. (1977). *Delivery of community leisure services: An holistic approach*. Philadelphia, PA: Lea and Febiger.

Sessoms, H. D., Meyer, H., & Brightbill, C. (1975). *Leisure services: The organized recreation and park system*. Englewood Cliffs, NJ: Prentice-Hall.

Statistics Canada. (1988). *Labour Force Annual Averages, 1981-1988*. (Catalogue 71wy7nm88529).

Chapter Eight

Recreational Travel and Tourism

Overview

PURPOSE

The purpose of this chapter is to explore travel and tourism as a leisure experience, and to describe the scope of tourism activity in Canada. It discusses the reasons for which people travel and the benefits they derive therefrom. Also discussed are the impacts of leisure travel on host and guest leisure opportunities and choices.

LEARNING OBJECTIVES

At the completion of this chapter, you should be able to:

1. define tourism and distinguish it from other forms of leisure activity,

2. describe the nature and scope of tourism in Canada,

3. understand why people travel, and

4. identify the impacts of tourism on other forms of recreation.

Recreational Travel and Tourism

The case was made earlier in this book that recreation is a subset of leisure. Unfortunately, many leisure service practitioners and scholars think or act as if that it is the only subset. There are other leisure subsets—some are quite distinct, and some are related to each other. Tourism is another subset of leisure that has some unique features and, at the same time, shares some characteristics and structures with recreation. Mieczkowski (1981) illustrated the relationship between leisure, recreation, and tourism by placing recreation entirely within the realm of leisure, and positioning tourism as being sometimes purely recreational, sometimes non-recreational leisure, and sometimes non-leisure. He distinguished between local recreation (i.e., activities we engage in while in our home environment), non-local recreation (i.e., recreational activities we pursue away from home), and business and personal travel (i.e., non-recreational activities away from home).

In comparing local recreation to the leisure dimension of tourism (i.e., non-local recreation), many similarities are readily observable. For example, the same tool or tools from a variety of academic disciplines can be applied to the study of both recreation and the tourism phenomenon, common psychological mechanisms are involved in recreation and tourism experiences, and common meanings and roles are learned in both tourism and recreation settings. In addition, there are commonalities in form and function, perceived barriers to participation in either activity are similar or the same, and similar environmental factors influence expectations and perceptions of quality in the tourism or recreation experience.

Of course, there are also some important differences. For instance, spatial rather than social considerations influence tourism market definition, different "bottom line" indicators are applied to performance evaluation, and lead sector and government roles are different for tourism than they are for recreation. These similarities and differences will be examined later in this chapter.

Definition of Tourism

To facilitate further discussion of tourism as it relates to leisure services in Canada, it is important that the concept be defined. What exactly is this thing called tourism? Is it, as some have suggested, simply "recreation away from home" (Balmer, 1992) and, therefore, unworthy of separate attention?

The Canadian Parks/Recreation Association defines tourism as "both an industry and a dimension of leisure" (CP/RA, 1987). In so doing, this national organization has recognized that leisure service agencies and professionals have a role to play in tourism and that the economic aspects of tourism figure prominently in its development and management. Like many other provincial governments and provincial recreation associations, the Alberta government describes tourism as "the practice of people travelling outside their home communities for rest, recreation, sightseeing or business" (Alberta Tourism, 1986). This definition emphasizes the non-local nature of the tourism experience, and identifies recreation as one of the main purposes of travel. In their text on tourism, McIntosh and Goeldner (1986) define it as "the sum of the phenomena and relationships arising from the interaction of tourists, business suppliers, host governments, and host communities in the process of attracting and hosting these tourists and other visitors". The McIntosh and Goeldner definition stresses the importance of host/guest and supplier/consumer interactions in the tourism experience.

Taking these and other definitions into account, we suggest that tourism be thought of as the activities, interactions, and impacts of individuals or groups engaged in travel away from their home communities for leisure purposes. Note that this definition is presented in the context of a study of leisure services and is not consistent with that proposed by the World Tourism Organization (WTO) because it does not include individuals who are travelling for business purposes.

DEFINITION OF A TOURIST

When we think of tourism, we think of people on the move. We think of people who are away from home, enjoying free time, spending a little more money than usual, and engaging in a variety of activities which are not a part of their normal lifestyles. Based on the definitions of tourism presented earlier in this chapter, a tourist can be defined as an individual who is engaged in travel away from his or her home communities for leisure purposes. In some official definitions, an individual must also travel a minimum distance from home (usually 80 km) and stay overnight to be counted as a tourist. The World Tourism Organization distinguishes tourists from same-day visitors by defining a tourist as one who stays "at least one night in a collective or private accommodation in the place visited" (WTO, 1991). Since, by definition, the only difference between same-day visitors and tourists is the trip duration, our discussion of tourists in the context of leisure services will include both types of travelers.

RECREATION AND TOURISM COMPARED

As noted earlier, recreation and tourism have common characteristics. It was suggested that they are similar because the study of each phenomenon is most appropriately conducted through a multidisciplinary effort and because the same tool or tools from a variety of academic disciplines can be useful in understanding both recreation and tourism. Recreation and tourism can be examined from many perspectives. They can be thought of as transportation issues or they can be considered as matters for exploration within the context of geography. Both can be viewed as a business activity that is an important part of the economy, or they can be studied with respect to their impact on culture, politics, the environment, and education. Jafari (1983) identified sixteen academic disciplines that contribute significantly to our understanding of tourism. Table 8.1 (following page) lists those disciplines and identifies their potential contributions to both recreation and tourism.

It has also been suggested that common psychological mechanisms are involved in recreation and tourism experiences. The same psychological constraints that influence recreation participation also influence tourism activity. These constraints

TABLE 8.1
DISCIPLINARY CONTRIBUTIONS TO UNDERSTANDING RECREATION AND TOURISM

ACADEMIC DISCIPLINE	CONTRIBUTIONS TO RECREATION	CONTRIBUTIONS TO TOURISM
Sociology	Understanding of social needs and constraints as they relate to recreational activity.	Understanding of social influences on the tourism experience, and of tourism activity on social conditions.
Economics	Identification and explanation of the impacts of expenditure and investment in recreation on economic development.	Identification and explanation of the impacts of tourism expenditure and investment on economic development.
Psychology	Description of psychological constraints and benefits expected and derived from recreational experiences.	Description of motivations to travel and psychological benefits derived from experiences in unusual environments.
Anthropology	Understanding the role of recreation in the development and expression of culture and religion.	Description of host-guest relationships and the impact of tourism on man's perception of origins and destiny.
Political Science	Understanding the workings of political systems and enhancing the ability of recreation professionals to succeed in politically charged environments.	Understanding the implications of a world without borders. Assessing the tourism impacts of government policy, terrorism, and armed conflict.
Geography	Understanding the role of distance and spatial relationships in infrastructure development and recreation behaviour.	Understanding the role of distance and spatial relationships in infrastructure development and travel behaviour.
Ecology	Preservation and conservation of natural resources and environments used as recreation settings.	Identification, interpretation, and presentation of natural attractions. Preservation and conservation of tourism resources.
Agriculture	Development and promotion of recreation in the rural farm environment.	Development and promotion of rural tourism.
Parks and Recreation	Professional preparation of recreation leaders, managers, and researchers.	Development and management of recreation resources as tourist attractions.
Urban and Regional Planning	Planning and development of the recreation infrastructure and integrated systems.	Planning and development of the tourism infrastructure and integrated systems.
Marketing	Understanding the nature of the recreation product and how to price, deliver, and promote it. Developing a consumer focus to recreation service delivery.	Understanding the nature of the tourism product and how to price, deliver and promote it. Developing a consumer focus to tourism supply.
Law	Implementation of legislation to support or regulate recreation development and activity.	Implementation of legislation to support or regulate tourism development and activity.
Business	Business planning and management of recreation resources.	Business planning and management of tourism attractions and services.
Transportation	Understanding needs for and usage of transportation systems in providing access to recreation services.	Understanding tourist usage of transportation systems and needs with respect to access.
Hotel and Restaurant Administration	Training and management of workers as 'hosts' in recreation settings.	Training and management of workers in the hospitality industry.
Education	Development and promotion of a leisure ethic and leisure skills.	Developing appreciation for other cultures and environments.

include fear, anxiety, lack of confidence, and feelings of unworthiness. Similarly, common perceptions of benefit are maintained by tourists and those involved in non-tourist recreation. Such benefits include those listed by Crompton (1981) in his study of motivations for pleasure vacation. They are: escape from a mundane situation, self-exploration and evaluation, relaxation, prestige, regression, enhancement of kinship relations, social interaction, cultural enhancement, novelty and education.

Through both recreation and tourism, social meanings and roles are taught and learned. Early forms of tourism (e.g., the Grand Tour, the Thomas Cooke pilgrimages, etc.) and the beginnings of the play and recreation movement in North America displayed the potential of recreation and tourism in establishing social roles and giving meaning to the individual's social world. The Grand Tour was designed to help young European noblemen to "find themselves" and become "wise in worldly matters". Thomas Cooke arranged tours to help parishioners to attend special religious services that reinforced their faith, and the playgrounds, sand gardens and recreation programs of the late 1800s were designed to socialize the new Canadians and Americans who had come to be part of a society with different expectations, limitations and opportunities.

Recreation and tourism also have commonalities in form and function. In referring to recreation and tourism as partners in the community leisure service delivery system, Brayley (1991) emphasized that "conceptually, and as far as the individual traveller/recreation participant is concerned, the link between recreation and tourism is quite natural". Both involve people engaging in free-time activities for intrinsic rewards. Both require the same specialized leadership and facilities. Both serve to broaden understanding, enhance self-awareness, promote health, and increase the quality of community life. A thorough examination of the activities and objectives of both recreation and tourism suggests a level of philosophical and practical compatibility that can be exploited for mutual advantage. The aim of municipal recreation is essentially to satisfy the leisure needs of individuals and enhance community life. The aim of tourism is to satisfy the leisure needs of individuals and enhance community life. The only difference is that community, in the tourism context, is viewed on a broader scale. Recreation and tourism organizations use similar means and engage in similar activities in attempting to satisfy individual leisure needs. They provide recreation facilities, distribute information about leisure opportunities, advise people on activities, and offer leadership and supervision.

Earlier in this chapter, it was also suggested that perceived barriers to participation in tourism are similar to or the same as those that restrict recreation activity. Antecedent constraints such as lack of awareness, absence of interest, value conflict and lack of desire to commit to a course of action apply as much to recreation participation as they do to the decision to seek a particular tourism experience. These antecedent constraints are labelled intrapersonal (Crawford & Godbey, 1987). Interpersonal constraints (another category of antecedent constraints) such as reference group disapproval, lack of travel companion(s) or activity partner(s), family obligations and social expectations also apply equally to both recreation and tourism. Inasmuch as the act of travelling to an away-from-home environment is a defining characteristic of tourism, it is likely that there will be more structural barriers to be overcome by the tourist than by the recreation participant. Overnight travel requires additional financial, temporal, and information resources, but most structural barriers (including financial costs, transportation and access, time, and facilities) do influence recreation and tourism activity in similar ways.

A final similarity to be noted is the influence of environmental factors on expectations and perceptions of quality in the tourism or recreation experience. Environmental factors such as weather, crowding, cleanliness, security, aesthetics, noise, and hospitality are all important criteria used by recreation and tourism consumers in establishing performance expectations and in evaluating the quality of their experiences.

Clearly there are many similarities between recreation and tourism. The two phenomena are actually much more alike than management or bureaucratic structures in most public, private, or commercial leisure service organizations would suggest. They are not, however, entirely the same.

One important difference is evident in the market definition activities of typical recreation and tourism organizations. In tourism, spatial rather than social considerations influence the identification and segmentation of the market. Though this practice is slowly changing, most Canadian tourism markets are described in terms of their origin or destination, and less attention is given to their social needs and characteristics. Market promotions may be oriented to "the U.S. market" or to "the outbound European market". Canadian markets for recreation, on the other hand, are typically classified according to relevant social characteristics such as age, gender, marital status, education, or income. Recreation programs are, for example, offered to "lower income, single women" or to "well-educated, middle-class families". This difference is important because the way that we define markets influences the manner in which we respond to them.

It was suggested earlier that different "bottom line" indicators are applied to performance evaluation in tourism and recreation. This is true so far as commercial tourism and public or private not-for-profit recreation are concerned. Unlike some eastern European nations in their socialist years, Canada has no public tourism strategy. Tourism is viewed as a merit service, and is left to the commercial sector to promote and facilitate. This means that the success of tourism will be measured in terms of its economic activity rather than its social contribution. In contrast, recreation is strongly influenced by the public sector and its success is measured in terms of the contribution to health, happiness and the quality of community life that it makes. There are, of course, commercial recreation enterprises that are driven by the need to produce economic gain, but the Canadian recreation industry is dominated by social service agencies.

A third important difference between recreation and tourism in Canada is in the area of industry leadership. As has already been noted, the lead sector in tourism is the commercial sector. More specifically, the transportation and lodging industries play an important part in determining the level of tourism development and its sustainability. The roles of the public sector in tourism are frequently limited to those of attraction manager (as in the case of parks, recreational waters, historic sites, and cultural displays/events), general publicist (as exemplified by federal and provincial government advertising in foreign and domestic markets), or industry regulator (through the exercising legislative authority). For recreation, however, the lead sector is clearly the public sector and the role played by government is often that of direct providers of leisure services.

Recreation and tourism are similar in many ways. They are also different enough from each other that it would be an unfair simplification to assert that tourism is just "recreation away from home" or that recreation is just "tourism without going anywhere".

Why Do People Travel?

People travel away from home as tourists because of an expectation of receiving desired benefits. Through travel and recreational activity in an unusual setting, tourists expect to receive social benefits which may include meeting new people, experiencing new cultures, teaching or sharing skills, developing new skills, or strengthening friendships and family relationships. Tourists might also expect to receive physical benefits like improved health and beauty, or access to goods and services that can enhance their home environment. Emotional benefits to be gained from tourism experiences could include ego enhancement, novelty and intellectual stimulation, stress reduction and relaxation, or opportunities for spiritual edification.

Whatever combination of social, physical, or emotional benefits are needed or desired by tourists, there is a belief and expectation held by recreational travelers that certain activities or experiences at particular destinations can satisfy their needs. Valene Smith (1977) described six types of tourism based on the kinds of travel experiences that tourists seek at their destinations. He described *ethnic tourism* as traveling for the purpose of experiencing the culture of other people or participating in cultural or religious events that are significant to the traveler. Through these types of destination activities, the tourist seeks social benefits by re-establishing links with his or her ethnic heritage. A second type of tourism described by Smith also provides social benefits and is called *cultural tourism.* Destinations and activities chosen by cultural tourists reflect their need to experience or witness a vanishing or sheltered lifestyle. Visits to museums, restored homes and villages, costume festivals, and "old-fashioned" restaurants are their favourite activities. *Historical tourism* accommodates travelers who desire to appreciate and find glory in the past. Popular attractions for historical tourists are battle reenactments, monuments and cathedrals, museums, forts, and designated historic sites. The fourth type of tourism described by Smith was *environmental tourism.* Here the tourist travels for the purpose of appreciating and heightening sensitivity to people-land-nature relationships. Sometimes called "green tourism," "alternative tourism," or "ecotourism," this type of tourism activity addresses a consciousness and satisfies an emotional need that seems to be growing significantly in the last years of this century. Environmental tourists typically hike, take photographs, observe wildlife from afar, and practise minimal impact camping. Canada's national parks are favourite destinations for environmental tourists. *Business tourism* is characterized by job-related activities such as company retreats, conventions, meetings and seminars. The business tourist is motivated less by leisure interests, although business travel is often combined with other non-work related tourism activities. Travel may also facilitate *recreational tourism*. Mieczkowski (1981) suggested that most tourism is motivated by the desire to participate in recreational activities. Travel itself may be recreational, or the recreational nature of the trip may be observed in the tourists' activities at the final destination. Martin and Mason (1987) believe that recreational tourism will increase in importance and that "all types of tourists, both young and old, will be looking for tourist destinations and packages that offer more than just a chance to enjoy the weather, the surroundings, the view and the company. Activities, experiences, participation and learning will all be elements in the future tourism product."

People travel to realize specific benefits and satisfy a wide variety of needs. Their motivations for travel are often similar to those for recreation, but tourism will always offer some unique benefits and satisfy some peculiar needs.

The Scope of Tourism Activity in Canada

By the end of this century, tourism is expected to be the world's largest industry. It already employs one sixteenth of the world's work force and generates annual world-wide revenues of over 2.5 trillion dollars (Canadian). A 1,600 percent growth in annual international arrivals over the past four decades means that over 400 million international tourist trips are taken each year (Edgell, 1990). When this number is combined with the number of domestic (i.e., within the borders of the origin nation) trips, it is not surprising that tourism is of great interest to the leisure service industry.

Tourism in Canada is of great economic importance. Millions of people travel for pleasure purposes and, in so doing, contract for services or make purchases which support an extensive tourism industry. The tourism industry includes companies, individuals and organizations that provide travel and transportation services, lodging and accommodation, food and beverage services, entertainment and recreation, souvenirs and gifts, communications, and information services. Foreign visitors and Canadians traveling within Canada spent nearly 27 billion dollars on tourism products in 1990. More than 7 billion dollars were spent by international travellers, thus providing an important economic stimulus. Figure 8.1 illustrates the relative sizes of the shares of tourism receipts by each province and the territories. The provinces attracting most tourism revenue are Ontario, British Columbia, and Quebec which accounted for 70 percent of all tourism receipts in 1990.

Statistics Canada reported that, in 1991, there were 259,000 Canadians employed in Canada in tourism-driven industries (e.g., accommodation, air travel, travel services). A further 940,000 were employed in tourism-related industries such as food and beverage services, surface transportation, and amusement and recreation. It should be noted, however, that approximately half of the jobs in the tourism industry are seasonal or part-time positions.

Canadian residents travel extensively within their own country and abroad. In 1990, nearly 70 percent of Canada's population made an overnight non-business trip in Canada, and more than a third of those people travelled to another province during the trip. The United States was also a popular destination for Canadian travellers, with 19 million people crossing the border that year for overnight non-business purposes.

Not only do Canadians travel within their own country and abroad, but millions of residents of other nations visit Canada. In 1991, 37 million international visitors entered Canada. Most (91 percent) were travelers from the United States, but many visitors also came from the United Kingdom (579,000), Japan (478,000), France (325,000), and Germany (312,000). American tourists represent the absolute largest but a proportionally decreasing source of international visitors, even though as many as 14 percent of the U.S. population visit their northern neighbours each year.

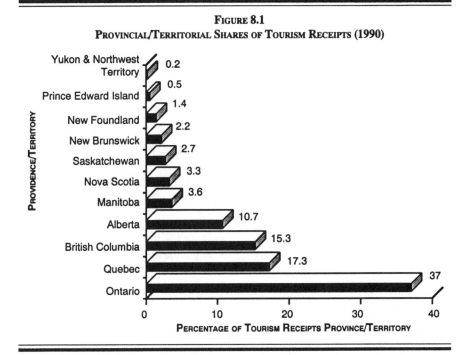

FIGURE 8.1
PROVINCIAL/TERRITORIAL SHARES OF TOURISM RECEIPTS (1990)

Tourism and the Recreation Service Provider

The national, provincial, and community recreation delivery system contributes to the tourism experience in several ways. Most importantly, it enhances the attractiveness of the destination by providing publicly accessible recreation areas, facilities, programs and services. Attractions such as parks, beaches, waterways, trails, nature reserves, golf courses, festivals, sporting events, museums, and scenic areas are, in many parts of Canada, managed by public or private not-for-profit recreation agencies. Other tourist attractions such as amusement parks, theatres, and specialized sports facilities are managed by commercial recreation enterprises. Without these public and commercial attractions, much of Canada's tourism potential and competitive advantage would be lost.

Sometimes, policy-makers and managers in public recreation agencies believe that being responsible to the taxpayer means that they must treat these local recreation resources as exclusive privileges for their constituents. "After all," they might argue, "why should *our* limited tax dollars be used to develop a park or operate a swimming pool that will be full of out-of-towners?" There's a glimmer of reason in this position, since most public recreation facilities and programs neither make a profit nor break even and, therefore, require the expropriation of local personal resources to facilitate their provision. The increasingly popular concept of market equity suggests that benefits should only accrue to those who pay the full price of a service (Crompton & Lamb 1986) and, since they don't contribute directly to the municipal tax coffers, tourists are thought to be unjustly advantaged when welcomed and given access to public recreation facilities and programs.

Of course, this position is weak because it ignores the indirect impact of tourist activity on the economy of the community. It is true that tourists don't pay the taxes which subsidize recreation services, but it is also true that they help to keep taxpaying businesses in business, contribute directly to the income of local taxpayers, and enhance recreation revenues through payment of user fees. The user fees collected from tourists help to reduce the need for tax revenue subsidization of recreation programs for local citizens. Not surprisingly, the Canadian Parks/ Recreation Association believes that "promoting and catering to tourism is a legitimate way for park and leisure service providers to earn revenues which can support other public services" (CP/RA, 1987).

In addition, the demand for services by tourists often creates new opportunities for the local population to enjoy those same services. Some recreation facilities, services, and programs are only feasible when local demand (and financial support) is supplemented by that of tourists.

The recreation service provider also contributes to the tourism experience because of the protective role it plays with respect to the physical environment. The presence of Banff National Park as a protected recreation resource *and* as an enduring tourism destination is in no way coincidental. Concern for quality local recreation environments enhances tourism opportunity, but it should also be noted that tourism initiatives have often protected special areas for recreation. Even the harshest critics of tourism must recognize that "conservation and the preservation of natural areas, archaeological sites and historic monuments have emerged as important spill-over benefits of tourism" (Mathieson & Wall, 1982).

Intuitively, it seems "right" for recreation service providers and the tourism industry to work together, but the motivation for such cooperation is ultimately going to be the perceived satisfaction of self-interest by both parties. When nurtured and allowed to flourish, the symbiotic relation between tourism and local recreation will yield an abundance of opportunities for all kinds of leisure and for important organizational objectives to be met.

Modern Vacation Behaviour

If your memory of family vacations involves images of two-week long summer excursions with Mom, Dad, the kids, and Spot the Wonder Dog in the station wagon, then you are probably older than most recent high school graduates. In the years of relative prosperity following the Second World War, family vacation behaviour was reasonably predictable and usually resembled that described above. The Baby Boomers (those people born in the late 1940s through the early 1960s) are forging a new model of vacation behaviour.

Family vacations in the 1990s often include a mixture of business and pleasure. Frequently, vacation destinations and schedules are chosen to facilitate some business activity of one or more family members. It would not be unusual, for example, for a young family to plan a spring vacation on Vancouver Island because one of the parents had a business meeting in Victoria. While there, the family might also include in its itinerary a tour of a major marina because the parent's line of work relates to pleasure boating.

The "Baby Boomer Break" or quick getaway is also a common style of vacationing in the 1990s. "One of the real trends in travel is that people are taking shorter vacations—and more of them" (Royal Bank, 1988). Not only is the duration decreasing and the frequency of vacations increasing, but impulse travelling (deciding to go on a holiday today and leaving tomorrow) is becoming more common.

Destination Development in the Great White North

Canada faces the challenge of having too little of at least two of the four Ss (sun, sand, sea, sex) that are generally considered to be essential ingredients of a successful mass tourist destination. Our weather is not always inviting, and relatively few people (with the exception of skiers and snowmobilers) prefer to travel to a cold climate for their holidays. National park development in northern areas and the growing interest in adventure travel and wildlife viewing may provide a window of opportunity for Canada's tourism industry. One of the challenges facing destination development in northern areas is the availability of varied cold weather recreation resources (especially activities and leadership).

Snowbirds

During the first three months of 1987, Canadians spent 18.9 million person-nights on vacation in the sun states of the U.S. Residents of those destinations refer to the Canadians who are fleeing the winter as "snowbirds" and welcome their contributions to the local economy. Snowbirds tend to be older (usually retired) and somewhat affluent, and they enjoy recreational pursuits that are not available during the winter in Canada (e.g., boating, walking, golf, tennis). Travel to these four areas accounted for almost half the winter travel outside Canada. Figure 8.2 (p. 136) illustrates the relative share the snowbird market attracted by California, Hawaii, Arizona, and Florida.

Snowbirds obviously have a major impact on recreation resource demands in the destination areas, but they also affect recreation resource utilization in their home communities. In their absence, the demographics of the home community changes and the provision of leisure services needs to account for that change.

Tourism and Canada's International Image

Canadians usually experience greater local acceptance when they travel abroad than do their immediate southern neighbours. Why? Perhaps because we, as a multicultural, bilingual nation symbolize tolerance, or because we have demonstrated

FIGURE 8.2
SHARES OF SNOWBIRDS IN THE FOUR MAJOR SUNBELT DESTINATIONS (1987).

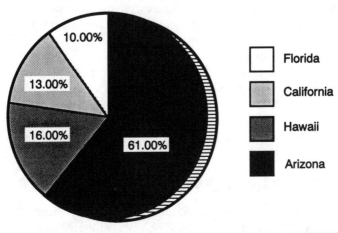

10.00%

13.00%

16.00%

61.00%

☐ Florida

▨ California

▨ Hawaii

■ Arizona

peaceful intentions by not exercising our ability to create nuclear weapons and maintain a strong army. Perhaps it is because we have demonstrated a sense of fairness and order through our support of the United Nations, or because our international business practices are relatively non-colonial in spite of our economic advantage. Whatever the reason, Canadian tourists are perceived to enjoy an enviable sense of security (as evidenced by the large number of Americans who deliberately display maple leaf buttons, pins or stickers while travelling in Europe and Asia).

Canada is also viewed by international travellers as a safe, beautiful, vibrant and interesting place to visit. The old image of a land of "moose, mountains and mounties" is fading and Canadian tourism promoters are finally beginning to capitalize on our positive international image.

> "For my part, I travel not to go anywhere, but to go. I travel for travel's sake. The great affair is the move."
>
> Robert Louis Stevenson

Summary

This introduction to the travel and tourism industry in Canada provides an important component in our understanding of the leisure services system. We have distinguished between tourism and other forms of leisure activity, described the nature and scope of tourism in Canada, examined the motivations of travellers, and identified the impacts of tourism on other forms of recreation. The travel and tourism field is one of growing interest to governments because of its economic potential. As a result, it will continue to be an area of considerable focus and while, careers per se are primarily those associated with the commercial recreation sector and government tourism agencies, growth opportunities among researchers seem likely.

STUDY QUESTIONS

1. Explain the differences between leisure, recreation, and tourism as noted in the work of Mieczkowski.

2. How was tourism and tourist defined in the chapter?

3. How are constraints that affect your leisure similar to those that affect your travel behaviour?

4. What is the relationship between recreation and tourism in terms of the activities of service providers?

5. Describe the three important differences between recreation and tourism.

6. Describe the six types of tourism based on Smith's work.

7. If asked, how would you describe the economic impact of the tourism industry in Canada?

8. Compare and contrast the types of tourism services that might have been offered in 1960 for families versus those that might be offered today.

9. Who are the "snowbirds" and where do they go?

10. How would you promote Canada to someone from Europe? Japan? Australia? United States?

References

Alberta Tourism. (1986). *Community tourism action plan, book 1.* Edmonton, AB: Author.

Balmer, K. (1992). Tourism: The other half of Canada's leisure industry. *Leisure Watch Canada, 1*(4), p. 1.

Brayley, R. E. (1991). Recreation and tourism: Partners in the community. *Recreation Canada, 49*(4), pp. 19-22.

Canadian Parks/Recreation Association. (1987). *National policy on recreation and tourism.* Ottawa, ON: Author

Crawford, D. W. & Godbey, G. (1987). Reconceptualizing barriers to family leisure. *Leisure Sciences, 9,* pp. 119-128.

Crompton, J. L. & Lamb, C. W. Jr. (1986). *Marketing government and social services.* New York, NY: Wiley & Sons.

Crompton, J. L. (1981). Dimensions of the social group role in pleasure vacations. *Annals of Tourism Research, 8*(4), pp. 550-67.

Edgell, D. (1990). *Charting a course for international tourism in the '90s.* Washington, DC: U.S. Department of Commerce.

Jafari, J. (1983). Anatomy of the travel industry. *The Cornell Hotel and Restaurant Administration Quarterly, 24*(1), pp. 71-77.

Martin, W. H. & Mason, S. (1987). Social trends and tourism futures. *Tourism Management, 8*(2), pp. 27-34.

Mathieson, A. & Wall, G. (1982). *Tourism: Economic, physical, and social impacts.* Essex, UK: Longman Scientific and Technical (p. 95).

McIntosh, R. W. & Goeldner, C. R. (1986). *Tourism principles, practices, philosophies.* New York, NY: John Wiley & Sons, Inc.

Mieczkowski, Z. T. (1981). *Some notes on the geography of tourism: A comment. Canadian geographer, 25,* pp. 186-91.

Murphy, J. F. & Howard, D. R. (1977). *Delivery of community leisure services: An holistic approach.* Philadelphia, PA: Lea and Febiger.

Murphy, P. E. (1985). *Tourism: A community approach.* New York, NY: Methuen.

Royal Bank (1988). And away we go: Travelling at home and abroad. *The Royal Bank Reporter,* (Spring, 1988).

Smith, V. (1977). *Hosts and Guests.* Philadelphia, PA: University of Pennsylvania Press.

WTO (1991). *Definitions and Classifications,* briefing document for delegates to the International Conference on Travel and Tourism Statistics. (Ottawa, OT: June 24-28, 1991). Madrid, Spain: Author.

Chapter Nine

Recreation for Persons with Special Needs
by
Michael J. Mahon, The University of Manitoba

Overview

PURPOSE

The purpose of this chapter is to provide an introduction to the opportunities which are presently available to persons with special needs related to recreation and leisure, the conceptual foundation for such opportunities, and most importantly, the changes which are necessary to ensure that opportunities for persons with special needs continue to grow.

LEARNING OBJECTIVES

At the completion of this chapter, you should be able to:

1. understand the basic terminology used within the field of recreation and leisure related to persons with special needs,

2. have a working knowledge of the history of recreation services for persons with special needs in Canada,

3. grasp the significance of the contemporary cornerstones of service delivery for individuals with special needs,

4. have an understanding of the various service delivery models which exist for the provision of general recreation and therapeutic recreation services for persons with special needs,

5. be acquainted with the most prominent intervention strategies within both a community recreation and therapeutic recreation environment, and

6. have an appreciation for the critical issues which exist in the 90s related to individuals with special needs and the provision of recreation services.

Recreation for Persons with Special Needs

Substantial changes in the conceptualization and provision of recreation and leisure services for individuals with special needs has occurred during recent years. Many of these changes are a reflection of the slow transition in attitudes which has occurred in society with respect to persons with special needs. A great deal of this reconceptualization is a reflection of our realization that individuals with special needs are indeed *people* with similar needs and aspirations as the rest of society. An underlying theme of this chapter is that recreation and leisure service professionals must consider the *individual* with the special need, before focusing on their disability.

One way in which we will achieve this theme is through the use of "people first" language throughout the chapter. At all times, we will refer to "individuals with special needs" as opposed to such labels as "disabled people," "the disabled or handicapped," "the retarded," etc. The use of "people first" language will help to ensure that we always keep in mind that discussions are centered on individuals as opposed to stereotypes.

Terminology

There is often a great deal of confusion among students, professionals, and lay people regarding the meaning of terms such as special needs, disabled, handicapped, etc. This is not surprising given the preponderance of terms used today to describe similar if not the same types of people, situations, and settings. In order to have a basic understanding of the most typical terms used within the field of recreation and leisure, a number of definitions are provided within this section.

SPECIAL NEEDS/SPECIAL POPULATIONS

The term special populations is an umbrella term used to describe groupings of individuals who are not typically considered a part of the mainstream (Austin & Powell, 1981). This classification is most often used to describe people with disabilities, older adults, individuals who are economically deprived, and even at times to describe individuals of particular cultures perceived as "in need". A problem with the term "special population" is that it tends to connote that people who fit within these "populations" are homogeneous. This is far from the truth. In keeping with this chapter's focus on the individual, the term which we will use throughout this chapter is "individuals with special needs". This term is meant to be as broad as that of the term special populations, yet at the same time, centres on the "individual". As such, throughout this chapter when referring to individuals with special needs we will be including a broad range of individuals, who, for a variety of reasons, require extra support to ensure that they are able to benefit from recreation and leisure programs and services. For the most part, this term is intended to include the following types of people:

- individuals with disabilities (e.g., mental retardation, cerebral palsy, spina bifida, learning disabilities),
- older adults,
- individuals who are economically deprived, and
- individuals from cultures who have been historically underserved and/or segmented from Canadian society (e.g., native Canadians).

DISABILITY/HANDICAP

It is quite common for the terms disability and handicap to be used interchangeably in the everyday vernacular. Though they may have come to mean the same thing for many people, there is an important distinction to be made between these two terms. Thorburn and Marfo (1990), using the classification system of the World Health Organization as a basis for their argument, suggest that the term disability refers to the individual's loss of functional ability which is caused by an impairment, whereas a handicap is a disadvantage limiting fulfillment of normal roles, which is the result of the impairment and disability. Kennedy, Smith and Austin (1991) present a similar argument. They suggest that the distinction which can be made between the two terms is that:

the word disability refers to a specific impairment or disorder, whereas a handicap results from actions of the person with the disability or by society. (p. 29)

The importance of the distinction between these two terms relates to the need for society as a whole to fight "handicapism," which refers to attitudes and practices that lead to unequal and unjust treatment of people with disabilities. It is critical for us to understand that an individual who has a disability is not necessarily handicapped.

SPECIAL RECREATION/ADAPTED RECREATION

These two terms have been used by various agencies to describe what are, in most cases, the same services. Kennedy, Smith and Austin (1991) indicate that the term special recreation:

has recently emerged to describe recreation and leisure provisions that accommodate recreation participation by members of special populations groups, and particularly by persons with disabilities. (p. 31)

Meyer (1981) points out that the word special relates to the type of services, and not to the individual. That is, special recreation focuses on the unique nature of the accommodations required to assist an individual in participating in a recreation activity. In Canada, a very typical description for the branch of a municipal recreation department that caters to the needs of individuals with special needs is "adapted services". For example, the City of Winnipeg employs "adapted recreation specialists" responsible for facilitating the recreation needs of persons with disabilities. The term adapted recreation is for the most part synonymous with that of special recreation. The one significant difference between the terms adapted and special is that the latter, while not intending to, tends to emphasize the "differentness" of the individual who benefits from such services. The term adapted is in many ways more neutral, and as a result tends to contribute much less to the labelling of persons with special needs as "different".

THERAPEUTIC RECREATION

A great deal of debate has occurred as to what the term therapeutic recreation means. It is beyond the scope of this chapter to enter into a long discussion on the issues within this debate. The definition of therapeutic recreation which is subscribed to herein is best described by Bullock (1987):

> Therapeutic recreation is the purposive use of recreation by qualified professionals to promote independent functioning and to enhance optimal health and well-being in persons with illnesses and/or disabling conditions. (p. 203)

As you can see by this definition, it is the purpose of the service which distinguishes whether it is "therapeutic recreation" or recreation services. Bullock (1987) in the same passage argues that:

> Therapeutic recreation is not any and all recreation services for persons who are disabled. Merely being disabled does not qualify a person to receive "therapeutic" recreation services...To call recreation services "therapeutic" because they involve a person or a group of persons with a disability is doing a disservice to the person who is being served. (p. 203)

Given this definition of therapeutic recreation, it is appropriate to suggest that recreation for persons with special needs fit within two broad categories: (a) general recreation services for persons with special needs, and (b) therapeutic recreation services. Both will be addressed in the remainder of this chapter.

The History of Recreation Services for Individuals with Special Needs: A National Perspective

Information related to history of recreation services for individuals with special needs in Canada is scant. That which is available primarily refers to the past three decades. This is not altogether surprising, given that the majority of services in Canada for individuals with special needs were initiated during this time. Up until the 20th century, the primary provider of recreation services for individuals with special needs were families. For the most part persons with disabilities and others with special needs remained at home and spent the majority of their time indoors, shut out from society.

The introduction of institutional care for individuals with mental retardation and mental illness in the 1800s resulted in the provision of some recreation services for such individuals (Avedon, 1974). It was not until the middle of the 20th century, however, that recreation services within the community began to develop. Prior to the late 1960s, most of these services were offered by voluntary agencies.

A significant turning point for individuals with special needs in Canada was the amendment of the *Human Rights Act* in 1974 which prohibits discrimination against persons for a position of employment for reasons of physical or mental disability. Though this did not specifically relate to recreation and leisure, it served notice to the Canadian public that persons with disabilities "have rights". During this same year Peter Witt (1974) reported on a study, "The Status of Recreation Services for the Handicapped" commissioned by Recreation Canada (then a unit of Fitness and Amateur Sport Canada). Witt reported that national associations such as the then Canadian Association for the Mentally Retarded and the Canadian Mental Health Association strongly promoted the value of recreation and leisure, but that the municipal providers of recreation often did not provide such services. Of the 663 communities surveyed across Canada, only 145 reported any programs available for persons with disabilities. Institutions for persons with disabilities were much stronger providers of recreation services, with 235 of 442 institutions surveyed reporting the availability of recreation programs.

As a result of the Witt (1974) study, a flurry of activity took place related to enhancing leisure opportunities for persons with special needs. From 1975 to 1979 seven provinces and the Northwest Territories acquired financial support from Recreation Canada to assist in the establishment and operation of councils on recreation for special groups. During this same time period the Canadian National Institute for the Blind (CNIB), the Canadian Mental Health Association (CMHA), the Canadian Rehabilitation Council for the Disabled (CRCD), and the Canadian Association for the Mentally Retarded (CAMR) received federal funding to cooperate in creating the National Inter Agency Recreation Project (NIARP). The purpose of this project was to seek methods to improve the status of leisure services for their clients nationwide. In 1978, the NIARP was disbanded. At this same time the Canadian Parks/Recreation Association established the Committee on Recreation for Disabled Persons. This was partially in response to the ending of the NIARP. Unfortunately, little funding was attached to this committee.

In 1981 the United Nations designated the "International Year of the Disabled". This was a watershed year in Canada. The Federal Government also at this time released "Obstacles," a report of the special committee on the disabled and handicapped. One hundred and thirty recommendations appeared in the report of the subcommittee which had travelled across Canada to facilitate the development of this report. These recommendations were subsumed under 20 central areas, one of which was titled Sports, Recreation, and Leisure. This section of the document outlined the following two recommendations: (a) To provide a greater number of recreational programs and enhanced information regarding recreation opportunities for persons with disabilities, and (b) To integrate disabled persons into existing sports activities. It is unfortunate that the second recommendation focused only on sport as opposed to the integration of persons with disabilities into all *recreation* and sport programs. In addition to the recommendations which related specifically to recreation and sport, a number of others had significant impact on the delivery of recreation services. The most critical were those that related to human and civil rights, income and public accessibility. Obstacles updates were produced in 1985 and 1987. Also in 1981, Lyons (1981) published a follow-up to the Witt (1974) study. She reported that since 1974 leisure services for people with special needs in Canada had grown considerably. However, Lyons reported that services tended to be provided on demand rather than as the result of a general policy of inclusion. In many cases the demand came from advocacy groups such as the Canadian Association for the Mentally Retarded (now the Canadian Association for Community Living). The general climate at a municipal level tended to be one of "passive provision," with little advocacy for individuals with special needs by municipal recreation departments.

In 1986, the Jasper Talks conference took place in Jasper, Alberta. These talks, co-sponsored by Fitness Canada, the Canadian Association for Health, Physical Education, and Recreation, and the University of Alberta, brought 40 selected delegates and 30 resource people together from across Canada to review past efforts, evaluate the current situation and plan for the future related to adapted physical activity in Canada. A Blueprint for Action was subsequently released which charted the direction for the federal government related to this area. Subsequent to the production of the Blueprint for Action, in 1990 the Canadian government in conjunction with 15 national partners (including such organizations as Canadian Parks/Recreation Association, Canadian Red Cross Society, Canadian Special Olympics, YMCA, and the Learning Disabilities Association of Canada) created an arms-length organization called the Active Living Alliance: For Canadians with a Disability. The mandate of this alliance is to improve physical activity opportunities and experiences for people with disabilities. This initiative represents a commitment on the part of the Canadian Federal Government to help facilitate the participation of individuals with special needs in active recreation opportunities. It is important to note that the Active Living Alliance has been criticized because of ts somewhat narrow focus on physical activity, as opposed to a broader focus of ecreation.

A number of other events had lasting impact on the lives of Canadians with special needs during the decade of the 1980s. Probably the most significant of these was the heroic attempt on the part of Terry Fox to run across Canada. On April 12, 1980, Terry Fox set out from St. John's, Newfoundland in an attempt to be the first person with a disability to run across Canada. His story became a national news item. Tragically, Terry had to stop just outside of Thunder Bay, Ontario on September 1, 1980 because of a reoccurrence of the cancer which had earlier caused the loss of his leg. His subsequent death ignited a wave of support to find a cure for cancer, as well as for the rights of Canadians with a disability to a healthy and active lifestyle. More recently, in 1986, the journey of Rick Hanson, a wheelchair athlete from British Columbia, served to heighten the awareness of Canadians of the abilities of individuals with a disability. Hanson wheeled more than 35,000 km through 33 countries and Canada over the course of 21 months on his Man in Motion World Tour. The central objective of this tour was to facilitate the understanding that concentrating on abilities, and not disabilities, is what allows all individuals to move forward and grow stronger. These are but a few of the most notable occurrences within the history of recreation for persons with special needs at a national level.

Contemporary Cornerstones of Services for Individuals with Special Needs

In their introduction to the text *Recreation Integration*, Hutchison and Lord (1979) state that:

> The notion that individuals who are disabled can participate fully in their communities, has been met with controversy and avoidance in North America ... Intolerance and devaluation of individuals who are considered different have resulted in physical and social barriers which are difficult to overcome. (p. 3)

The injustices which Hutchison and Lord describe in their book, have not disappeared altogether in the 90s. However, a number of critical concepts introduced over the course of the past 30 years have begun to impact on the attitudes of society and the barriers described by Hutchison and Lord. The most notable of these are the notions of self-determination/self-advocacy, social role valorization/normalization, and integration. We will address each of these in relation to the delivery of recreation programs and services for individuals with special needs.

SELF-DETERMINATION AND SELF-ADVOCACY

Recently, individuals with and without disabilities have embraced the concepts of self-advocacy and self-determination. Williams and Schultz (1982, p. 89) indicate that self-advocacy "means that individually or in groups (preferably both), they (individuals with disabilities) speak to or act on behalf of themselves, or on behalf of others". In many ways, the evolution of the concept of self-advocacy represents a climax to the revolution of rights for persons with special needs. During these past thirty years a great deal has been written regarding how to facilitate equal rights for individuals with special needs, yet until very recently, much of what has been proposed has been done by non-disabled individuals. The self-advocacy movement represents the beginnings of people who are disabled themselves voicing their perceived rights and needs.

Ward (1988) suggests that self-determination consists of two critical components: (a) the attitude which leads people to define goals for themselves, and (b) the ability to take the initiative to achieve these goals. The amount of self-determination possible for any person depends not only on factors within a person, but on opportunities outside a person. One of the most significant ways in which we can empower individuals with special needs to become more self-advocating is by allowing them to make their own decisions.

Together the concepts of self-advocacy and self-determination are crucial for us to consider in relation to recreation and leisure for persons with special needs, especially as they relate to choice. Mahon and Bullock (1992) have suggested that one of the most significant ways people with special needs can be empowered within the domain of leisure is through allowing them to make decisions for themselves related to their recreation participation. Recently, a number of studies have been conducted within the field of therapeutic recreation related to the area of decision making and leisure and persons with mental retardation (Mahon & Bullock, 1992; Mactavish & Searle, 1992; Hawkins, Freeman, & Mash, 1991; Dattilo, 1986). This focus is congruent with the definitions of leisure proposed by a number of scholars (Iso-Ahola, 1980; Neulinger, 1974). Iso-Ahola (1980) suggests that the critical regulator for what people define as being leisure is perceived freedom. That is, if an individual perceives that he or she is free to choose when, where, and how they participate in an activity (or do not for that matter) they will tend to define that state as leisure (see earlier discussion in Chapter Three). Conversely, if that same individual is not given such a choice they will tend to define the same experience as anything but leisure. Thus, it would seem that the ability to choose or to exercise decision making, may be the principal determinant as to whether an individual experiences leisure.

Normalization and Social Role Valorization

The principle of normalization was first defined by Nirje (1970). Since then, following a comprehensive interpretation by Wolfensberger (1972), this principle has become an internationally influential paradigm which has served as the cornerstone of service delivery (including recreation) for persons with disabilities (Howe-Murphy & Charboneau, 1987). The principle of normalization was defined by Wolfensberger as the:

> Utilization of means which are as culturally normative as possible, in order to establish and/or maintain personal behaviours and characteristics which are as culturally normative as possible (p. 28).

There has been some confusion over this term, as many have focused on the word "normal" in attempting to understand its application to the recreation service delivery system. It is important to understand that the intent of normalization is not to transform persons with disabilities into "normal individuals". Rather, the principle should be interpreted as a process for facilitating the creation of recreation environments and experiences for persons with disabilities which are typical of all people. Thus, this process has a final end goal of individuals engaging in culturally normative leisure experiences. As a result of the misrepresentation/interpretation of the normalization principle, Wolfensberger (1983) reconceptualized the principle into the theory of *social role valorization*. The foundation of this theory, which is highly correlated with that of normalization, is:

> . . . that the most explicit and highest goal of normalization must be the creation, support, and defense of valued social roles (emphasis added) for people who are at risk of social devaluation, p. 234).

Thus, social role valorization theory advocates for each individual's right and responsibility to assume a valued social role in society, and society's obligation to allow individuals to pursue that role without constraint. Certainly one of the role's which is valued within North American society is that of the person "at leisure". The media abounds with images of individuals enjoying a variety of recreation pursuits, and typically these individuals are presented in such a manner, as to suggest that their recreation participation is of value. Recently, Bullock and Howe (1991) and Rancourt (1989) have suggested that it is incumbent upon the therapeutic recreation professional to facilitate the outcomes most crucial to the achievement of valued social roles, which are according to Wolfensberger (1983), an enhanced social image and enhanced personal competence.

RECREATION INTEGRATION

One of the outcomes of the adherence to the principle of normalization should be the opportunity for social integration, which consists of both social interaction and social acceptance (Bullock & Howe, 1991). An area in which social integration can take place is within a recreation and leisure setting. Fullwood (1990, p. 3) defines integration in this way:

> 'Integration' is based on the word 'integrity' which can mean 'to be yourself amongst others, able and allowed to be yourself among others'. It does not mean 'making identical or even 'making similar', and neither does it mean making people conform, pass a certain standard or be 'more normal' . . . integration does mean allowing people to be the same if they want, through giving them the same chances and choices in their lives . . . as well as the right to be different.

Lord (1983), in his seminal article "Reflections on a Decade of Integration" suggested that integration has meant different things to different people, and has been subject to progressive ideas as well as some distortions. According to Lord, in many cases service delivery agents have proposed opportunities for integration, which he describes as false alternatives. Two of the false alternatives which have been proposed within the field of recreation as viable integration alternatives to segregation, are:

1. *Integrated Programs.* Recreation departments have responded to the demands for integration by creating an integrated program.

2. *Non-disabled People placed in Segregated Programs (Reverse Integration).* Many recreation systems have used this strategy to satisfy their integration mandate, by arguing that the persons with a disability are able to interact with non-disabled people, without having to 'disrupt' the system.

It is important to recognize that these alternatives are examples of recreation systems responding to a perceived push towards integration through the creation of contrived integrated opportunities. The notion of integration within a recreation setting must be recognized as an individual process for facilitating the choices of an individual with respect to the setting within which they wish to participate. In and of themselves these integration alternatives are by no means bad. They should not, however, be utilized by service providers simply as a means to satisfy a mandate for integration.

The three constructs which have been presented within this section provide an important framework within which all community recreation and clinically based personnel should deliver services. As should be evident to you by now, none are mutually exclusive. The concept of self-determination in leisure is strongly related to normalization and social role valorization. An individual who is capable of making decisions with respect to leisure and carrying out his or her decisions, will be perceived by society as having a valued social role. At the same time, the notion of self-determination is related to Fullwood's (1990, p. 3) definition of integration, in which she suggests that integration connotes "giving them the same chances and choices in their lives". This interconnected framework provides the foundation for the last two sections within this chapter which provide an overview of the existing service delivery models and intervention strategies used within the fields of therapeutic recreation and community recreation for persons with special needs.

Service Delivery Models

The provision of recreation services to persons with special needs in Canada is facilitated by a number of different service delivery systems with varying models for providing such services. We can loosely group the breadth of service models which exist across Canada into three categories:

1. Community Based Recreation Programs,

2. Clinical Therapeutic Recreation, and

3. Community Based Disabled Sport Programs.

We will describe each of these systems within this section. It is important to note that the vast majority of recreation programs for persons with special needs in Canada are community-based programs. The delivery of recreation services occurs primarily at a local or municipal and a provincial level. Typically, that which occurs at a national level falls under the category of advocacy and coordination. We will concentrate on the area of service delivery and following this briefly describe the most significant aspects of the national advocacy/coordination system.

COMMUNITY-BASED RECREATION PROGRAMS

As noted above, the majority of recreation services provided to persons with special needs in Canada exist within the community as opposed to institutional or hospital settings. More importantly, the majority of these programs do not have a therapeutic emphasis, but are more in keeping with mainstream community recreation programs in which the central goal is to facilitate recreation participation. This is also in keeping with the trend in our national health care system (of which many persons with special needs are a part), towards what Witt (1977, p. 13) describes as a movement away from: "institutionalization, medically dominated practices, notions of prescription, and notions of passive patients."

The majority of community-based programs and services for individuals with special needs can be described as either:

1. Adapted recreation programs offered by a municipal recreation system or a voluntary non-profit organization, or

2. Programs/services offered by a municipal recreation system or a private agency which exist for the benefit of all citizens (including those with special needs).

A great deal of discussion has taken place during the past twenty years related to which program models are most beneficial for the population under consideration. Many have suggested that it is crucial for communities to facilitate the inclusion of individuals with special needs in existing community-based recreation programs or enable them to engage in independent leisure pursuits (e.g., going out for dinner or to a show) (Bridge & Hutchison, 1988; Lord, 1983; Hutchison & Lord, 1979; Melchers, 1976). Such proponents argue that this is in keeping with the principles of normalization and integration. One of the most noted Canadian models proposed as a process for facilitating this goal is the Model for Recreation Integration by Hutchison and Lord (1979) (Figure 9.1). The key to this model is that integration is considered a process. Three factors are deemed necessary considerations in this process: upgrade, educate, and participate. All three must be considered in relation

FIGURE 9.1
A MODEL FOR RECREATION INTEGRATION PROPOSED BY HUTCHISON AND LORD (1979)

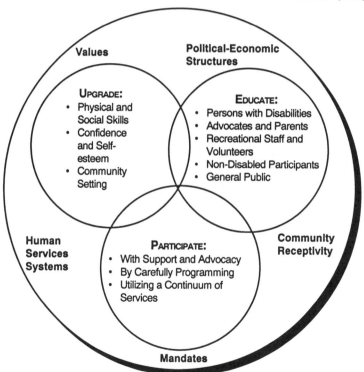

From: Hutchison, P. & Lord, J. (1979). *Recreation integration: Issues and alternatives in leisure services and community involvement.* (page 45, A Model for Recreation Integration). Reprinted with permission from Leisurability Publications, Inc.

to the individual, as well as society. More recently the authors of this model have criticized all such models, including their own, because they create an illusion on the part of society and the person with a special need that there are certain readiness factors which must be present before an individual can be integrated into the community (Hutchison & McGill, 1992; Lord, 1983). This is a complex debate regarding the appropriateness of continuum-based approaches to integration. For a full appreciation of the issues, the reader is directed to Hutchison and McGill (1992), Fullwood (1990), Howe-Murphy (1979), Bullock (1979), and Hutchison and Lord (1979). Nonetheless, the Hutchison and Lord (1979) model provided one of the earliest comprehensive descriptions of how to facilitate the integration of individuals with special needs into community-based programs, and is still very relevant today.

Since the introduction of this and other integration models by Canadian-based professionals and organizations (Alberta Recreation & Parks, Special Recreation Services Section, 1981; Hunter, 1981; Arsenault & Wall, 1979; Lyons & Reynolds, 1978) a number of initiatives have been introduced across Canada in an attempt to facilitate recreation integration at a local/municipal level. One municipal recreation example is the approach taken by the City of Dartmouth (Nova Scotia) Parks and Recreation (Landry, 1989). This department has fostered partnerships and co-operative ventures with many organizations and agencies with the aim of increasing community-based recreation opportunities for people with special needs. A six component value framework gives direction to the deliver system (see Figure 9.2). The city employs a 'recreation integrator' who's job it is to facilitate a personalized, individualized integration process. This process uses a leisure education approach to facilitating each individuals' recreation needs. During the process the integrator helps each participant to explore their interests, barriers, and resources, and to deal with such practical issues as transportation, access, and available programs.

FIGURE 9.2

A VALUE-BASED FRAMEWORK FOR THE INCLUSION OF PERSONS WITH SPECIAL
NEEDS IN COMMUNITY-BASED RECREATION PROGRAMS AND SERVICES
(Adapted from Landry, *Journal of Leisureability*, 1989)

1. Recreation is a fundamental right of all citizens.
2. All people have the right to develop a good understanding of leisure and recreation.
3. All people have a right to routines or a way of life typical to other people in the community.
4. All people have the right to community programs which are age- and culture-appropriate.
5. All people have the right to make recreation choices based upon their needs and interests.
6. All people have the right to the necessary supports for recreation participation.

A similar approach to facilitating integrated recreation opportunities is taken by the City of York (Ontario) Parks and Recreation Department (Hearst, 1989). In 1989 this department did away with any staff positions dedicated to creating special recreation opportunities. At that time all full-time staff were given the responsibility for the provision of integrated opportunities. Like Dartmouth, the City of York helps staff to facilitate these opportunities by employing integration staff to do such things as work directly with participants initially during the integration experience, facilitate interaction between participants who are disabled and non-disabled, help adapt programs when necessary, and work cooperatively with program staff. As a support to this integration initiative, the department provides recreation integration leadership training to staff. Other municipalities and provincial governments have begun to move towards an integration model for the delivery of recreation to persons with special needs. In 1986, the Surrey, British Columbia Parks and Recreation Commission renamed their "Specialized Programs" section to "Recreation and People with Special Needs Sections," and placed one such section in each community recreation office. By doing this, community recreation staff became responsible for ensuring the availability of recreation programs "for all," in contrast to this being the responsibility of a few "specialty" staff. The St. John's (Newfoundland) Department of Parks and Recreation released a policy statement on the integration of people with special needs in 1989. This statement indicated that people with special needs have the same need for recreation as does the population at large.

FIGURE 9.3
PROMOTIONAL MATERIAL FOR THE 1991 BRIDGING THE GAP AWARD PRESENTED BY THE NEWFOUNDLAND AND LABRADOR PARKS/RECREATION ASSOCIATION AS ONE MEANS OF FACILITATING ITS POLICY TO CREATE INTEGRATED RECREATION OPPORTUNITIES

Newfoundland & Labrador Parks/Recreation Association

BRIDGING THE GAP

AWARD

The NLP/RA Committee on Leisure services & Disabled Persons is pleased to announce the "Bridging the Gap Award". This Award is specifically designed to recognize the efforts of volunteers who have made significant contributions to the development of recreational opprtunities for persons with a disability in an integratred setting.

Reprinted with permission from Newfoundland and Labrador Parks and Recreation Association Committee on Leisure Services and Disabled Persons from "Bridging the Gap" promotion advertisement.

Historically, the more typical approach to providing services for persons with special needs has been through adapted recreation programs. These types of programs are often made available by municipal recreation departments, local YMCAs, Red Cross adapted aquatics programs, older adult day programs, etc. Municipal parks and recreation departments most often employ one or more staff who are responsible for the creation of programs which cater to individuals with special needs. Typically such programs are geared to a specific element of the special needs population, for example individuals with mental retardation, or older adults.

The argument which is most often made for such programs is that they cater to the specific needs of the client population. In the case of individuals with mental retardation, this may mean that a physical activity program has adapted activities to enable full participation by all. Programs for individuals with visual impairments offered by local chapters of the Canadian National Institute for the Blind are specifically geared to visually-impaired individuals. Another argument which is often made for such programs is that many individuals with special needs prefer them.

It is important to consider adapted programs in relation to the earlier discussions on self-determination, choice, and integration. Individuals with special needs should have the opportunity to make informed choices between integrated programs and adapted recreation programs. It is critical that recreation professionals not make assumptions in either direction with respect to each individual. Given this, it is incumbent upon municipal recreation agencies and community-based not-for-profit agencies to carefully consider the entire community and their needs before determining the types of programs which will or will not be offered. For example, if a municipality decides to delete an adapted swim program, they must determine whether all the needs of those who had attended the program in the past will continue to be met. In the final analysis, it is likely that more municipalities and agencies will move towards an integration-based model for service delivery. The challenge to all such agencies will be to ensure that programs remain accessible to persons with special needs.

CLINICAL THERAPEUTIC RECREATION PROGRAMS

The existence of institutional recreation programs has diminished over the course of the last two decades with the advent of deinstitutionalization (Reynolds, 1978). Institutions for individuals with mental illness and mental retardation which have been severely downsized in terms of client numbers, have correspondingly reduced the extent to which recreation is provided. In addition, the emphasis in community-based hospitals has begun to shift to shorter stays, day hospital services, and more in home care (Searle & Mahon, 1991). Given this, the provision of recreation within a hospital/institutional setting is or should be shifting in emphasis.

Much of what exists related to the provision of therapeutic recreation services in Canada has its roots in the United States. There is no formal national professional organization in Canada for individuals who describe themselves as therapeutic recreation specialists (TRS). The focus of the Canadian Parks/Recreation Association is primarily on community recreation for persons with special needs. There are, however, a number of provinces including Alberta, British Columbia, Ontario, and Nova Scotia which have some type of therapeutic recreation association. The majority of individuals working in therapeutic recreation (TR) in Canada have tended to hold membership in either the National Therapeutic Recreation Society (NTRS), the American Therapeutic Recreation Association (ATRA), or have had no formal linkages to a national therapeutic recreation association. Much of what is offered by way of therapy in either an institutional or community-based clinical setting has evolved from the theoretical and conceptual frameworks of one or other association.

In 1981 the NTRS adopted the Leisurability (Peterson & Gunn, 1978) philosophy and model as its official therapeutic recreation position. The purpose of the Leisurability model of therapeutic recreation is:

> ... to facilitate the development, maintenance, and expression of an appropriate leisure lifestyle for individuals with physical, mental, emotional, and social limitations. Accordingly this purpose is accomplished through the provision of professional programs and services which assist the client in eliminating barriers to leisure, developing leisure skills and attitudes, and optimizing leisure involvement (Peterson & Gunn, 1984, p. 321).

The Leisurability Model consists of three components: Therapy, Leisure Education, and Recreation Participation. According to Peterson and Gunn (1984), the purpose of the therapy component of the model is to improve functional behaviours which can allow the individual to become involved in meaningful recreation experiences. As such, therapy is necessary when an individual has certain functional limitations. Typically the functional behaviours which the TRS and individual address are those which have been identified as goals by an interdisciplinary team. Leisure education, the second component of the model, is provided to an individual in order to facilitate recreation skill acquisition, develop knowledge related to leisure, and to enable the individual to clarify their leisure attitude. Most importantly, leisure education is provided to facilitate the eventual *independent* leisure functioning of a person. The content areas which a leisure education curriculum may focus on are: concepts of leisure, leisure resources, leisure barriers, leisure skills, decision making in leisure, and leisure action planning (Mahon & Bullock, 1992).

The purpose of the final component of the model, recreation participation, is to provide opportunities which allow voluntary client involvement in recreation. Peterson and Gunn (1984) argue that it is important for TR to offer such opportunities because it is often necessary to adapt programs and equipment to allow for active participation by given individuals. The inclusion of this component in a therapeutic recreation model does not have the full support of the TR community. Austin (1991) argues that it is the responsibility of the special recreation programmer to offer such programs as opposed to TR. In contrast, Bullock (1987) argues that it is not the responsibility of the special recreation programmer, so much as the *recreation programmer*, to offer recreation opportunities for all individuals, including those with special needs.

FIGURE 9.4
THE LEISURABILITY MODEL

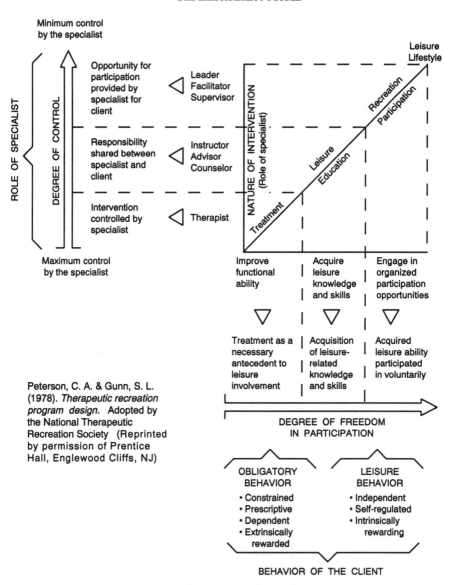

Peterson, C. A. & Gunn, S. L. (1978). *Therapeutic recreation program design*. Adopted by the National Therapeutic Recreation Society (Reprinted by permission of Prentice Hall, Englewood Cliffs, NJ)

Typically, the components of therapy and leisure education are offered within a clinical setting in Canada under the auspices of therapeutic recreation. In most institutions (either short-term or long-term care) opportunities for recreation participation are offered by recreation activity specialists. In many cases, such individuals have not had training in therapeutic recreation. The rationale for the provision of activity-based services by paraprofessionals is to offer diversion from the every day routine of institutional living. Because of the community-based orientation which prevails across Canada, it is also very uncommon for recreation participation outside of an institution to be facilitated by a TRS. Much controversy continues to exist related to the future of the activity specialist and the therapeutic recreation specialist within Canada. In most cases, the activity specialists are more organized, and in larger numbers than the therapeutic recreation specialist. The lack of professional ties by many professionals in TR continues to be an issue. We will discuss this issue further in the final section of this chapter.

COMMUNITY-BASED DISABLED SPORT PROGRAMS

The final component of the recreation delivery system for persons with special needs is that of Disabled Sport. This component has similar features to the community recreation delivery system. Both provide opportunities for individuals with special needs within the community. A crucial difference, however, relates to the mandate of each. While the community recreation delivery system has a mandate to offer a variety of recreation opportunities, ranging from painting classes to instructional aquatic courses, disabled sport programs have the provision of sport training and competitive sport opportunities as their central mandate.

Sport in relation to persons with disabilities has historically been misunderstood by the general population, service providers, the media, and at times care providers (Kennedy, Smith, & Austin, 1990). For example, historically articles related to athletes with a disability were not found in the sports pages of a local newspaper, but were most often treated as a human interest story. The needs and motivations of athletes with a disability were often viewed as different than those of athletes without a disability. More recently, however, society and those in the sport community have come to realize that individuals with disabilities have similar needs, aspirations, and drives related to participation in sport. This has resulted in some very exciting opportunities developing for persons with disabilities in the area of sport.

The somewhat recent realization of the rightful place of disabled athletes in the world of sport has resulted in the development of what is today a very comprehensive delivery system of sport for persons with disabilities. Kennedy, Smith, and Austin (1990, p. 239) suggest that there are some common goals shared between most sport programs for persons with disabilities. All such programs tend to:

- provide a method of informing the public about the unique abilities that participants possess;
- promote independence, sport skill development, and increased physical fitness among their participants;
- promote maximum participation by offering local or regional events but also provide for recognition of outstanding performances through national and international competition;
- have some system of classification, such as degree of disability, to make the competition in events as fair as possible;

- use a classification system as a method of increasing participation opportunities among individuals with severe disabilities; and
- offer some unique competitive events, or modified activities, that provide the participant with a chance to display special skills not usually associated with non-disabled competition.

In Canada, disabled sport mirrors that of generic sport in terms of the organizational hierarchy. Most disabled sport programs such as the Canadian Special Olympics, the Canadian Wheelchair Sport Association, and the Canadian Blind Sport Association are recognized by the Canadian Government's Fitness and Amateur Sport Branch. Each is a national non-profit organization which has counterpart provincial organizations. Many provincial sport organizations are also recognized as Provincial Sport Governing Bodies (PSGB) for the disability group they cater to, in the same way in which a basketball association is a PSGB. Some provinces have an umbrella body which advocates for disabled sport as a whole to their provincial government. One example of this is the British Columbia Sport and Fitness Council for the Disabled. This body, established in 1982, has a mandate "to increase participation in sport and physical recreation by disabled persons in all regions of the province" (J. A. Virtue, personal communication, October 7, 1991). Each disabled sport group provides competitive outlets from a local level to an international level for its athletes. Some organizations such as the Special Olympics and Wheelchair Sport are highly developed with impressive service delivery networks, coach training programs, and competitive schedules, while others are still at a developmental stage.

As the disabled sport movement has grown stronger, it has received strong criticism from some because many programs segregate athletes with disabilities from athletes without a disability (Hourcade, 1987; Brasile, 1990). For the most part it is true that disabled sport programs are segregated. One must recognize, however, that the very nature of competition and sport typically results in 'segregation' based upon ability level. All sport in Canada is divided into levels based upon ability, the seriousness of the competitors, etc. Disabled sport is no different. If an athlete with a disability is to be afforded the opportunity for fair competition, then they typically must compete against disabled athletes of their own ability level. Kennedy et al. (1990) also point out that sport competition is but one element of an individual's life. If an individual chooses to participate in a disabled sport program this does not preclude them from being integrated at work, during other recreation experiences, at school, etc.

Recently, many disabled sport programs have begun to develop parallel competitive opportunities for athletes with disabilities. For example, Manitoba Special Olympics enters athletes who are of high-school age in a Special Olympics class in the Manitoba Provincial "A" High School Athletics Meet. Parallel competitive opportunities allow athletes to compete against those of their own ability level, yet interact socially with athletes without a disability. This model holds great promise for the future.

NATIONAL RECREATION ADVOCACY/COORDINATION SYSTEM

The majority of services for individuals with special needs are provided for at a local, municipal, or provincial level. There are, however, some key national/federal bodies which advocate for and/or coordinate recreation services for persons with special needs. The most recently formed body which fits this description is the Active Living Alliance: For Canadians with a Disability. The mandate of this body is to promote and support active living by persons with a disability. Since its inception, this umbrella organization has developed such programs as a self-advocacy training program, and a leadership development model. The Canadian Association for Community Living (formerly the Canadian Association for the Mentally Retarded) is a major advocacy body for persons with intellectual impairments. This organization has a long history of advocating for recreation for individuals with a disability and developing training materials for volunteers and professionals working in this area. One of their most noted training programs is "Play for Plays Sake". Other organizations which have provided both advocacy and national coordination of programs and services for individuals with special needs are the Canadian Red Cross Association, the Canadian Federation of Sport Organizations for the Disabled, YMCA, Fitness Canada and the Canadian Parks and Recreation Association. Organizations such as these not only provide necessary coordination and advocacy, but through their national image, lend credence to the need for society to be aware of the rights of individuals with special needs related to recreation.

Intervention Strategies

There are numerous intervention strategies which have been used within the field of recreation to help facilitate participation by individuals with special needs. Many of these intervention strategies are utilized by a variety of disciplines ranging from psychology to special education, and are not the sole property of the professional working in a recreation and leisure setting. The distinction, however, is that they are used by recreation and leisure professionals to facilitate independent leisure behaviour by individuals with special needs. Within this section, we will highlight a few of the most prominent intervention strategies.

LEISURE EDUCATION

This intervention strategy is most often described as a comprehensive process employed to enhance the quality of a persons life through the development of leisure attitudes, knowledge and skills for recreation participation (Driscoll, Bullock & Bedini, 1991). Most leisure education models focus on the areas of leisure awareness, attitudes, leisure skills, social interaction, decision making, and leisure planning and initiation. Leisure education programs have been introduced to a variety of persons with special needs, including those with mental retardation, physical disabilities, older adults, and youth and adults in conflict with the law. Programs have been introduced through both one-on-one and group instruction. A number of techniques such as behaviour management, task analysis, counselling, and individualized prescription are used within this process. Though the literature on the benefits of leisure education is fairly scant, the positive effects of this intervention strategy have been reported related to social-psychological outcomes (Searle & Mahon, 1991; Shary & Iso-Ahola, 1989; Zoerink, 1988), leisure decision-making instruction (Mahon & Bullock, 1992), attitudes (Aguilar, 1987) and levels of leisure awareness (Mahon & Bullock, 1992).

Leisure education has been used within various aspects of the service delivery system. The Independent Living Resource Centre in Winnipeg, Manitoba, one of the first of its kind in Canada, uses leisure education as one of the integral parts of it's independent living facilitation process. Clients with physical disabilities are introduced to a leisure education program similar to the one described above to help facilitate transition into an independent living setting. The process is meant to help such individuals develop an enjoyable and healthy living environment through focusing on more than the vocational and daily living needs of the client. Other settings in which leisure education has been introduced are hospitals, group homes, adult day programs, and municipal recreation departments. A discussion of leisure education in the context of the recreation programming is presented in Chapter Twelve.

LEISURE COUNSELLING

Much debate has centered on the distinction between leisure counselling and leisure education. Both have been described as including the other. Chinn and Joswiak (1981, p. 6) provide one of the most clear distinctions in suggesting that:

> The leisure counselling process, then, a subset of leisure education, facilitates the process of problem solving, decision making, and conflict management regarding leisure interests, awareness, values, and opportunities.

We believe leisure counselling to be a problem-centered approach which utilizes verbal facilitation techniques to assist an individual in dealing with perceived and/or real leisure related problems.

ACTIVITY ANALYSIS

When an individual engages in any activity, their participation is dependent on three behavioural areas: physical, cognitive, and affective. For example, participation in a game such as checkers, normally considered a mental game, also makes demands on other aspects of the individual. Cognitively, the players must understand rules and strategy. Physically, the game requires sight, as well as the ability to grasp and move a small object. Affectively, checkers demands control of emotions and concentration. In addition, beyond these behavioural areas, it is important to consider the social or interactional skills required for participation in various recreation activities. In checkers, an individual must be able to deal with close contact with one other individual in what is often an intense level of interaction. The process of activity analysis allows an instructor to break down and examine a given

activity to determine the behavioural and social requirements for successful participation (Peterson & Gunn, 1984). Once an instructor has this knowledge, he or she
is better able to direct individuals towards activities to which they are most suited.
Activity analysis also helps the instructor and person with a special need to identify
the parts of activities which require adaptation and modification to facilitate
meaningful participation.

WILDERNESS ADVENTURE PROGRAMS

An exciting development in camping programs for individuals with special needs
has been the recent emphasis on wilderness adventure programs. These types of
programs are exciting for any individual who enjoys action, and the outdoors, and
are similarly exciting for persons with special needs. While each has their own
format, most programs are derived from a model developed by Outward Bound in
the early 1960s for working with youth with special needs (Kennedy, Smith, &
Austin, 1990). Wilderness Pursuits is one example of this type of program. A small
non-profit organization, Wilderness Pursuits has a mandate to provide wilderness
experiences ranging from three days to two weeks for individuals with any type of
disability. Participants are taken on a canoe/camping experience which necessitates
that they learn to work in a group, experience the stresses of the wilderness and group
living, and the physical strain of being in the out-of-doors at all times. This
organization has worked with individuals with all ranges of disabilities with great
success. The purpose of the program is to develop skills, a greater sense of self, and
to facilitate social integration between a variety of people.

ACTIVITY-BASED THERAPIES

This intervention approach represents a significant segment of any therapeutic
recreation program. Activity-based therapy is a term used to describe a treatment-
oriented program which utilizes a specific activity or a group of activities to facilitate
the improvement of an individuals physical skills, cognitive, social, and/or psychological functioning. One example of a specific activity-based therapy is pet therapy.
This intervention provides individuals with the opportunity to interact with pets in
either a group or individual session. The purpose of this activity may be to enable
the individual to experience the feeling of warmth and affection while in a sterile
environment, or may be to foster a feeling of control by providing the individual the
opportunity to care for a particular animal. Other types of activity-based therapies
are horticulture therapy and music therapy.
    Each of the different activity therapies are often used to foster similar types of
behaviours and feelings. It is important that an individual is given the choice,
however, of which type of activity they wish to experience. It is also important that
the activity therapy provided relate to possible leisure pursuits an individual might
enjoy once they leave the therapeutic environment. Horticulture therapy may be used to
foster a feeling of competence, by allowing an older adult to take care of plants within a
hospital unit. At the same time, teaching this same adult to take care of plants may well
lead to them caring for plants when they return home as a personal leisure pursuit.

OTHER INTERVENTIONS

A number of other interventions have been utilized within both a therapeutic recreation environment and a community-based setting. For example, cognitive behavioural techniques have been utilized to facilitate decision making and leisure participation by individuals with mental retardation in a community-based setting (Mahon & Bullock, 1992). Reminiscence therapy has been utilized extensively with older adults and adults with Alzheimer's in therapeutic recreation programs. Given the growing interdisciplinary nature of the human services field, recreation will continue to utilize new approaches, often borrowed from other disciples, to help facilitate independent leisure participation by individuals with special needs. It is impossible to overview all such strategies within this chapter. The reader is directed to Wuerch and Voeltz (1982), Peterson and Gunn (1984), Schleien and Ray (1987), Dattilo and Murphy (1987), and Austin (1991) for additional information on intervention strategies.

The 1990s and into the Year 2000

At the beginning of the chapter it was suggested that services for persons with special needs have progressed fairly rapidly during the past three decades, yet a great deal of ground still needs to be covered before all individuals are truly a part of the mainstream in recreation and leisure. The challenge for professionals during the last decade of the 20th century and into the 21st century is to empower individuals with special needs to achieve this goal. A number of recent trends in the fields of health care, education and recreation may help to facilitate this goal.

One of the trends which can have significant impact is the movement towards interdisciplinary planning for persons with special needs. This approach tends to facilitate the treatment of the individual with a special need as a whole person, as opposed to a segmented being. Recently, in both institutional and community-based settings, the recreation professional has begun to play a significant role in the interdisciplinary planning process. The ability of recreation professionals to interact with physicians, psychologists, nurses, educators, etc., can facilitate the inclusion of leisure goals in independent program plans in a variety of settings.

Earlier in this chapter, the trend toward shorter hospital stays, day hospitals, and more community based care was highlighted. This is often described as an inevitable yet nonetheless desirable outcome of the evolution of our health care system. A concern which arises, however, is the inability of therapeutic recreation to provide meaningful interventions with an individual with the advent of shorter hospital stays. A solution is to create transitional therapeutic recreation programs which are able to work with an individual as they move back into the community. Searle and Mahon (1991) demonstrated that leisure education could be utilized in a Municipal Day Hospital setting in Winnipeg to support the transition of older adults from a hospital to community based living arrangement. Further work is needed to investigate strategies for facilitating transitional TR.

The final issue of significance related to recreation for persons with special needs is the ongoing question of whom should provide recreation services. Many have recently suggested that it is the responsibility of the general recreation professional to provide such services in a community-based setting (Lord, 1983; Bullock, 1987). Given this, it is important for recreation curriculum at a university and community college level to provide the necessary training to such prospective professionals. Hutchison (1983) developed curriculum guidelines for colleges and universities which provide the necessary direction for this to occur. A second part of this issue relates to the provision of therapeutic recreation services. It is crucial for clinical recreation professionals to become more self-determining with respect to their future. Given the shrinking budgets of many hospitals, it is unlikely that hospital administrators will continue to advocate for therapeutic recreation specialists. The issue to be determined is whether to create a Canadian-based association, link up with a counterpart in the United States, or face a slow but sure disintegration of the place of the Therapeutic Recreation Specialist in a clinical setting.

Summary

Individuals with special needs have historically been underserved within the field of recreation and leisure. Over the past three decades, however, recreation professionals and society in general have slowly begun to realize the inequities which have existed, and have started on the slow road to change. This chapter has presented a wide scope of material in an attempt to introduce you to some of the critical considerations in the provision of recreation opportunities to individuals with special needs. The challenge of providing meaningful opportunities in recreation for persons with special needs is to do so in a manner which allows for individual choice and self-determination. We can best achieve this by keeping in mind the _person_ who happens to have a special need.

1. Define the terms handicapism, normalization, and self-determination in your own words, and then create a case example of a recreation program which is exemplary in dealing with all three concepts.

2. Distinguish between adapted recreation programs and disabled sport programs. What are some similarities between these two types of programs?

3. Contrast the intervention strategies of leisure education and activity-based therapy.

4. List some practical strategies you would use as a recreation programmer in order to integrate a child with mental retardation into a community-based swimming program.

5. Prepare a case to support the statement that "All individuals with disabilities should be afforded the opportunity to participate in community-based recreation programs, no matter what the cost."

References

Aguilar, T. E. (1987). Effects of a leisure education program on expressed attitudes of delinquent adolescents. *Therapeutic Recreation Journal, 21*(4), pp. 43-51.

Alberta Recreation and Parks: Special Recreation Services Section. (1981). *Mission: Recreation integration.* Edmonton, AB: Alberta Recreation and Parks: Special Recreation Services Section.

Arsenault, D. & Wall, A. E. (1979). *Service continuum for recreation.* Edmonton, AB: Alberta Association for the Mentally Retarded.

Austin, D. R. (1991). Therapeutic Recreation: Processes and Techniques. Champaign, IL: Sagamore Publishing.

Austin, D. R. & Powell, L. G. (1981). What you need to know to serve special populations. *Parks and Recreation, 16*(7), pp. 40-42.

Avedon, E. M. (1974). *Therapeutic recreation: An applied behavioural approach.* Englewood Cliffs, NJ: Prentice-Hall.

Brasile, F. M. (1990). Wheelchair sports: A new perspective on integration. *Adapted Physical Activity Quarterly, 7*(1), pp. 3-11.

Bridge, N. J. & Hutchison, P. (1988). Leisure, integration, and community. *Leisurability, 15*(1), pp. 3-15.

Bullock, C. C. (1987). Recreation and special populations, In A Graefe and S. Parker (Eds.), *Recreation and leisure: An introductory handbook* (pp. 203-208). State College, PA: Venture Publishing, Inc.

Bullock, C. C. & Howe, C. Z. (1991). A model therapeutic recreation program for the reintegration of persons with disabilities into the community. *Therapeutic Recreation Journal, 25*(1), pp. 7-17.

Driscoll, L. B., Bullock, C. C., & Bedini, L. A. (1991). *The Wake leisure education program: An integral part of special education.* Chapel Hill, NC: The Center for Recreation and Disability Studies of the Curriculum in Leisure Studies and Recreation Administration, The University of North Carolina—Chapel Hill.

Chinn, K. A. & Joswiak, K. F. (1981). Leisure education and leisure counseling. *Therapeutic Recreation Journal, 15*(4), pp. 4-7.

Dattilo, J. & Murphy, W. D. (1987). *Behavior modification in therapeutic recreation.* State College, PA: Venture Publishing, Inc.

Dattilo, J. (1986). Computerized assessment of preference for severely handicapped individuals. *Journal of Applied Behavior Analysis, 19*, pp. 445-448.

Fullwood, D. (1990). *Chances and choices: Making integration work.* Baltimore, MD: Brookes.

Hawkins, B. A., Freeman, P., & Mash, C. (1991). Leisure interests and preferences of aging adults with mental retardation: An exploration of choice-making determinants. *Proceedings of the 1991 Leisure Research Symposium.* Baltimore, MD: National Recreation and Park Association.

Hearst, C. (1989). Making integration a reality: City of York Parks and Recreation. *Leisurability, 16*(1), pp. 3-7.

Hourcade, J. J. (1989). Special Olympics: A review and critical analysis. *Therapeutic Recreation Journal, 23*(1), pp. 58-65.

Howe-Murphy, R. (1979). A conceptual basis for mainstreaming recreation and leisure services: Focus on humanism. *Therapeutic Recreation Journal, 13*(4), pp. 11-18.

Howe-Murphy, R. & Charboneau, B. (1987). *Therapeutic recreation intervention: An ecological perspective.* Englewood Cliffs, NJ: Prentice-Hall, Inc.

Hunter, J. (1981). Leisure education: Its role in the recreation integration process. *Recreation Canada Special Issue,* pp. 76-78.

Hutchison, P. & Lord, J. (1979). *Recreation integration: Issues and alternatives in leisure services and community involvement.* Ottawa, ON: Leisurability Publications, Inc.

Hutchison, P., & McGill, J. (1992). *Leisure, integration and community.* Concord, ON: Leisurability Publications.

Hutchison, P. (1983). *Curriculum guidelines for Canadian colleges and universities: Leisure and disabled persons.* Ottawa, ON: Canadian Parks/Recreation Association.

Iso-Ahola, S. (1980). *The social-psychology of leisure and recreation.* Dubuque, IA: Wm. C. Brown.

Joswiak, K. J. (1989). *Leisure education: Program materials for persons with developmental disabilities.* State College, PA: Venture Publishing, Inc.

Kennedy, D. W., Smith, R. W., & Austin, D. R. (1991). *Special recreation: Opportunities for persons with disabilities.* Dubuque, IA: Wm. C. Brown.

Landry, J. (1989). Making leisure available in Dartmouth. *Leisurability, 16*(1), pp. 3-7.

Lord, J. (1983). Reflections on a decade of integration. *Journal of Leisurability, 10*(4), pp. 4-11.

Lyons, R. (1981). A profile of municipal services for special populations in Canada. *Journal of Leisurability, 8*(4), pp. 14-24

Lyons, R., & Reynolds, R. (1978). *How to improve community leisure opportunities for disabled people.* Halifax, NS: Recreation Council for the Disabled.

Mactavish, J. B. & Searle, M. S. (1992). Older individuals with mental retardation and the effect of a physical activity intervention on selected social psychological variables. *Therapeutic Recreation Journal, 26,* pp. 38-47.

Mahon, M. J. & Bullock, C. C. (1992). Teaching adolescents with mild mental retardation to make decisions in leisure through the use of self-control techniques. *Therapeutic Recreation Journal, 26,* pp. 9-26.

Melchers, R. (1976). Community action: Recreation and disabled persons. *Leisurability, 3*(4), pp. 4-10.

Meyer, L. (1981). Three philosophical positions of therapeutic recreation and their implication for professionalization and NTRS/NRPA. *Therapeutic Recreation Journal, 15*(2), pp. 7-16.

Neulinger, J. (1974). *The psychology of leisure.* Springfield, IL: Charles C. Thomas.

Nirje, B. (1970). The normalization principle: Implications and comments. *Journal of Mental Subnormality, 16,* pp. 62-70.

Peterson, C. A., & Gunn, S. L. (1984). *Therapeutic recreation program design: Principles and procedures.* Englewood Cliffs, NJ: Prentice-Hall.

Rancourt, A. M. (1989). Older adults with developmental disabilities/mental retardation: Implications for professional services. *Therapeutic Recreation Journal, 23*(1), pp. 47-57.

Reynolds, R. P. (1978). The changing role of leisure services in residential facilities: Implications and challenges. *Leisurability, 5*(3), pp. 34-37.

Schleien, S. J., & Ray, M. T. (1988). *Community recreation and persons with disabilities.* Baltimore, MD: Paul H. Brookes.

Searle, M. S., & Mahon, M. J. (1992). Leisure education in a day hospital setting: The effects on selected social-psychological variables among older adults. *Canadian Journal of Community Mental Health, 10*(2), pp. 95-109.

Shary, J., & Iso-Ahola, S. E. (1989). Effects of a control-relevant intervention on nursing home residents' perceived competence and self-esteem. *Therapeutic Recreation Journal, 23*(4), pp. 7-16.

Thorburn, M. J. & Marfo, K. (1990). *Practical approaches to childhood disability in developing countries.* St. John's Newfoundland: Memorial University

Ward, M. J. (1988). The many facets of self-determination. *National Information Center for Children and Youth with Handicaps, 5,* pp. 2-3.

Williams, P., & Schoultz, B. (1982). *We can speak for ourselves: Self-advocacy by mentally handicapped people.* London, England: Souvenir Press (E & A) Ltd.

Witt, P. A. (1977). Recreation therapy: Who cares. *Leisurability, 4*(4), pp. 13-15.

Witt, P. A. (1974). *The status of recreation services for the handicapped.* Ottawa, ON: Department of National Health and Welfare.

Wolfensberger, W. (1972). *The principle of normalization in human services.* Toronto, ON: National Institute on Mental Retardation.

Wolfensberger, W. (1983). Social role valorization: A proposed new term for the principle of normalization. *Mental Retardation, 21*(6), pp. 234-239.

Wuerch, B. B., & Voeltz, L. M. (1982). *Longitudinal leisure skills for severely handicapped learners: The Ho'onanea curriculum component.* Baltimore, MD: Paul H. Brookes.

Zoerink, D. A. (1988). Effects of a short-term leisure education program upon the leisure functioning of young people with spina bifida. *Therapeutic Recreation Journal, 22*(3), pp. 44-52.

Outdoor Education and Ethical Outdoor Leadership
by
Karen M. Fox, The University of Manitoba

Overview

PURPOSE

The purpose of this chapter is to discuss the philosophical foundations of outdoor education and recreation, describe some specific programmatic applications of outdoor education, and connect the outdoor leadership to a larger context of humans' ethical relationship to natural areas.

LEARNING OBJECTIVES

At the completion of this chapter, you should be able to:

1. identify and describe the components of outdoor leadership,

2. compare and contrast outdoor education and interpretation, and

3. discuss current issues within the outdoor recreation and education field.

Outdoor Education and Ethical Outdoor Leadership

Outdoor recreation is intimately connected with the quality of the setting or natural environment. From a professional perspective, the objective is to support the integrity of the ecosystem while providing a quality outdoor recreation experience. Such an objective requires knowledge and skills in (1) outdoor leadership and followership, (2) outdoor education and/or interpretation, and (3) environmental ethics.

Outdoor leadership began with a focus on the requirements and competencies (often called "hard skills") of leading trips or activities within natural settings. Such competencies would include such things as rock climbing, canoeing, cross-country skiing, and first aid. When outdoor trip programs began to emphasize individual and group development (e.g., team building or individual psychological development), other competencies such as group dynamics, communication, and good judgement abilities (often called "soft skills") were also included for leadership competencies. Current issues for outdoor leadership include environmental ethics, meeting the needs of various populations (e.g., ethnic groups, people with disabilities, and women), transference of learning from the outdoor trip to other situations, and verification of a leader's capabilities.

Outdoor education and interpretation are the processes that help connect people with the setting so they may understand, respect and appreciate the complexity of the natural world and humans' relationship to the natural world. In outdoor education programs, a participant may take a nature hike, learn to canoe or make moccasins, build a bird house, perform a wildlife inventory, or participate in an "earth ceremony". In an interpretation program, a participant may watch a re-enactment of a historical event, learn how to protect a specific site or practice minimum impact camping, or take a self-guided tour.

Environmental ethics address the values surrounding the human/natural environment relationship. Environmental ethics include guidelines for minimum impact camping, discussions about the relationships among species, ethical decision making that affects outdoor recreation programming, and involvement in political processes to protect specific natural lands.

Leadership and Followership for Outdoor Recreation

Traditionally outdoor leadership has been defined as those people who lead trips in the outdoors. Within this framework, the major focus has been to enunciate a set of skills that can be taught and evaluated for competency. Drawing from surveys of existing trip programs, Priest (1979) and Ford and Blanchard (1985) have developed models that include a set of "hard skills" and "soft skills" that are necessary for competent outdoor leaders. The "hard skills" are essential for being able to lead a trip, teach specific skills, develop trust between leaders and followers, and to insure safety. The "soft skills" are vital for achieving specific individual and group development goals, teaching such concepts as environmental ethics, and insuring the safety of the group.

Training programs for outdoor leaders were developed to achieve these objectives. Building upon a model of outdoor leadership developed by Ford (1988), Figure 10.1 shows some of the elements of ethical outdoor leadership.

FIGURE 10.1
COMPOSITE OF OUTDOOR LEADERSHIP ELEMENTS

Knowledge About
Activities
Natural Environment
People
Ethics
Equipment
Resource Management

Skills In
Leadership
Followership
Outdoor
Teaching/Mentoring
Counseling
Group
Social Interaction   **Attitudes**
Supervision   Concern for Environment
Discussion   Love & Respect for People
Regard for Community
Inclusiveness
Compassion, Vulnerability
Ethical Disposition
Critical Thinker
Maturity

McAvoy (1987) enumerated six components related to this integrated concept necessary for an educational program of outdoor leadership:

1. develop judgment and decision-making abilities. This is seen by most experts as the most important component of leadership training that insures the safety of participants and the continuation of an outdoor program;

2. develop skills in outdoor living (e.g., backpacking, rock climbing);

3. develop ability to guide group interaction or support what is called "expedition behaviour";

4. develop competency in individual and group safety techniques;

5. develop an awareness and appreciation for natural environments and minimum impact camping; and

6. develop skills in planning and administering a comprehensive risk recreation programs including funding, personnel supervision, equipment maintenance, and teaching methods.

Historically, the field of outdoor recreation has primarily relied upon the leadership model of Hersey and Blanchard (1977) or the situational leadership model. This model has application because of the changing nature of participants and environment in the outdoor recreation setting. As seen in Figure 10.2, Hersey and Blanchard see leadership as a changing interaction between two variables: group maturity or skill level, and leader behaviour. However, it is only one model and others are necessary for an enhanced vision of leadership and followership in outdoor recreation if we are to respond to current changes and demands for inclusion of women or indigenous leadership patterns, people of varying abilities, and more respectful ways of relating to nature.

PLACE FIGURE 10.2
SITUATIONAL LEADERSHIP MODEL

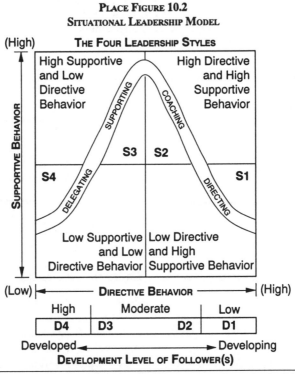

From: Hersey, P. H. and Blanchard, K. H. (1977). *Management of organizational behavior: Utilizing human resources*, p. 164. Reprinted by permission of Prentice Hall, Englewood Cliffs, NJ.

Outdoor recreation professionals are building upon these initial efforts to respond to current changes such as outdoor trip programs for people with disabilities, various ethnic backgrounds, and women. Schleien and McAvoy (1989) research demonstrated the benefits for people of varying abilities who participate in integrated adventure outdoor trips and the related leadership skills necessary to insure safety and support integration among the participants. Leaders of integrated groups are constantly balancing factors such as terrain, ability levels, expectations, safety, and group morale. In addition, the leader must establish patterns for integrated decision making or question answering because the status of individuals is often dependent upon their ability to participate in these processes. Mitten (1985) develops another perspective based upon adventure trips for women. She describes the importance of creating a trip environment where participants feel safe both emotionally and physically, travel in the wilderness for its own sake, and view leadership as a role, not a personality trait. Such a framework includes an environment that participants feel safe both emotionally and physically, responds to differences in client needs, travels in the wilderness for its own sake, and sees leadership as a role not a personality trait.

These changes in trip objectives, participants, and leadership roles demand a re-assessment of the competencies for outdoor leadership. An adaptation of Shapiro's (1989) definition of ethical leadership may provide another perspective—people dancing over ever-changing terrain to often-changing music while trying to balance group and individual needs: human and non-human needs, freedom of choice, trip requirements and safety with compassion and caring, competency with mere rule-following, conscience with inaction and unexamined practices.

Since the goal of outdoor trips revolve around group and individual develop-ment and a positive relation to the environment, the relationship between an ethical outdoor leader and follower is important. This is especially true since one of the basic goals is that outdoor recreation and education provide the affective elements in the development of environmental ethics and outdoor leisure pursuits that will affect several arena's of an individual's life. If an individual is to transfer the skills, learning, and attitudes to other areas of his or her life, then the functions, education, and support of ethical outdoor followers during the outdoor experience is crucial and is normally not discussed...Figure 10.3 (page 174) summarizes the "hard" and "soft" skills needed by outdoor recreation leaders.

The quality of natural areas is deteriorating because of events during an outdoor trip (i.e., number of visitors and camping practices) and beyond the scope of an outdoor trip (i.e., acid rain and development practices). There is a potential that we might lose trips into these natural areas because the quality of the environment is decreasing and/or the numbers of people recreating are increasing and making certain types of outdoor recreation impossible (e.g., experiencing solitude). For instance, visitors to the Nahani National Park will most likely encounter other visitors each day along the river compared to only 10 years ago when it was considered a "wilderness, solitude" adventure. If we are to protect some of these areas, the efforts of a diverse group of people are required and will include park superintendents and wardens, outdoor educators, chief executive officers of busi-nesses (e.g., Outward Bound, ecotour programs, and extractive industries), outdoor recreators, and members of citizen groups. It is important that the profession begin to view leadership and followership in outdoor recreation and education in a larger context and see outdoor recreation and education programs as part of a process to establish a relationship with nature and create new behavioural strategies for protecting these areas far beyond the confines of an outdoor trip.

FIGURE 10.3
SUMMARY OF "HARD" AND "SOFT" SKILLS

OUTDOOR LEADERSHIP SKILLS

HARD SKILLS	SOFT SKILLS
Knowledge of equipment	Knowledge of leadership styles
Knowledge of environment	Communication techniques
First aid and emergency skills	Group-dynamics
Wilderness weather factors	Maturity and good judgement
Wilderness trip safety factors	Expedition behaviour
Proficiency in outdoor pursuits:	Knowledge of human development:
rock climbing	group facilitation skills
whitewater kayaking	group process
canoeing	counseling techniques
cross-country skiing	motivation techniques
winter camping	Teaching/mentoring

Outdoor Education and Interpretation

Outdoor education and interpretation are vital components to outdoor recreation because they provide the philosophical and theoretical basis and the method for teaching the participants to interact with natural areas wisely, respectfully, and knowledgeably in order to protect and maintain the quality of the natural areas *and* the outdoor recreation experience. Outdoor education is teaching or learning about the outdoors, in the outdoors, for the outdoors. Interpretation is normally associated with specific institutional structures, such as Canada Parks Service, and with specific objectives: (1) to provoke visitors' curiosity and interest; (2) to promote the policies of the institution including visitor behaviour management; and (3) to promote environmental citizenship. Both outdoor education and interpretation are firmly grounded in the concepts and philosophies associated with experiential education.

EXPERIENTIAL EDUCATION

Experiential education derives its philosophical and theoretical foundations from various disciplines including philosophy, psychology, education, and sociology. Chickering (1976) defines experiential education as:

> learning which occurs when changes in judgments, feelings,
> knowledge or skills result for a particular person from living
> through an event or events . . . (p. 63).

From an outdoor education perspective, experiences must include (Walsh & Golins, n.d.):

1. Organized programs with problem-solving tasks (experiences) that promote education objectives. Not all experience is necessarily education.

2. Experiences are introduced incrementally in terms of complexity and consequence.

3. Experiences are recognizable as problems and limited in time and space.

4. Experiences can be solved with the use of previous experience and knowledge plus the skills that have been taught incrementally.

5. Experiences have real consequences for the participant.

6. Experiences are holistic and require the fullest complement of response (i.e., mental, emotional, and physical) of the participant.

For example, an outdoor education program might include learning to rock climb because the risk element facilitates both individual and group development. A participant can learn very quickly which handholds are better than others and the specific skills and strengths of each of the other participants. A nature centre may provide a specific program on snakes that allow participants to touch a snake in a safe manner and learn about the value of snakes within an ecosystem context. Each program is limited by time, provides essential information and experiential contact, relates experience to cognitive understanding (processing) and provides an opportunity for a more positive interaction with natural environments.

As Drengson (n.d.) summarizes, experiential learning "... is a holistic process, where conceptual, linguistic and perceptual elements are blended with direct impressions of the environment (p. 90). Experiential learning goes beyond merely seeing and doing because it includes cognitive, personal, and cultural elements that help interpret and provide significance to the experience.

Therefore, experiential learning must include a processing component. Often the processing component of an activity is overlooked even though research (Lederman, 1984) indicates that it is the most crucial element for a successful experiential education experience. The basic framework for processing an experience involves three steps (Rohnke, 1977):

1. *WHAT*: Identifying what happened (e.g., What did you see or hear? What were the steps of the activity?)

2. *SO WHAT*: Describing what the participants felt or experienced (e.g., What did you feel? What was important to you? What did you learn?)

3. *NOW WHAT*: Predicting how the activity can help the participant or change future actions (e.g., How can you use this information? What will it change for you in the future?)

OUTDOOR EDUCATION

As stated earlier, outdoor education is about, for and in the outdoors and began as an element of school camping programs in the 1940s. Outdoor education differs from environmental education which encompasses teaching about the quality and quantity of all aspects of the environment and does not have to occur in the outdoors. The concept of outdoor education implies that outdoor education is a process—that is creating the opportunity for the participant or learner to answer questions by analysis, synthesis, and logical reasoning (the discovery approach). Outdoor education is a method of teaching in the outdoors that emphasizes the goals of conservation, attitudes of appreciation, understanding and expression, basic skills for leisure-time pursuits in the outdoors and ethical treatment of the natural world and others.

It is helpful to think about outdoor education in terms of:

WHAT: Outdoor education is about the outdoors and natural resources. Therefore, it includes facts and specific knowledge such as the interconnections within a ecosystems, uses of particular resources, and identification of plants and animals.

HOW: Outdoor education uses outdoor recreation activities (e.g., games that require participants play the roles of animals and plants) to teach about the interconnections in the natural environment as well as specific outdoor living skills such as backpacking and identifying edible plants. Therefore, as a participant, you may participate in a game that assigns roles of animals or plants to demonstrate the interaction and connection of an ecosystem.

ME: Outdoor education is directed at increasing personal awareness, exploration, creativity, personal growth, and self-realization of an individual in relation to the natural world. The participant is involved and engaged not merely receiving information and is constantly challenged to relate this experience to his or her own life.

WE: Outdoor education includes group process activities such as development of social skills, cooperative strategies, and connection with the natural environment.

Outdoor education can occur in a school setting and will be primarily curriculum-oriented. Specific topics or activities are chosen because they support the learning process within a specific topic such as science, English or physical education. Therefore, students may learn how to make moccasins as a part of a social studies class, to perform an inventory of an ecosystem as part of a science class, or write about specific outdoor experiences in an English class.

Outdoor education can occur in an outdoor camp or residential nature centre. In this setting, the objective is still wise use, understanding or appreciation of the natural environment and may include information relevant to school curricula. However, the audience of an outdoor camp or nature centre is more diverse and demands a definite recreational component. Therefore, programs in these settings will include skill teaching such as bird-watching or building bird houses, recreational skills such as swimming, snowshoeing or cross-country skiing, and programs with emotional content such as vision quests or earth ceremonies.

Finally, outdoor education also occurs as a part of an outdoor trip. The philosophy and methods of outdoor education pervade all teaching on an outdoor trip—from teaching specific skills such as lighting a stove to identifying trees and plants to appreciating the majesty and diversity of a specific area. It is through combining teaching information, involving the entire individual, and enhancing one's awareness of the natural environment that an outdoor leader hopes to affect change in a participant so that she or he views the wilderness more positively, will learn specific skills, is able to return to the wilderness on their own, and will protect those areas in all aspects of their lives. One example of an outdoor recreation program is depicted in Figure 10.4.

FIGURE 10.4
THE REDISCOVERY PROGRAM: AN EXAMPLE OF AN OUTDOOR RECREATION PROGRAM

The Rediscovery Program is a specific outdoor education model that serves the needs of native as well as non-native youth within an authentic cultural context. The original Haida Gwaii Rediscovery Camp began in the Queen Charlotte Islands and the program elements build on Native knowledge about their culture and nature. The original camp was established in 1978 to serve a broad range of ages, boys and girls, native and non-native, the privileged and underprivileged, those in a state of crisis and those well-adjusted. The goals of the program are "to discover the world within oneself, the cultural worlds between people, and the wonders of the natural world around us". The program elements contain activities and games that heighten awareness of the environment and facilitate group cooperation and teaching traditional Native skills and knowledge. (Henley, 1989).

INTERPRETATION

Interpretation is normally associated with people employed by specific agencies to plan and implement interpretive programs. Interpretive programs are events that are designed to explain, interpret specific protected sites and promote the management policies of a specific agency. These positions are most commonly found in federal and provincial parks, museums, and nature centres. Officially, interpretation probably began in Canada in the 1940s when the Province of Ontario began the first officially organized program of guided walks, campfire talks and natural history presentations. This was followed by programs in British Columbia and the federal National Parks Branch in the 1960s. Within the *National Parks Act*, education is one of the objectives of a national park and the Canadian Parks Service has been dedicating more effort to focusing on the beneficial relationship between outdoor recreation and education. Recreation, therefore, is seen not only as a means of enjoying the park, but also a means of gaining a better understanding of the park's natural values. In addition, visitor education appears to many people and agencies as preferable to regulation or in addition to regulation because education makes regulations more acceptable and workable. With the advent of the Green Plan (the federal government environmental policy), this objective has been expanded to include a concept of "educating for environmental citizenship" since it is painfully obvious that all Canadians must take responsibility, not simply the Department of Environment (DOE) or the Canadian Parks Service (CPS), for the quality and protection of natural areas.

For most agencies in Canada, interpretive programs reflect two complementary perspectives: (1) to provoke curiosity and appreciation in the visitor, and (2) to promote specific management objectives. Freeman Tilden (1957) of the U.S. Parks Service was an advocate for "not instruction, but provocation". Tilden included all those educational activities that reveal meaning and relationships through the use of original objects by first-hand experience or illustrative media rather than simply communicating factual information. In Canada, Yorke Edwards (cited in Foley & Keither, 1979) in his paper "What is park interpretation?" presented this philosophy when he states:

> So while entertaining, we give directions, hand out information, and educate a bit, and even spread a little beneficial propaganda and if we do it right we will inspire a few people so that the park becomes a special place to them and their lives will never be the same again.

Sharpe (1982) presents the other theme—management objectives—when he discusses two additional objectives for interpretation: (1) to accomplish specific management goals such as minimizing human impact and encouraging specific, minimal impact practices; and (2) to promote the public's understanding of the agency's goals and objectives in preserving a specific historical or natural site. In most agencies in Canada, the interpretive programs reflect both themes. This melding of two philosophies is reflected in the four categories of interpretation as described by Foley and Keith (1979):

(1) **Tool for attitude change:** Interpretation can provide the opportunity for people to develop an awareness of the value of natural areas, intelligent opinions and attitudes about the relationship of humans to natural areas, and affective experiences that bring people closer to the vitality of natural areas.

(2) **Resource management tool:** Interpretation can educate visitors about appropriate behaviours that help preserve natural areas, enhance the quality of the outdoor recreation experience, and reduce the need for enforcement actions by park personnel. For instance, if visitors understand that stripping the bark off birch trees will kill the trees and reduce the aesthetics of campsites, then visitors are less likely to commit such actions and park personnel can spend less time enforcing regulations and spend less money on saving trees or reconstructing campsites.

(3) **Educational tool:** Interpretation can offer information and enlarge the information base of the visitor. This activity is included within the *Parks Policy* and is often desired by visitors because the knowledge adds to their experience and ability to utilize the resource of the park. For instance, the Batoche National Historical Site presents a multimedia presentation about Louis Riel that both informs the audience and provokes careful consideration of various interpretations of the significance of the events.

(4) **Recreational/Inspirational experience:** Interpretation can enhance the visitor's experience and may be one of the direct benefits sought by many visitors. There are a growing number of visitors who desire and even demand that natural areas be preserved so that they can broaden their experiences and maintain their psychological balance through

contact with the natural world. Interpretation may fulfill this function by providing opportunities and means to establish and maintain a connection between emotional aspects of humans and their natural heritage.

Today, with growing recognition that fundamental behavioural changes are required for public patterns of environmental consumption and use, encouraging personal stewardship of our natural lands is occurring through a variety of programs including the Green Plan. This change signals a more promising future for interpretation as a method of environmental communication, cementing the relationship between outdoor recreation, education and resource management.

ETHICS FOR PEOPLE AND THE ENVIRONMENT

Outdoor recreation and education revolve around a relationship between (1) humans and the natural environment, and (2) humans and humans. Ethics, in general, are systems of beliefs, guidelines, and rules that govern the relationship between individuals and groups of people. Environmental ethics extends systems of beliefs, guidelines, and rules to address the relationship between humans and the natural world. Minimum impact camping techniques is a response to the environmental ethical issues within the relationship between humans and the natural environment.

The attitude of resource protection does not provide a strong rationale for the long-term protection of undisturbed ecosystems because the ecosystem then becomes merely the arena for the outdoor recreation activity and as such is dispensable (Reid, 1979). Aldo Leopold (1949) wrote "that land as a community is the basic concept of ecology, but that land is to be loved and respected is an extension of ethics (p. viii)". In this light, ethical environmental behaviour becomes the demonstration of our care and concern for humans and natural areas and includes all of us in the web of life (Cheney, 1987; Kheel, 1985; Warren, 1990).

In addition, a participant's positive relationship with the environment is also dependent upon a positive relationship with the outdoor leader and other participants. Such a relationship must be built upon trust and integrity which requires an outdoor leader to consider carefully a variety of ethical issues. These ethical decisions are made even more complex as outdoor programs include people from, among many, different cultural and racial backgrounds, physical and mental abilities, sexual affectation, and socioeconomic levels (Hunt, 1990).

Examples of ethical issues in outdoor recreation and education are plentiful: interface between wildlife and humans; impact of recreational activities on the environment; issues of power between outdoor leaders and participants; access issues across gender, ability, class, and ethnic differences; the issue of survival of indigenous cultures as a part of designation of national parks; the damaging effects of recreational and ecotourism practices upon women who are dependent upon natural environments not normally valued by cash economies. Figure 10.5 provides a process for developing an environmental ethic among leisure service practitioners.

FIGURE 10.5

A MODEL FOR DEVELOPING AN ENVIRONMENTAL ETHIC

In 1990, the Government of Canada prepared the original Green Plan document after extensive, cross-country consultations with thousands of citizens and stakeholder groups. As part of the framework, Environment Canada defines itself as helping Canadian citizens and stakeholders make responsible decisions about the environment that benefit both the present and future generations. To that end, Environment Canada will contribute to the knowledge, skills and values that Canadians need to make environmentally responsible decisions and promote environmental stewardship. Leo H. McAvoy (1990) describes five steps toward developing and implementing an environmental ethic by park and recreation professionals.

1. **Formulate a code of environmental ethics:** An environmental ethic code should insist on environmental protection and preservation as one of the primary goals and differentiate between levels of morally good recreation pursuits and activities.

2. **Provide education about moral goodness of recreation pursuits, identification with the natural environment, and responsibility of stewardship:** In order for ethical behaviour to occur, it must be accompanied by feelings of understanding and identification with the environment. Education and interpretation can help make nature meaningful to the individual.

3. **Determine the amount of care necessary to sustain the natural world and humans of all cultures, races, abilities, and backgrounds:** When we propose new park and recreation developments or analyze the impacts of activities, we must complete in-depth environmental assessments to understand the natural processes, the impacts upon people and environment anticipated, alternatives strategies, and methods of mitigation.

4. **Procure general acceptance of environmental ethic:** Procuring general acceptance of an environmental ethic is a long and challenging process. This is an opportune time to increase public interest and develop support for environmental interpretation, education, and environmentally sensitive recreation programs and facilities. As mediators between the natural environment and humans, we are obliged to educate the public regarding their activity choices that are in harmony with what is good for the environment and humans. We, as park and recreation professionals, must provide ethical leadership and followership.

5. **Nurture dreams of a better future:** We must give ourselves and the people we serve a vision of a future that will be better than today—a vision of living more in harmony with a clean, beautiful environment and a diverse human community.

The Future of Outdoor Recreation and Outdoor Education

Since the 1960s, participation in outdoor recreation and education has increased. The increase in participation has two different results: an increase in appreciation and valuation of natural areas and an increase in deterioration of those areas as a direct result of use. Fortunately, the population's awareness of the need to wisely use and protect natural resources has also increased. Therefore, outdoor recreation professionals will face numerous challenges in the coming years to protect natural areas, provide quality outdoor recreation and education experiences, and to encourage support for outdoor recreation from all Canadians. Some of these issues will include items 1-4 following:

(1) Protection and support of natural areas: Outdoor recreation and education is dependent upon quality natural areas. The responsibility for protecting and sustaining such areas must be assumed by resource managers, outdoor recreation and education leaders and followers, *and* citizens in general. The task goes well beyond legal designation to working collaborative with many diverse peoples, developing outdoor education programs, and working within various arenas such as recreation, business, political, educational.

Ecotourism is a merging of the interests of tourism, ecological awareness, and outdoor recreation that is becoming more popular. Examples include: programs that allow people to spend their vacations working on ecological research projects; adventure trips to areas not normally accessible or the habitat of rare and endangered species; or spiritual quests following the philosophy and models of indigenous sacred rites. Ecotourism has both promises and pitfalls. Through exposing people to various natural areas and outdoor adventures, the individual's awareness and environmental commitment may be enhanced. On the other hand, such programs also increase the impact upon natural areas, have often had disastrous results for local cultures and peoples, and does not guarantee a change to a more environmentally concerned lifestyle. Since ecotourism is firmly rooted in business ethics that stress profit, many of its critics point to the fact that profit still holds a priority over protection of the resource and that this endeavour supports valuing natural areas only in terms of value for humans. Since ecotourism is one way for establishing awareness and personal attachment to diverse ecosystems, the challenge is to promote strategies that respect cultural diversity and protects natural areas.

The concept of national parks and outdoor recreation is grounded in North American culture and higher class values. As the fields of ecology, biology and botany have demonstrated, the concept of protecting natural areas is beneficial for more reasons than class, national pride, or recreational benefit. However, it is difficult, if not impossible, to separate these issues as we strive to protect natural areas in northern Canada or around the world. These natural areas are often inhabited or used by local, indigenous populations. These natural areas may provide the only place that people who have been displaced can grow food and survive. These natural areas may exist in countries that cannot feed their population and hence protecting an animal that can feed children seems cruel and unethical. In the future, the protection and maintenance of natural areas must be seen within social, cultural and legal contexts. In addition, history has demonstrated that protection of natural areas is dependent upon commitment from users and local neighbours as well as agency personnel. If people from other cultures and countries are to support the designation, protection, and maintenance of natural areas, then the management, control, and participation in outdoor recreation and education must reflect the diversity of cultures, values, and nations. The challenge is to develop management strategies that include diverse perspectives and provide for quality outdoor recreation experiences.

(2) Nurturing a connection between humans and natural areas: Outdoor recreation and education programs have long emphasized the technical skills and personal and group development. It is becoming increasingly apparent that other domains such as ethical leadership and followership or spiritual connections need to be included if participants are to achieve their own expectations and relationships with natural areas. The challenge is how to define or characterize such skills, develop training programs for outdoor leaders, and evaluate the quality of the programs and leaders.

The entire perspective of outdoor recreation and education is primarily based upon the value of natural areas as related to human leisure interests. As stated earlier, the value of natural areas exceeds such a limited view and there is a need to develop a more comprehensive and respectful view of the natural world. We may be saying something terribly sad about our world and ourselves if our outdoor recreation perspective is based totally on our needs rather than on a view that respects and allows the natural world to live because of its own needs. The challenge is to make visible the foundations of environmental ethics in outdoor recreation and design programs that explore alternative environmental and cultural perspectives.

(3) Strengthening the transfer of the learning in outdoor recreation and education to other arenas of life: Outdoor recreation and education professionals have long believed in the benefits of outdoor recreation and have provided much anecdotal evidence to support their claims. Research about the benefits and success of outdoor recreation programs is in its infancy. The need for more complete and rigorous research about the results of the programs, the ability to transfer across situational boundaries, the most appropriate research strategies for outdoor recreation and education, and the lasting effects of such programs is sparse and very necessary if we are to document the benefits of the programs, values of natural areas, and the benefits for environmental sensitive behaviour. For the field to develop a coherent picture of the components of outdoor recreation and their significance related to individual participants and programs, research must be increased and continued over longer periods of time.

(4) Sustaining a professional competency level and integrity: As the elements within an outdoor recreation and education program change and the participants represent more diverse backgrounds, the qualifications and training of outdoor leaders will, by necessity, also change. In addition, there are other competency issues related to safety, acquisition of new skills, and ethical issues that need to be discussed.

Programs that are conducted in natural environments face a variety of safety issues. There is simply no way to control all elements and things like weather are always an unknown factor. Most programs have developed procedures and strategies to ensure the safety of all participants but the unknown element of nature is always present. One of the most vital elements of safety (and most difficult to teach and assess) is good judgment by the leader. In recent years, problem of legal liability has gained prominence among outdoor trip leaders. The issue of competency is one that concerns all professionals in the field and has led to proposals for certification.

However, certifying complex skills (e.g., judgement, group leadership and integrating people of varying abilities) is difficult at best. Most professionals seem to prefer an evaluation of overall programs rather than specific leaders or leadership skills. The challenge is to develop a system that helps maintain quality without endangering the necessary flexibility and creativity required in outdoor recreation and education.

Summary

The field of outdoor recreation and education is complex and requires the outdoor recreation professional to be competent in several areas. First, the outdoor recreation professional must understand the systems of flora and fauna and appreciate the multiple values and benefits of natural areas. Second, the outdoor recreation experience combines a variety of motivations, expectations, benefits, and conditions which include risk, quality environmental settings, and psychological benefits such as self-confidence, solitude, and self-awareness. Third, systems of management for both outdoor recreation experience and the natural areas are a crucial element in today's world of outdoor recreation and education. Fourth, outdoor recreation and education revolves around a relationship between humans and the natural world. Hence, there must be opportunities to learn about the individual actors as well as the synergistic relationship between actors and how to behave appropriately and respectfully so that the natural areas can survive and the outdoor recreation experience can be enhanced. Finally, there is a need for ethical outdoor leadership and followership so that all people can participate in outdoor recreation and education, benefit from the protection and management of natural areas, and appreciate and value the existence of natural areas for the world and our own survival.

STUDY QUESTIONS?

1. Outdoor leadership includes the categories of "hard" and "soft" skills. Define each category and give three examples.

2. Define outdoor education and interpretation. What is the basic difference between the two perspectives?

3. List the six components necessary for an educational program for outdoor leadership. Identify which of the components relates to "hard" or "soft" skills.

4. What are two current issues that are affecting the role of the outdoor leader?

5. Give two reasons why this author argues for discussing outdoor followership as an important component of outdoor leadership.

6. Describe the philosophy of experiential education and how it relates to outdoor recreation?

7. List the three areas where outdoor education is most likely to occur and describe the different emphasis of each area.

8. What are the two complementary perspectives within interpretive programs?

9. Discuss the four categories of interpretation as described by Foley and Keith.

10. Discuss why outdoor education is essential if we are to change people's behaviour toward natural areas.

11. Discuss two of the current issues related to outdoor recreation and education and identify two programs within your community that implement programs to resolve these issues.

References

Cheney, J. (1987). Eco-feminism and deep ecology. *Environmental Ethics, 9*(2), pp. 115-145.

Chickering, A. (1976). Developmental change as a major outcome. In M. Keeton, *Experiential learning*. (pp. 62-107). San Francisco, CA: Jossey-Bass Publishers.

Drengson, A. R. (n.d.). What means this experience? In R. J. Kraft & M. Sakofs (Eds.). *The theory of experiential education*. Boulder, CO: Association for Experiential Education.

Edwards, Y. R. (1965). *What is park interpretation?* A paper originally given in Manning Park to the Parks Branch Training School. Mimeo.

Foley, J. P. & Keith, J. A. (1979). Interpretation in Canadian National Parks and related reserves—To what end? In J. G. Nelson, R. D. Needham, S. H. Nelson, & R. C. Scace (Eds.). *The Canadian National Parks: Today and Tomorrow Conference II. Vol. I*. Waterloo, ON: Faculty of Environmental Studies, University of Waterloo, pp. 179-189.

Ford, P. & Blanchard, J. (1985). *Leadership and administration of outdoor pursuits*. State College, PA: Venture Publishing, Inc.

Ford, P. (1988). The responsible outdoor leader. *Journal of Outdoor Education, 9*, pp. 4-13.

Freeman, M. M. R. (1979). Traditional land users as a legitimate source of environmental expertize. In J. G. Nelson, R. D. Needham, S. H. Nelson, & R. C. Scace (Eds.). *The Canadian National Parks: Today and Tomorrow Conference II, Vol. I*. Waterloo, ON: Faculty of Environmental Studies, University of Waterloo, pp. 345-361.

Henley, T. (1989). *Rediscovery: Ancient pathways—New directions*. Vancouver, BC: Western Canada Wilderness Committee.

Hersey, P., & Blanchard, K. H. (1977). *Management of organizational behavior: Utilizing human resources*. Englewood Cliffs, NJ: Prentice Hall.

Hunt, J. (1990). *Ethics in experiential education*. Boulder, CO: Association for Experiential Education.

Kheel, M. (1985). The liberation of nature: A circular affair. *Environmental Ethics, 7*(2), 135-149.

Lederman, L. C. (1984). Debriefing: A critical reexamination of the post-experience analytic process with implications for its effective use. *Simulation & Games, 15*(4), pp. 415-431.

Leopold, A. (1949). *A Sand County almanac and sketches here and there*. New York, NY: Oxford University Press.

McAvoy, L. H. (1987). Education for outdoor leadership. In J. F. Meier, T. W. Morash, and G. E. Welton (Eds.). *High adventure pursuits*, (pp. 459-467). Columbus, OH: Publishing Horizons.

McAvoy, L. H. (1990). An environmental ethic for parks and recreation. *Parks and Recreation, 25*(10), pp. 68-72.

Mitten, D. (1985). A philosophical basis for women's outdoor adventure programs. *Journal of Experiential Education, 8*(20), pp. 20-24.

Priest, S. (1979). *Preparing effective outdoor pursuit leaders.* Eugene, OR: University of Oregon Press.

Reid, R. A. (1979). The role of national parks in nature preservation. In J. G. Nelson, R. D. Needham, S. H. Nelson, & R. C. Scace (Eds.). *The Canadian National Parks: Today and Tomorrow Conference II, Vol. I.* Waterloo, ON: Faculty of Environmental Studies, University of Waterloo, pp. 3-15.

Rohnke, K. (1977). *Cowstails & cobras.* Hamilton, MA: Project Adventure.

Schleien, S. J. & McAvoy, L. H. (1989). *Learning together: Integration persons of varying abilities into outdoor education centers.* Minneapolis, MN: Therapeutic Recreation/Outdoor Education Integration Grant Project, University of Minnesota.

Shapiro, G. L. (1989). Ethical leadership & liberating education. *Global Perspectives.* St. Paul, MN: University of St. Thomas.

Sharpe, G. (1982). *Interpreting the environment.* New York, NY: John Wiley & Sons.

Tilden, F. (1957). *Interpreting our heritage.* Chapel Hill, NC: The University of North Carolina Press.

Walsh, V. & Golen, G. (n.d.). *The exploration of the Outward Bound process.* (Available from Colorado Outward Bound.)

Warren, K. J. (1990). The power and promise of ecological feminism. *Environmental Ethics, 12*(2), pp. 125-146.

Chapter Eleven

Outdoor Recreation and Management in Canada

by
Alex Zellermeyer, Canadian Parks Service
and
Karen M. Fox, The University of Manitoba

Overview

PURPOSE

The purpose of this chapter is to describe the significance of natural places for outdoor recreation, the components of the outdoor recreation experience, and the policies and structures for managing natural areas for ecological integrity and the outdoor recreation experience.

LEARNING OBJECTIVES

At the completion of this chapter, you should be able to:

1. identify and describe the components of outdoor recreation,

2. explain how and why outdoor recreation depends upon ecological integrity,

3. identify the major national and international environmental initiatives for protected area management, and

4. discuss why a knowledge of protected area management mechanisms, public involvement and multijurisdictional co-operation is important for the outdoor recreation professional.

Outdoor Recreation and Management in Canada

Outdoor recreation is "all those activities of a recreational nature resulting from our interest in the environment and our relationship to its elements" (Sessoms, 1984, p. 238). Outdoor recreation, according to the Fitness Canada Report (1988), is those activities that lead to interaction with the natural environment, develop a rapport with natural elements, and generate an understanding and appreciation of Canadian cultural, natural, and historical perspectives.

The outdoor recreation professional is often an intermediary between the participant and the natural environment and is responsible for protecting the environment for current and future generations as well as enhancing the quality of the recreational experience of the participant through leadership, education, interpretation, and management of facilities, environment and recreational experience. In effect, there exists an "obligation to influence" outdoor recreation participants to share in the stewardship of our supporting environments upon which the recreation experience depends.

This chapter explores three dimensions of outdoor recreation: the significance and value of natural environments, the outdoor recreation experience, and the management of natural environments for ecological integrity and sustainable outdoor recreation.

The Lure of the Place

Participation in outdoor recreation has increased because few environments can equal the natural environment for its ability to offer a pleasurable experience. Outdoor recreation takes place in areas that have a variety of labels: wilderness, wildlands, parks, natural areas, forests, bioregions, ecosystems, protected areas, and endangered spaces to name a few. The basic concept that underlies all of these labels is a specific area that allows for human interaction with natural or "primeval" processes and often, but not always, has a minimal amount of human intrusion. The value of these protected areas goes far beyond the recreational experience or economic importance of the resources themselves.

One value of these large areas is related to ecological integrity and biodiversity. It has become clear that all peoples are a part of and are dependent upon the natural world in some way—energy is needed to fuel our industries and heat our homes; food is necessary to keep us alive and healthy; water is the vital element of our bodies; beautiful vistas lift our spirits and our souls; wilderness is the essence of Canada's national identity; ecosystems hold the future medicines that will cure illness or support sustainable technologies such as wetland wastewater treatment plants.

The natural areas of Canada are immense and varied, contributing to the quality of life in Canada and the world. Canada is one of the few countries in the world that contains large pristine natural areas such as the tundra of the Northwest Territories, the Canadian Shield of central Canada, and the Rocky Mountain Cordillera of western Canada. Canada has the largest total coastline in the world and the second largest continental shelf.

Many people (Nash, 1967; Hargrove, 1989; Merchant, 1980; Griffin, 1978) have speculated about the fascination and appreciation of natural areas. The appreciation of wilderness may have its beginnings in the matriarchal and pantheistic practices of early times (Merchant, 1980) and revived more recently because of the increase in densely populated centres. In addition, the increase in participation in outdoor recreation may be a reaction against urban living which has been and is the fate of increasing proportions of Canadians. Protection of natural areas began to surface as the myth of endless abundance was discredited and traditions such as the Judeo-Christian stewardship, aboriginal spirituality of connection, and scientific ecology of interrelated systems gained more credence (Nash, 1967; Plant, 1989; Rowe, 1990; Leopold, 1949). Whatever the historical antecedents, natural areas play a vital role in the lives of all Canadians.

Holmes Rolston III (1986) enlarges the list of values of natural areas to include: (1) a life support value that refers to our dependence upon biosystems; (2) a scientific value related to the wealth of knowledge held within natural entities and systems; (3) an aesthetic value that elevates humans beyond their personal needs; (4) a life value or reverence for life that is commended by every great religion; (5) diversity and unity values that recognizes the complementary dimensions of seemingly contradictory concepts; (6) stability and spontaneity values that demonstrate the connection as well as the freedom within natural systems; and (7) a sacramental value that recognizes the ability of nature to generate poetry, philosophy, and religion and at the deepest educational levels creates awe and humility in humans.

The Honourable Hugh Faulkner (1979) reinforced the more philosophical discourse of Rolston III, when he stated at the Canadian National Parks: Today and Tomorrow Conference II in 1978:

> "They are unique places where one can have solitude and simple peace and quiet. They are areas where the craving for adventure and for self-reliance can be satisfied. We often discover a great deal about the natural world and something about ourselves when we confront the wildlands. Our descendants will need this experience no less than we do; no less than our ancestors did before us (p. 7)."

The multiple values of these natural areas creates unique challenges for the outdoor recreation professional and partially explains the lure of such places to participants in outdoor recreation and education.

The Outdoor Recreation Experience

The outdoor recreation experience can be defined or described from different standpoints much like the definition of leisure itself. For instance, outdoor recreation activities include backpacking, cottaging, canoeing, kayaking, rock and mountain climbing, bird-watching, scuba diving, recreational vehicle use in natural areas, and expedition travel. The outdoor recreation experience may comprise such elements as risk, adventure, solitude, connection with natural environments, social interaction, rest and relaxation. People experience the outdoors individually, in groups, and through institutions such as camps, commercial tours, travel agencies, and specialized programs designed for special interests and issues such as youth-at-risk, women, business executives and people with special needs.

Outdoor recreation uses a specific medium (the natural environment) for personal and group growth, healing, revitalization, and inspiration. For instance, adventure outdoor recreation uses elements of real or perceived risk within activities such as rock climbing or whitewater rafting for personal or group development such as the enhancement of self-esteem or cooperation skills. Vision quests and outdoor programs designed for people with chronic illness or incidents of abuse build upon the concepts of the healing and revitalization properties of natural environments and cultures closely related to the natural environment. Ecotourism provides opportunities for people to travel to new, different, sometimes endangered environments. All of these outdoor activities depend upon a natural setting for achieving their particular outcomes.

Scholars and practitioners in outdoor recreation have spent decades researching and analyzing the motives, behaviour, and activities of people engaged in outdoor recreation in hopes of defining, understanding, and influencing outdoor recreation patterns so that natural areas are protected and the outdoor experience is enhanced. This section discusses the concept of risk or adventure outdoor recreation, the benefits of outdoor recreation, and an overview of the several models of outdoor recreation programs.

RISK OR ADVENTURE OUTDOOR RECREATION

Although not all outdoor recreation contains risk, it is a major component of most activities and/or most people's perception of outdoor recreation. The element of risk not only attracts people to specific activities but also provides the component that supports the achievement of many of the benefits of outdoor recreation.

Risk activities in outdoor recreation are self-initiated activities, which generally occur in natural environments, that contain real or perceived uncertain and potentially harmful consequences thus providing the opportunity for intense levels of cognitive and emotional arousal (Hollenhorst & Ewert, 1989). These activities may range from high rope courses in residential camp settings to free rock climbing in a wilderness area.

Many forms of outdoor recreation contain components of real risk or the potential for physical harm. Examples of real risk (i.e., situations that actually expose the participant to the possibility, even probability, of being hurt or having a close call (Ewert, 1989) are changes in weather, natural environments, or difficult whitewater rapids where individuals have lost their lives. This potential is offset or controlled through safety procedures, training, and skill levels which separates something difficult from something that is foolhardy. Houston (1968) states that "experienced climbers understand, enjoy, and seek risk because it presents a difficulty to overcome and can be estimated and controlled. [The climber] equally abhors danger because it is beyond control" (p. 56).

Since risk is directly related to control through procedures or skill, the perception of risk may vary among people. What may be perceived as risky to a novice, may appear simple to an expert because of the difference in skill level or understanding of the safety procedures. For instance, many participants view activities at heights as risky even though most are relatively safe because of safety procedures and equipment. This is an apparent risk because it is an "illusion" of danger or the possibility of being injured. Therefore, activities at heights, such as high rope courses (see Figure 11.1) or rock climbing, are frequently used in outdoor adventure programs to provide the experiential reality of risk for learning and growth.

It is the element of real or apparent risk that provides the opportunity to test specific skills or hypothesis about the natural world, oneself, or the group. In this situation with uncertain outcomes, the achievement of a specific goal, if only surviving the incident, provides the events that can, through reflection and processing, nourish personal and social change.

FIGURE 11.1

ROPES COURSE EXPLAINED

A maze of cables, plastic pegs, platforms, thimble eye bolts, PVC rod, logs, and boards provide challenge and "perceived risk" that results in a physical activity course. The goals of such courses are to combine a joyful sense of adventure, challenge that moves people beyond previously set limits, and satisfaction for solving problems in a cooperative group context. A Ropes Course is designed developmentally, logically, imaginatively, and safely to support individuals and groups to successfully negotiate progressively more difficult challenges. The specific goals of a Ropes Course are:

(1) To increase the participant's sense of personal confidence
(2) To increase mutual support within a group
(3) To develop an increased level of agility and physical coordination
(4) To develop an increased joy in one's physical self and in being with others; and
(5) To develop an increased familiarity and identification with the natural world (Rohnke, 1977).

THE BENEFITS OF OUTDOOR RECREATION

Scholars and researchers in outdoor recreation have identified benefits in four areas: personal, social or group, physical, and spiritual (See Table 11.1, Page 192). It is these potential outcomes that attract so many people and programs to outdoor settings and activities and lead to management strategies to enhance and sustain outdoor recreation experiences.

Successful outdoor programs include elements that support growth in all four areas. McAvoy (1987) states that a successful outdoor recreation program includes challenging environment, challenge for individuals and group, opportunity for decision making, skill development, environmental awareness and appreciation, and time for group interaction. It is the interaction of these components that support learning from the risk activity and achieving specific benefits or outcomes. In addition, others (Hammel, 1986; Lederman, 1984) indicate that processing the experience by discussing what happened and how it relates to the individual or group is vital for learning to occur and is related to the concept of experiential education discussed in Chapter Nine.

MODELS OF OUTDOOR RECREATION PROGRAMS

There are numerous models of outdoor recreation and this chapter will present several of the most common: established residential camps; adventure programs that emphasize risk activities; commercial operations such as ecotours; and special programs for specific populations.

Residential camping became popular in the 1940s and has been a major force in providing opportunities for children and young people to experience the out-of-doors. The major providers of camps have been such organizations as YM-YWCAs, Girl Guides, Boy Scouts, and religious groups. In most cases these camp programs were focused on social interaction, team building, and learning specific value frameworks.

TABLE 11.1
SOME POTENTIAL BENEFITS OF OUTDOOR RECREATION

PSYCHOLOGICAL	SOCIAL	PHYSICAL	SPIRITUAL
Self-concept	Compassion	Strength	Inspiration
Confidence	Group Cooperation	Coordination	Solitude
Self-efficacy	Respect for Others	Cardiovascular	Contemplation
Sensation-Seeking	Outdoor Education	Outdoor Skills	
Value Clarification	Communication Behaviours	Sensory Awareness	Connection with Nature
Diversion	Group Problem Solving	Improved Health	Understanding Myths
Problem Solving	Leadership and Followership	Catharsis	

Adventure programs, such as those offered by Outward Bound and the National Outdoor Leadership School, provide an experience within designated natural areas such as national parks. They emphasize adventure as a means for developing leadership in the world. These programs are based primarily upon a military, male model of facing fear and risk. Kurt Hahn was the "moving spirit" behind Outward Bound, the first of these programs, which began in Britain during World War II. Hahn described the purpose of the initial endeavors as "...to train citizens who would not shirk from leadership and who could, if called upon, make independent decisions, put right action before expediency and the common cause before personal ambition" (James, n.d., p. 41). The idea was to use natural environments such as mountains as a classroom to produce better people, to build character, to instill that intensity of individual and collective aspiration on which society depends for its survival. Hahn stated that the goal was to ensure "the survival of an enterprising curiosity, an undefeatable spirit, tenacity in pursuit, readiness for sensible self-denial, and, above all, compassion" (James, n.d., p. 41).

Commercial outdoor programs are those organizations that provide opportunity for others to experience the outdoors for a price and primarily emphasizes recreation. In recent years, the increase in environmental awareness and the ability to travel great distances has supported the development of ecotourism. Since these programs depend upon a quality outdoor experience, part of the operating procedures as well as some client education revolves around protection of the environment. For instance, it is often the river guides that ensure specific minimum impact camping techniques are followed by all clients.

Finally, there have emerged specific programs designed for the needs of special populations such as people who are physically challenged, youth at risk, women who have been abused, people with chronic illness and people of different cultures. These programs may be an overlay of other models (such as the adventure programs of Outward Bound) or develop new models to address specific needs of the members of special populations. For instance, women who have been abused may need program elements to help them heal and to regain their self-confidence rather than completing a risk activity (Mitten, 1985). Other programs may focus on benefits of natural environments such as healing or spiritual revitalization or the ability to foster cooperation among members rather than risk activities.

Protection, Preservation, and Use of Natural Areas in Canada

Outdoor recreation can only occur in the outdoors and many activities can only occur in areas that have a minimum amount of human intrusion and development. Therefore, an essential element for outdoor recreation is the management of natural areas so that the quality of the biosystem is protected and preserved first for its own sake, and then in relation to humans and the quality of the outdoor experience.

THE VALUE OF CANADIAN NATURAL AREAS: INTERNATIONALLY RECOGNIZED LANDS

In most cases, the quality of the outdoor recreation experience is based upon a quality natural environment. Hence, a crucial element for outdoor recreation is the management of natural areas so that the quality or "integrity" of ecosystems is preserved. In short, the setting or venue of outdoor recreation, the very core of the outdoor recreation profession, is inextricably tied to the health of the environment.

Although we often think only in terms of national benefits and priorities, natural areas contribute to the quality of life, ecological integrity, recreational opportunities, and environmental stewardship of the world as well as Canada. People from other countries travel to Canada to see its natural wonders and experience its remaining wilderness. The tundra, plains, old growth forests and vast bodies of fresh water contribute to the health of the planet, mediating global temperatures and other complex atmospheric processes, and providing habitats for many species of migratory wildlife. The joint management and cooperative agreements between governments and aboriginal First Nations are adventures into new land-use relationships and management strategies that are important worldwide if we are to protect natural areas. For the outdoor recreation professional, it is important to know at least some of the major components of the framework of conservation both nationally and internationally.

CANADA'S ROLE IN INTERNATIONAL CONSERVATION

There are several major international organizations, conventions and initiatives directed toward conserving natural and cultural heritage areas and biodiversity on a global scale. These are summarized in Table 11.2.

PROTECTED AREA MANAGEMENT WITHIN CANADA

In Canada, protected area management can be broadly categorized under four levels of government: federal, provincial (or territorial), municipal and aboriginal. Generally, a natural area must be large enough to not only protect habitats (a relatively easy task), but sustain habitats (a difficult task), and provide quality recreational experiences.

Canada has many different kinds of protected areas and management systems: national and provincial parks, historic sites, wildlife management areas, wilderness rivers, marine parks, outdoor recreation parks, near urban parks, ecological reserves and others. Some are huge areas of Canada such as Wood Buffalo National Park (44,000 km²), larger than Denmark in size. Others may be small sites protecting a rare orchid patch or a wildlife species breeding area such as the Narcisse snake pits of Manitoba.

Levels of protection for these special areas vary as greatly as the jurisdictions and designations. To complicate matters even more, below the federal level, similar designations may differ in management details from province to province, reflecting the individual legislation of each jurisdiction. Nevertheless, all protected areas contribute towards the achievement of global environmental integrity. They act as models for the management of ecological and cultural resources. For the recreation professional, they provide not only important settings for the profession, but opportunities for delivering fundamental benefits of outdoor recreation to people and hopefully, in the process, affecting their behaviour so that environmental stewardship becomes a personal concern of all citizens.

The recognition that protection of specific, designated areas alone is not enough to guarantee sustainability is driving managers to move toward ecosystem-based management. Increasingly, this ecosystem-based management approach towards protected areas requires a cooperative, often multiple jurisdiction approach. Science has shown us that no spot on the globe is untouched by our collective actions. Boundaries and fences alone cannot protect or sustain ecosystems or guarantee their integrity. The source of threats, such as acid rain, may be hundreds or even thousands of miles away. The construction of a British Columbia dam on the Peace River is threatening the long-term survival of the

TABLE 11.2
INTERNATIONAL AGREEMENTS AND PROTECTED AREAS IN CANADA

- **International Union for the Conservation of Nature (IUCN).** The IUCN (founded in 1948) involves over 120 governments and hundreds of non-government organizations (NGOs). The IUCN provided the leadership that gave rise to such major environmental milestones as the World Conservation Strategy, the World Charter for Nature and the World Commission for Environment and Development (Brundtland Report).

- **World Conservation Strategy.** The main objectives of the 1980 World Conservation Strategy, embraced by over 30 countries, are (1) to preserve genetic diversity, (2) to maintain essential ecological processes, and (3) to ensure that the utilization of species and ecosystems is sustainable. These strategic concepts underlie almost every national environmental effort.

- **Brundtland Report.** Perhaps the most pivotal international environmental effort of the century will prove to be the 1987 World Commission on Environment and Development (chaired by Norwegian Prime Minister, Gro Brundtland), commonly called the Brundtland Report. Most significantly, the report established once and for all the inextricable link between economic development and environment. In addition to concluding that the protection of species and ecosystems is a prerequisite to sustainable development, the Commission recommended that a global network of protected areas be established, confirming the importance of protected areas in global conservation.

- **World Charter for Nature (1982).** This charter called for the protection of unique and representative samples of the world's ecosystems and habitats of endangered species and was adopted by the United Nations in 1983.

- **World Heritage Convention.** What do the great pyramids of Egypt and India's Taj Mahal have in common with Wood Buffalo and Nahanni National Parks in Canada? All four are World Heritage Sites under the World Heritage Convention (1972). Over 100 countries have signed this UNESCO (United Nations Educational, Scientific and Cultural Organization) convention to protect specific sites that are considered to be important to the heritage of all humankind.

- **Man and the Biosphere Program (MAB).** As opposed to the World Heritage Sites Program (which concentrates on distinct unique sites of great international importance), MAB was launched by UNESCO to create an international network of representative biosphere reserves of the world's major ecological systems (including the patterns of human use adapted to them). Each MAB reserve includes a protected "core" of undisturbed lands (often a national park) surrounded by areas that are used by people to meet human needs. Hence the program encourages exchange and cooperation between different land jurisdictions and users. Canada has six Biosphere Reserves. The protected cores of these areas are: Waterton Lakes National Park (Alberta), Riding Mountain National Park (Manitoba), Long Point National Wildlife Area (Ontario), Niagara Escarpment (Ontario), Mont. St. Hilaire Nature Conservancy (Quebec), and Charlevoix (Quebec).

- **Ramsar Sites.** Ramsar, Iran was the site of a 1971 Agreement on the Conservation of Wetlands of International Importance. The ecological importance of wetlands is immense for many reasons including their role in migratory bird breeding and water conservation. Canada has the largest area of Ramsar sites (over 130,000 km²) in the world, reflecting the little known fact that Canada also possesses 24 percent of the world's wetlands and 15 percent of the worlds fresh water. Delta Marsh on Lake Manitoba (one of North America's largest waterfowl breeding and staging areas) is an example of a Ramsar site.

Peace-Athabasca delta, one of the world's great wetlands in Wood Buffalo National Park in northeastern Alberta. Thus, the heart of a national park, its prime waterfowl and wildlife breeding area, is threatened from afar. Protection inside boundaries is insufficient. Ecosystem-based management means that all the jurisdictions which have the power to affect a resource, and all the stakeholders (public and private) who have an interest in its use and preservation, must work together towards a common goal of ecological integrity and sustainable use. There is no other way to avoid the "tragedy of the commons". As a key stakeholder, the outdoor recreation professional has a major role to play in this ecosystem-based management framework. It is a challenge for outdoor recreation professionals and managers that demands a blending of a range of professional talents, conceptual frameworks and ethical considerations and requires the use of opportunities for public participation and cooperation among numerous agencies, levels of governments, organizations and interest groups. The outdoor recreation professional must be conversant with all of these elements.

Coordination among and between government levels occurs in four major areas:

1. Agreements for the establishment of protected areas.

2. Development of strategic (management) plans for protected areas.

3. Implementation of plans and programs in areas of mutual concerns.

4. Development of program policies for each level's mandates.

The Forks Agreement in Winnipeg, establishing the Forks National Historic Site and an extensive area of river bank development for historic interpretation, recreation and commerce, is an example of a project that crosses multiple levels of government (in this instance, federal, provincial, and municipal).

FEDERAL LEVEL: THE DEPARTMENT OF ENVIRONMENT

Canada's major programs that involve the management, protection and use of nationally significant areas essential for outdoor recreation fall under the jurisdiction of the federal Department of the Environment (DOE). The department includes services such as the Canadian Parks Service (CPS) and the Canadian Wildlife Service (CWS).

CPS manages the largest national park and historic site system in the world. Since 1885, from a 26 km² land base around a hot spring at Sulphur Mountain in what would become Banff National Park, the system has grown to over 215,000 km², roughly 1.8 percent of the total area of the country. It is interesting to consider that the start of one of the world's great park systems, a leader in protected areas management, was essentially born around an outdoor hotspring planned as a natural "pleasure and playground" for people.

Historically, people saw the management of protected areas containing a tension, some would say an inherent conflict, between the notion of protection/preservation and use, regardless of how minimal or benign that use may be. As early as 1920, James B. Harkin, first Commissioner of the Dominion Lands Branch, developed a vision of protection and use of natural areas when he stated:

> "The day will come when the population of Canada will be ten times as great as it is now, but the national parks ensure that every Canadian . . . will still have free access to vast areas possessing some of the finest scenery in Canada, in which the beauty of the landscape is protected from profanation, the natural wild animals, plants, and forests preserved, and the peace and solitude of primeval nature retained."

In response to controversies over a hydroelectric dam built in Banff National Park in 1923, the government passed the *National Parks Act* in 1930 prohibiting future hydroelectric dams, logging or mining in national parks. This action heralded the modern era of preservation as the conceptual basis of national park management. Today, the *National Parks Act* remains the principal legislation protecting and guiding Canada's national parks and historic sites. The Act differs markedly from provincial policies and legislation which often overlay resource conservation and resource extraction. The guiding principle for the CPS is the dedication clause which states:

> The National Parks of Canada are hereby dedicated to the people of Canada; for their benefit, education and enjoyment, subject to the conditions of this Act and the Regulations, and the National Parks shall be maintained and made use of so as to leave them unimpaired for the enjoyment of future generations.

Increasing post-war urbanization, industrial and tourism development coincided with a rise in environmental awareness and especially wilderness advocacy in the 1960s. In response to this growing conflict between the use and preservation of national parks, the government developed a National Parks Policy in 1964. Periodically updated (e.g., in 1979) this policy is the detailed interpretation of the *National Parks Act* at the park and site level for such varied topics as tourism, facility development, appropriate use, aboriginal rights and zoning for use and protection. Developed with very broad public participation and involvement, the CPS Policy is a reflection of modern societal values, expectations and guidelines by which people expect their government to abide in managing their parks and sites. The latest CPS Program Policy, the conceptual umbrella of CPS, is based on the internationally accepted principle that environmental (ecological) and cultural heritage resource integrity must be the basis of all decision making.

How are national parks established in Canada? A System Plan classifies Canada into 39 distinct terrestrial "Natural Regions" (See map 1, page 198). Each region displays a particular combination of Canada's geology, landforms, wildlife, and vegetation. The intent of the CPS program is to establish at least one national park within each of Canada's 39 Natural Regions. Of the 39 regions, 16 (primarily in Canada's Arctic, British Columbia and Quebec) remain unrepresented. The commitment under the Green Plan (the federal government policy on the environment) is to have 5 new national parks by 1996 and 13 more agreements in place so as to complete the national parks system by the year 2000. National parks are created in provinces by negotiating agreements and transferring rights of administration and control to the federal crown. The *National Parks Act* requires all national parks to be federal lands. In the territories, federal land withdrawals for national park purposes are made through specific negotiated conditions with territorial governments, and as equal partners, aboriginal peoples within whose homelands these parks are established.

Besides the national parks program, CPS is also responsible for nationally significant cultural heritage sites. This is the responsibility of National Historic Sites Branch of CPS. Cultural heritage sites are planned around historic themes such as native history, fur trade, and prairie settlement. These themes and their prioritization

MAP 1
CANADIAN HERITAGE RIVERS SYSTEM

The
Thirty Mile
(Yukon River)

Alsek
River

South
Nahanni
River

Thelon
River

Kazan
River

Soper River

Seal River

Athabasca
River

Clearwater
River

Main
River

Kicking
Horse
River

North
Saskatchewan
River

Bloodvein
River

Margaree
River

Missinabi
River

Jacques-Cartier
River

St. Croix
River

✳ Nominations accepted
by the Board
(not yet designated)

Note: Only rivers in national parks are
eligible for Canadian Heritage River
status in Alberta and British Columbia

Boundary
Waters

French
River

Grand River

0   Miles   500

of significance is based on the National Historic Sites System Plan and is the functional equivalent of a National Park System Plan. These sites of national historic significance are also designated by the Minister of the Environment under the *National Parks Act*. There are over one hundred designated National Historic Sites in Canada that protect a land area. Some of them are quite large such as Chilkoot National Historic Park (British Columbia and Yukon), which commemorates the Klondike gold rush and is an extremely important international hiking trail. Hundreds of other sites fall under the authority of other governments below the federal level. Although many are national historic sites, unlike national parks, they are not required to be federally owned or controlled.

Another program significant for the outdoor recreation professional is the Canadian Heritage Rivers System (CHRS). CHRS is a cooperative program of the federal government and eight provinces and two territories as of 1992. The objectives of the CHRS are to give national recognition to the important rivers of

MAP 2
NATIONAL PARK NATURAL REGIONS

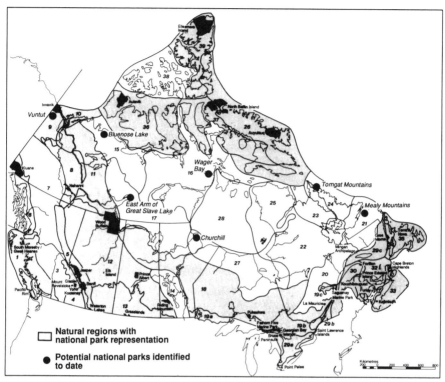

Natural regions with national park representation

● Potential national parks identified to date

Western Mountains
1. Pacific Coast Mountains
2. Strait of Georgia Lowlands
3. Interior Dry Plateau
4. Columbia Mountains
5. Rocky Mountains
6. Northern Coast Mountains
7. Northern Interior Plateaux and Mountains
8. Mackenzie Mountains
9. Northern Yukon Region

Interior Plains
10. Mackenzie Delta
11. Northern Boreal Plains
12. Southern Boreal Plains and Plateaux
13. Prairie Grasslands
14. Manitoba Lowlands

Canadian Shield
15. Tundra Hills
16. Central Tundra Region
17. Northwestern Boreal Uplands
18. Central Boreal Uplands
19. a. West Great Lakes—St. Lawrence Precambrian Region
    b. Central Great Lakes—St. Lawrence Precambrian Region
    c. East Great Lakes—St. Lawrence Precambrian Region

20. Laurentian Boreal Highlands
21. East Coast Boreal Region
22. Boreal Lake Plateau

23. Whale River Region
24. Northern Labrador Mountains
25. Ungava Tundra Plateau
26. Northern Davis Region

Hudson Bay Lowlands
27. Hudson-James Lowlands
28. Southampton Plain

St. Lawrence Lowlands
29. a. West St. Lawrence Lowland
    b. Central St. Lawrence Lowland
    c. East St. Lawrence Lowland

Appalachian
30. Notre Dame-Megantic Mountains
31. Maritime Acadian Highlands
32. Maritime Plain
33. Atlantic Coast Uplands
34. Western Newfoundland Island Highlands
35. Eastern Newfoundland Island Atlantic Region

Arctic Lowlands
36. Western Arctic Lowlands
37. Eastern Arctic Lowlands

High Arctic Islands
38. Western High Arctic Region
39. Eastern High Arctic Region

Canada so as to ensure their long-term management to preserve their natural, historical and recreational values. A CHRS Board, made up of representatives from member provinces and territories, reviews nominations to see if they meet CHRS selection criteria. Upon acceptance, the Board recommends to the federal Minister of the Environment that a river be designated a Canadian Heritage River. Map 2 (page 199) shows Canada's Heritage Rivers, over 2,500 km of protected heritage waterways. Manitoba's Bloodvein, the Yukon's Alsek and Ontario's Mattawa are examples of Canadian Heritage Rivers.

The Canadian Wildlife Service (CWS) administers two types of federally managed wildlife areas: migratory bird sanctuaries and national wildlife areas. The authority for designating and protecting wildlife areas and sanctuaries is given by the *1973 Canada Wildlife Act*. In total, these two types of conservation lands protect almost as much area as Canada's national parks although they are far less well-known. The Queen Maud Gulf Bird Sanctuary in the Northwest Territories is the largest protected area in Canada (62,000 km^2). However, the bulk of Canada's national wildlife areas and migratory bird sanctuaries, especially in southern Canada, are small. Moreover, unlike the more stringent legislation of the *National Parks Act*, the *Canada Wildlife Act* allows grazing, farming and other extractive uses on a case-by-case basis. Nevertheless, they are important accessible areas for compatible outdoor recreation activity based on environmental study and enjoyment.

FIRST NATIONS OR ABORIGINAL GOVERNMENTS

Aboriginal peoples were the first inhabitants of Canada. However, it was not until the 1982 *Constitution Act* (section 35.1) that the inherent aboriginal rights of native peoples were recognized in law. Today, native governments are playing a significant and growing role in the establishment, protection and management of vast areas of protected lands in Canada.

In areas where comprehensive land claims have been negotiated between aboriginal governments (e.g., the Tungavik Federation of Nunavut of the eastern Arctic) and Canada, large areas of aboriginal lands have been set aside as national parks. In exchange for designation and protection of lands as national parks, aboriginal peoples receive preferential economic rights (e.g., tourism opportunities, training and employment) and continuation of their traditional land use including hunting and gathering. Most importantly, aboriginal peoples are involved in the direct co-management of these areas. Hence, they are key players in the decision-making process that establishes management systems for not only natural resource management, but also visitation and activity patterns, facility development, and all other aspects of outdoor use.

Increasingly, as Canada comes to negotiate and establish the specific details of aboriginal rights with specific First Nations, aboriginal peoples will be playing a more significant role in natural area management and conservation. The fundamentally ecology-based world view and environmental ethics of aboriginal peoples towards land use will make them important partners in the management and use of protected areas. As such, their role in the future of outdoor recreation development in Canada, while yet to be developed, is unquestionable.

PROVINCIAL AND TERRITORIAL GOVERNMENT

Within the boundaries of provinces and territories, the power to influence areas directly related to outdoor recreation rests with generic equivalents of a Ministry of Forests, Department of Natural Resources, Ministry of Parks, or Recreation and Tourism. Generally, outdoor recreation-related responsibilities will be grouped with agencies that deal with land use (forestry), tourism, culture and economic development reflecting the multifaceted nature and implications of outdoor recreation development.

A fundamental difference between territories and provinces is that the vast majority of lands in the territories are federal crown lands administered under the *Territorial Lands Act* (1950). Private ownership is infinitesimal. Hence, land disposition is essentially a federal concern. However, increasing transfers of powers to territorial governments (e.g., forestry and wildlife) and the settlement of land claims with aboriginal peoples involving vast areas of the north points to the evolving maturity of territorial and aboriginal governments towards something approximating provincial status. As this chapter is being written, the Inuit of the Eastern Arctic (represented by the Tungavik Federation of Nunavut) have ratified the formation of an Inuit homeland called Nunavut with a predominantly Inuit government. This vast area will likely become Canada's newest territory with widespread powers in land use management. The ongoing settlement of comprehensive claims in Canada's north has kept the development of a territorial protected lands system at an embryonic stage. However, with advances in recent land claim settlements, protected areas such as Hershel Island Territorial Park on the Beaufort Sea and Kekerten Territorial Historic Site in Cumberland Sound (Baffin Island) show the growing development of territorial protected areas management. These areas could only have been established with the full support, cooperation, and involvement of the indigenous aboriginal people of the region.

In contrast, the provinces, by virtue of the transfer of resources (e.g., the *1930 Land Transfer Act*), have ownership of surface and subsurface rights for the purposes of land disposition. Some provincial parks systems, such as British Columbia's, trace their origins to the early years of the 20th century (e.g., Strathcona Provincial Park established in 1921). Today, these systems are extremely diverse and are aimed to anticipate the future and changing needs of citizens and society in general. Hence, provincial parks and recreation areas provide an extremely important role in the conservation/recreational lands relationship. In general, provincially protected lands are designed for more intensive use along the outdoor recreation spectrum reflecting the need to serve a broad range of users. In addition, many provincial parks allow resource extraction although more and more provinces are now designating parks where maintenance of natural values is paramount and extraction activities are prohibited.

Often, provincial parks are within easy reach of urban populations and provide quality accessible and affordable outdoor recreation opportunities. Alberta's "Kananaskis Country", near Calgary on the east slope of the Rockies, comprises a number of recreation and wildlife management areas (including Lougheed Provincial Park). This area provides a broad spectrum of recreation opportunities from downhill skiing and golf to wilderness recreation and back country horse use.

Most provinces and territories have or are developing comprehensive land use planning and conservation strategies. Unlike past detailed planning efforts, often done in sectorial isolation, the trend today is towards "strategic" planning efforts that involve all sectors, and integrating broad-based and long-term considerations. This approach strives to ensure that values and benefits arising from outdoor recreation are considered along side of those from traditional extraction activities, and, in this way, balancing the decision making process concerning land use.

MUNICIPAL GOVERNMENTS

Local or municipal governments are often overlooked in discussions of outdoor recreation and yet they play an extremely important part in the outdoor recreation field. The specific role of regional or municipal parks is to provide regional and community-based outdoor recreation opportunities. They complement the work of provincial protected lands and other recreation suppliers largely by concentrating on providing outdoor recreation activities close to population centres. Such areas are often designed with local or regional residents in mind. Although not exclusively so, their largest role is often in the provision of day use activities as opposed to the more extended recreation patterns of areas such as national parks.

These "local" protected areas also have a long history of evolution. As early as 1583, a small area of land near St. John's Harbour was used as public space. By the early 1800s, parks devoted to recreation were common features in Niagara-on-the-Lake, Toronto, Kingston and Hamilton. Their primary function was to serve as retreats from densely developed environments.

In recent years, municipalities and regional organizations have developed strategies for protected areas that approximate the spectrum if not the scale of provincial and federal efforts. For instance, the Capital Regional District of lower Vancouver Island and the Gulf Islands (a regional group of several district municipalities and electoral areas) has a well-developed regional parks organization. Their system plan includes a variety of areas that span the range of activity from intensive outdoor recreation to activities that require large undisturbed areas suitable for nature appreciation and recreation based on low density and opportunities for solitude. Unlike provincial and federal efforts, these areas arise from opportunistic or activity-related criteria for their designation as opposed to systematic landscape based representation. More than other levels, municipal and regional parks are generally areas that have been established specifically for outdoor recreation purposes.

NON-GOVERNMENT ORGANIZATIONS (NGOS)

A fundamental societal shift since the second World War is the recognition that governments are no longer perceived as having the sole responsibility for the identification, establishment, protection and use of protected areas or environments.

The growth of private non-government organizations, commonly called NGOs, is remarkable for their variety and philosophy, reflecting society's willingness to take on personal stewardship responsibilities for natural areas, responsibility for their advocacy and their use.

Some groups have specific interests and play an advocacy role such as the Canadian Parks and Wilderness Society, the Western Wilderness Society and the Canadian Nature Federation. Some are international organizations with Canadian branches such as the Sierra Club. Other groups, such as the Nature Conservancy of Canada, are involved in the actual purchasing and preservation of ecologically significant areas through private funding.

The rise in public environmental advocacy is nowhere better reflected than in the remarkable growth of the "cooperating association" movement. Increasingly, private citizens and groups want to contribute their time and efforts to enhance the viability and management of protected areas. These non-profit volunteer partnership programs undertake the revenue generation activities that are cycled back into the provision of services for their specific park or site. Cooperating associations promote community relations, interpretation, and awareness. Info-Nature Mauricie Cooperating Association in Quebec gives interpretation programs and operates sales outlets and back country hostels in La Mauricie National Park. Friends of the Trent-Severn Waterway Cooperating Association in Ontario manage several sales outlets, produce specialty publications, and sponsor special events such as an antique boat rally. For financially beleaguered governments at all levels, these Cooperating Association Programs are nothing short of vital. Their ability to develop new products and services and to generate revenue that goes directly back to benefit the protected area, with a minimum of operational overhead, is generally unmatchable by governments.

Some organizations, such as Ducks Unlimited, combine a recreational interest in hunting with conservation and habitat protection. Others combine an interest in regional environmental advocacy, preservation and ecology with compatible recreation (e.g., Alberta's Bow Valley Naturalists, the Federation of Ontario Naturalists, and Prince Edward Island's Island Nature Trust). These can be multifaceted groups, often working in an environmental or advocacy network with other provincial, federal and even international groups to achieve common goals.

Finally, there are the organizations that are devoted to outdoor recreation and understand the need to establish, protect and manage lands so that their primary activity interest is sustained. Groups such as the Alpine Club of Canada and the Canadian Recreational Canoe Association are examples of such organizations.

These NGOs and ENGOs (environmental non-government organizations) are extremely powerful when collectively mobilized. As coalitions, they can significantly influence governments not only because of their numbers and ability to organize, but also because of their fundamental grass roots origins reflecting societal values and expectations to which democratic governments, at all levels, are duty bound to react. No better example of this power exists than the organization of a national coalition by dozens of ENGOs that joined forces with First Nations, particularly the Haida of Gwaii Haanas (Queen Charlotte Islands), to force the federal and British Columbia governments to stop the logging of South Morseby

Island. The over $100 million dollar price tag to extinguish the logging rights and provide for other regional developments, including a national park, shows the leverage commanded by a national will for environmental management.

MANAGEMENT STRATEGIES FOR NATURAL AREAS AND RECREATION

Traditionally, managers of natural areas and outdoor recreation experiences are faced with two complementary, often contradictory, elements related to the activity and the setting in which it occurs: namely, providing or managing the outdoor recreation activity while maintaining the integrity of the natural setting in which it occurs. Clearly there is a direct line relationship between the two. A degradation of the setting results in a direct decline in the quality of the outdoor recreation experience.

The outdoor recreation manager must constantly balance the two elements considering such diverse aspects as site selection (e.g., campgrounds and trails), potential for deterioration, spatial needs and densities for solitude, sanitation and maintenance needs and many more related to the nature of the user, the activity and the setting.

To assist in conceptualizing and managing such diverse aspects of the outdoor recreation and protected area interface, outdoor recreation practitioners and scholars versed in the management of natural areas, have devised several conceptual and managerial strategies for approaching these issues. Outdoor recreation management receives information from three sources—people who use or have interest in the area, the natural environment, and management organizations.

In the past, outdoor recreation management has focused on the visitor—who the visitor is, what the visitor wants, needs and expects, and how the behaviour of the visitor impacts upon the environment. However, the fate of natural areas can be affected by people who are not typically classified as visitors—travel agents who sell tour packages, politicians who vote for or against budget allocations, and future generations who may or may not be able to experience the outdoor experience. It is important to understand that the fate of any natural area is not limited to the people who use the area directly for backpacking, vacations at the cottage, or cross-country skiing even though they provide the core of interested and committed people. Holistic approaches to protected areas use and management (as evidenced by the use of initiatives such as ecosystem based management and ecotourism) recognizes the inherent need to be more integrative with all stakeholders, not just the most obvious.

The natural environment provides the arena for all outdoor recreation and without a quality environment, a quality outdoor experience is simply not possible. Therefore, part of the responsibility of an outdoor recreation professional is to protect and maintain the quality of the natural environment. This requires a knowledge of ecology, recreation impact patterns on soils and vegetations, water quality parameters, wildlife behavioural patterns, and basic ecosystem management principles such as the role of fire and deadwood for the health of ecosystems.

Finally, the outdoor recreation professional is part of a management system. The management system provides the finances to support activities such as interpretation and research about recreational patterns, a power base for protection and negotiations with other groups and agencies, and a system of professionals who have expertise in specific areas necessary to protect natural areas and enhance outdoor recreation experiences.

Within this general context, there are several conceptual and management strategies used to help outdoor recreation practitioners and scholars understand and influence the patterns of outdoor recreation to provide quality experiences and protect natural areas. It must be remembered that managers of outdoor recreation do not provide an outdoor recreation experience or supply benefits. Managers of outdoor recreation provide opportunities for participants to produce experiences and/or benefits for themselves (by their own production functions) by using those opportunities and integrating their responses to them into their own lives both during and after participation (Driver, Brown & Peterson, 1992). We will consider five major strategies: carrying capacity (including social carrying capacity), satisfaction models, Recreational Opportunity Spectrum (ROS), Limits of Acceptable Change (LAC), and benefits analysis.

CARRYING CAPACITY

The concept of carrying capacity was derived from range and wildlife management and holds an appealing simplicity (and pitfall!). If some specific use level actually indicates the beginning of environmental deterioration and unsatisfactory recreational experiences, then outdoor recreation managers can state that an area is exceeding its carrying capacity when it exceeds this level and implement appropriate protective management actions. However, it has been difficult to develop a straightforward understanding of the use-impact relationship. For instance, some environmental settings demonstrate substantial deterioration even at low use levels. In other locations, the resources are very resilient and can withstand substantial use patterns. In addition, there is the phenomenon entitled "it depends": when it rains, some impact is more damaging than when it is dry. To complicate matters even more, simple "site hardening" (e.g., hard trails, boardwalks) can allow the substantial increase in physical carrying capacity, but overwhelm the capacity of other systems (e.g., facilities, services). Carrying capacity is almost never only one simple parameter.

A parallel concept is that of social carrying capacity. Social impact parameters (e.g., campsites, erosion, water quality), recreational use levels, and individual, activity, and site factors affect use/impact relationships. For instance, many backpackers seek solitude in contrast to many people who raft or canoe. For the solitary backpacker encountering one person creates a sensation of "crowding" where people on a raft may not perceive any "crowding" even when they encounter 20 other river parties. Basically, the conceptual framework of carrying capacity requires outdoor recreation managers to ask "How much use is too much?" Even with its limitations, the concept of carrying capacity shapes much of the thinking of outdoor recreation professionals.

RECREATIONAL OPPORTUNITY SPECTRUM (ROS)

People seek out a variety of outdoor recreation experiences that range from motorized activity such as motocross to non-motorized, solo activities such as cross-country skiing. The Recreational Opportunity Spectrum is a concept that attempts to encourage diversity in outdoor recreation. It is a formalized management guideline that was developed simultaneously by two groups of researchers. Clark and Stankey (1979) focus on providing a diversity of settings that will lead to a correspondent diversity of outcomes. For example, a single park might include a back country area that excludes motorized vehicles and sets limits on number of people which would create an opportunity for more adventurous and solo activities. Another area in the same park may provide developed campgrounds for recreational vehicles and family activities.

LIMITS OF ACCEPTABLE CHANGE (LAC)

Stankey, McCool and Stokes (1984) developed a framework within which decisions could be made about the conditions that will be permitted in a particular natural area. The premise behind LAC is that change (both environmental and social change) is a natural, inevitable consequence of recreation use. If recreation managers accept this premise, the question becomes, "How much change is acceptable?"

BENEFITS ANALYSIS

Recently, Driver, et al. (1992) have proposed managing outdoor recreation using a benefits-based management approach. This approach is based primarily on objective information about beneficial and detrimental consequences of alternative actions. Benefit is defined as a change that can be viewed advantageous or an improvement to an individual, group, society or other entity. In addition, a benefit can also be improving a condition or prevention of a condition becoming worse. This approach extends the analysis of benefits of outdoor recreation to include values such as environmental integrity and quality, historical significance, wildlife protection, and national identity.

Conclusion

The field of outdoor recreation and education is complex and requires the outdoor recreation professional to be competent in several areas. First, the outdoor recreation professional must understand the systems of flora and fauna within natural areas and appreciate the multiple values and benefits of natural areas. Second, the outdoor recreation experience combines a variety of motivations, expectations, benefits, and conditions which include risk, quality environmental settings, and psychological benefits such as self-confidence, solitude, and self-awareness. Third, systems of management for both outdoor recreation experience and the natural areas are a crucial element in today's world of outdoor recreation and education. Fourth, outdoor recreation and education revolves around a relationship between humans and the natural world. Hence, there must be opportunities to learn about the individual actors as well as the synergistic relationship between actors and how to behave appropriately and respectfully so that the natural areas can survive and the outdoor recreation experience can be enhanced.

It is both the personal experience and the natural setting that provides this unique entity entitled outdoor recreation experience. Perhaps Sigurd Olson (1969) said it best in *The Lonely Land*:

> I also knew there were some things that would never be dimmed by distance or time, compounded of values that would not be forgotten; the joy and challenge of the wilderness, the sense of being part of the country and of an era that was gone, the freedom we had known, silence, timeliness, beauty, companionship and loyalty, and a feeling of fullness and completeness that was ours at the end.
>
> I repacked the outfit and placed each item carefully away. It would not rest too long. Sooner or later it would all come out again. The Reindeer Country was waiting; Athabaska, Great Slave, Great Bear, and the vast barren lands beyond them all. Another year perhaps and the lonely land would claim us once again.

STUDY QUESTIONS

1. Name the basic concept that underlies all areas where outdoor recreation occurs. Give three reasons why you think such a concept is important to outdoor recreation.

2. What are three values for natural areas other than recreation?

3. Describe the characteristics of an outdoor recreation experience and list three outdoor recreation activities.

4. What is the definition of risk in outdoor recreation? Why is the risk element important in outdoor recreation? How is risk controlled in an outdoor recreation experience?

5. Name the four areas of benefits for outdoor recreation.

6. Compare and contrast the four categories of outdoor recreation programs. Give an example for each category.

7. Compare and contrast the criteria for internationally recognized lands, federal, First Nations or aboriginal, provincial or territorial, and municipal lands. Give two reasons how these different perspectives help protect all natural areas and outdoor recreation in Canada.

8. Define ecosystem-based management and identify two reasons for using such an approach to manage natural areas, especially national parks.

9. What are the criteria and legislation for establishing a national park?

10. List and give examples of the three programs of the Canadian Park Service that are particularly related to outdoor recreation.

11. Identify four categories of non-government organizations and describe how they help protect natural areas and promote outdoor recreation.

12. How is social carrying capacity related to carrying capacity? Give two reasons why this concept is important to a manager of a natural area.

13. Compare and contrast ROS and LAC? Which do you think is a better perspective and why?

14. What is the definition of a benefit as used in benefit analysis for outdoor recreation?

References

Clark, R. D. & Stankey, G. H. (1979). *The recreation opportunity spectrum: A framework for planning, management, and research.* USDA Forest Service Research Paper PNW-98.

Driver, B. L., Brown, P. J., & Peterson, G. L. (1991). *Benefits of leisure.* State College, PA: Venture Publishing, Inc.

Ewert, A. (1989). *Outdoor adventure pursuits: Foundations, models, and theories.* Columbus, OH: Publishing Horizons, Inc.

Faulkner, H. (1979). The opening address. In J. G. Nelson, R. D. Needham, S. H. Nelson, & R. C. Scace (Eds.), *The Canadian National Parks: Today and Tomorrow Conference II* (pp. 3-14). Waterloo, ON: University of Waterloo.

A Fitness Canada Report. (1988). *On outdoor recreation: Final report.* Prepared by Eastwest Consulting.

Griffin, S. (1978). *Women and nature: The roaring inside her.* New York, NY: Harper & Row.

Hammel, H. (1986). How to design a debriefing session. *Journal of Experiential Education, 9*(3), pp. 20-26.

Hargrove, E. C. (1989). Foundations of environmental ethics. Englewood Cliffs, NJ: Prentice Hall.

Hollenhorst, S. & Ewert, A. (1990). The adventure model approach to risk recreation and planning management and research. In D. W. Lime (Ed.), *Managing America's Enduring Wilderness Resource: Proceedings of the Conference* (pp. 331-338). St. Paul, MN: Minnesota Extension Services.

Houston, C. (1968). The 1st blue mountain. In S. Klausner (Ed.), *Why men take chances* (pp. 49-58). New York, NY: Doubleday and Company.

James, T. (n.d.) Sketch of a moving spirit: Kurt Hahn. In R. J. Kraft & M. Sakofs (Eds.), *The theory of experiential education* (pp. 39-44). Boulder, CO: Association for Experiential Education.

Lederman, L. C. (1984). Debriefing: A critical reexamination of the postexperience analytic process with implications for its effective use. *Simulation & Games, 15*(4), 415-431.

Leopold, A. (1949). *A Sand Country Almanac and sketches here and there.* New York, NY: Oxford University Press.

McAvoy, L. H. (1987). Education for outdoor leadership. In J. F. Meier, T. W. Morash, and G. E. Welton (Eds.), *High Adventure Pursuits* (pp. 459-467). Columbus, OH: Publishing Horizons, Inc.

Merchant, C. (1980). *The death of nature: Women, ecology and the scientific revolution.* New York, NY: Harper & Row.

Nash, R. (1967). *Wilderness and the American mind.* New Haven, CT: Yale University Press.

Olson, S. (1969). *Lonely land.* New York, NY: Random House.

Plant, J. (Ed.). (1989). *Healing the wounds: The promise of eco-feminism.* Santa Cruz, CA: New Society Publishers.

Rolston, H., III. (1986). *Philosophy gone wild: Essays in environmental ethics.* Buffalo, NY: Prometheus Books.

Rowe, S. (1990). *Home place: Essays on ecology.* Edmonton, AB: NeWest Publishers

Sessoms, D. (1984). *Leisure services.* Englewood Cliffs, NJ: Prentice-Hall, Inc.

Stankey, G. H., McCool, S. F. & Stokes, G. C. (1984). Limits of acceptable change: A new framework for managing the Bob Marshall Wilderness complex. *Western Wildlands, 10*(3), 33-37.

Chapter Twelve

Programming Recreational Services

Overview

PURPOSE

This chapter has been designed to introduce you to recreation programming and to discuss its nature and significance as part of the services provided by leisure services practitioners. We describe the evolution of recreation programming, the emergence of theoretical models to better understand and plan for the recreation program experience, leisure education, and issues to be addressed by those involved in planning, developing and delivering recreation programs.

LEARNING OBJECTIVES

At the completion of this chapter, you should be able to:

1. describe the social significance of recreation programming,

2. appreciate the historical context of the various models used to develop and provide recreation programs,

3. describe and explain several theories which help us to understand the basis of recreation programming, and

4. describe and explain key issues facing recreation programmers in Canada.

Programming Recreational Services

The provision of recreation and leisure programs has been the foundation of the organized leisure service delivery system in Canada since its inception at the turn of the century. Among the very early efforts at organized leisure service programming were the turn-of-the-century initiatives of the National Council of Women (McFarland, 1970). This service group initiated summer playground programs in order to contribute to the healthy development of youth and to counter the boredom which the Council believed contributed to juvenile delinquency. This social advocacy role was eventually assumed by the local civic governments across the country. Recreation program planning has a long and important history in the social development of the nation and is, from the perspective of the consumer, among the most visible and deeply rooted roles that leisure service agencies play.

It is through recreation programming that individuals may acquire skills for use throughout their lifetime. It is through the organized recreation program that individuals may enhance opportunities for social interaction and avoid unnecessary social isolation, become more physically fit, stimulate their intellectual powers, demonstrate their artistic or creative self, learn about new things, and generally experience a more fulfilling life. Recreation program planners have the responsibility to meet the diverse and demanding needs of the community they serve. This crosses age, religious, employment, ethnic, and gender groups, as well as education and income levels. It addresses those of different marital status and level of ability (including those who may be physically or mentally handicapped).

Particularly important to the recreation program planner are the concepts of lifestyle and lifestage. Lifestyle, according, Sessoms (1985), is the way we express our lives. It is the sum of those behaviours and attitudes that characterize an individual's existence. Lifestyles are, however, dynamic and individuals grow and change in time. Our adolescent lifestyles evolve in response to changes in the environment, opportunity growth, and social pressures. We are often faced with more discreet circumstances in our life which lead to changes in lifestyle. These circumstances relate to but are not limited to careers, marital status, parenthood, and disease or illness.

Any discussion of lifestyle would be incomplete without reference to the inter-related issue of life stage. In their pioneering work, Rapoport and Rapoport (1975) examined the effect of family life cycle on recreation behaviour. It is clear from their work and from the work of those who have continued in this area that an individual's expectations, demands, desires and opportunities change as he or she moves into different family life stages. Thus, the high school student leads a different life than does the college student living away from home for the first time. Older adults whose children have grown up and moved away have a new life stage with which to cope and to which they must adapt. The older adult entering a personal care home or other institutionalized environment also enters a new life stage. Thus, the recreation program planner has the opportunity and responsibility to address not only variations in types of people as described earlier (i.e., married, poor, physically handicapped, etc.), but also variations in lifestyles and life stages.

The role of leisure in the social fabric of our society is substantive and important to sustaining our quality of life and improving it. Recreation program planners must be capable of meeting those needs in the community or face the problem of becoming obsolete or lacking in usefulness.

Why Do We Need to Plan Recreation Programs?

What is the point of studying recreation programming? After all, if I want to participate in a leisure activity all I need to do is find out where it is available and then go to it, or arrange to participate with my friends. For some activities and some individuals this may be correct. However, there are a great many individuals who seek to participate in leisure which requires greater structure and organization, facilities, specialized equipment, teams or partners, or other resources not necessarily available to them. Thus, the leisure service professional fulfills the important role of designing and developing those recreation experiences which individuals cannot create on their own, and exposing the public to new and creative leisure pursuits.

Research by Jackson and Searle (1985), Henderson et al. (1988), Shaw (1990) and others has shown that many individuals perceive themselves to be constrained in their recreation. The different kinds of constraints were examined in Chapter Four. Recreation programmers find this information useful as it sheds light on who is constrained and in what manner. In a study of Albertans, Searle and Jackson (1985) found that single women, the elderly, and the poor were among the most constrained from participating in their desired recreational pursuits. Other research by Henderson et al. (1988) has shown that women are constrained by some unique problems. For example, the issue of body image is far more prevalent among women as is the issue of privacy. The latter is particularly acute for those with young children, a husband, a career and a home to manage. Both intervening constraints (e.g., lack of money, lack of time, and lack of knowledge about where to participate) and antecedent constraints (e.g., constraining conditions such as education and prior experiences) have a significant impact on individual leisure behaviour. Recreation programmers must seek ways to reduce the effects of these constraints.

This expanding area of knowledge of constraints heightens concern in another related area. Why do people stop participating in activities? What causes people to continue or discontinue activities? These issues go even more directly to the ability of the organization to provide for the wants of the people it serves. Research in this area is still in its infancy, but clearly there are reasons for quitting related to what the program service offers, what resources an individual has, and what effect, if any, the program is having on the individual participant.

Resulting from a growing need to consciously meet the wants of the public, the process of recreation program planning has frequently been placed within the context of marketing. Adopting a marketing orientation should not be construed as a suggestion that recreation program planners become "hucksters" trying to sell "snake oil" solutions to complex personal and social problems. Marketing-oriented recreation programmers are not just sellers of something that they have devised and now hope to convince the public to accept. The marketing approach is one in which the consumer determines the success of the organization, not the organization itself.

This argument, well-explained in the work of John Crompton (1985), is based on the principle that the marketing approach to service delivery begins with an assessment of what consumers or clients want. It is from this assessment that services and programs flow. Thus, if the recreation program planner can accurately match the wants of the group he or she seeks to serve with available program resources, success will be achieved. This need to understand the recreation participant's needs is expressed well in the marketing literature which reinforces "to sell Jack Jones what Jack Jones buys, you have to see Jack Jones through Jack Jones' eyes".

Moreover, the marketing approach has the logical appeal of being more cost-effective. If recreation program planners take the time at the outset to determine the wants and the priorities of the public it seeks to serve, then there will be less wasted effort and more focused and effective use of limited resources. This may be an increasingly important issue as public and not-for-profit organizations seek to address the problem of shrinking resources and increasing demand for service. For those in the private, commercial sector, this is always an issue since money spent on ill-informed speculation is potentially lost profits and will limit the potential for continued success and corporate viability.

In summary, recreation program planning can be defined as the process of organizing recreation resources and opportunities for other people for the purpose of meeting their leisure needs. This program planning process is used in all sectors of the leisure service delivery system.

Evolution of Recreation Program Planning

Over time, the processes used to determine what recreation programs should be provided have changed. Rather simplistic approaches of years gone by have evolved into approaches that are driven by social science theory. Following is a discussion of the evolution of recreation program planning techniques and the contemporary theory that supports them.

COMPENSATION, BALANCED DIET AND CAFETERIA: EARLY MODELS OF RECREATION PROGRAMMING

Sessoms (1985) has described what could be called a compensation theory of programming which asserts that activities at work or school were assumed to be inherently passive and thus it was the role of the recreation programmer to provide more physical challenges. Nash, among others cited by Sessoms, introduced the balanced diet model of recreation program service provision. Nash's work was discussed in Chapter Three in the context of the philosophical foundations of leisure services. The model Nash developed (reproduced in Figure 12.1 for easy reference), suggested the need for recreation programmers to provide a range of services covering each of the important areas of human development (physical, social, spiritual, emotional). Nash also believed that a person could not achieve his or her potential and be fully developed without experiences in each of the levels of positive participation. Nash also developed a self-test to evaluate your balance within the range of recreation experiences (see the end of this chapter for a copy of the test called "How Do You Rate?"). You should be aware of the value choices inherent in Nash's chart of recreation experiences. Also, note the limitations regarding the applicability of the scale to people in special circumstances. Those who are ill or infirm would score lower but conditions may not allow for more active participation. Research (Henderson, 1990) has shown that young women who are mothers and primarily engaged in sustaining the home have little leisure time. Thus, there are serious limitations and clear values to which not all individuals will subscribe. Nonetheless, this was a popular model and is subscribed to by some today (depending upon their philosophy).

Brightbill (cited in Sessoms, 1985) used Nash's model in suggesting that the role of the parks and recreation department was to provide a recreation "cafeteria" featuring services from each of Nash's levels of participation. He suggested that the participant be allowed to select and participate in different activities at different levels. The move from the balanced diet approach advocated by Nash to the cafeteria style of Brightbill has continued to what is often referred to as the facilitation or enabling method of programming.

FIGURE 12.1
NASH'S HIERARCHY OF RECREATION PROGRAM

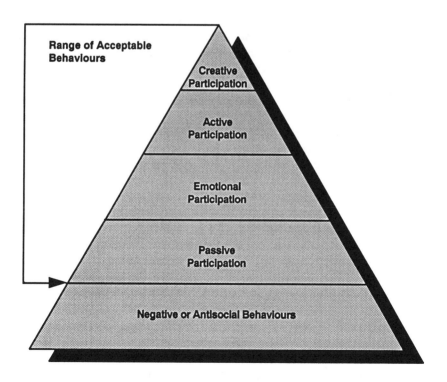

FROM DIRECT SERVICE TO FACILITATION

The facilitation method is often described using the word 'catalyst'. Essentially, the facilitation model or approach to recreation programming suggests that leisure professionals do not become a part of the leisure experience but, rather, serve to help people to act on their leisure desires and interests. This approach puts a premium on the professional's ability to lead. It is through his or her leadership that we achieve increased opportunities for conversation or communication which is what Ralston (cited in Gilhooly, 1991, p. 14) described as the "secret and forgotten soul of our community development initiatives". Dialogue leads to increased understanding and this begets programs which are reflective of the community's needs and interests.

Because of the intense interaction with the community and need for continual developmental activity, facilitation is often more expensive than other methods although it has commonly been mistaken by political decision-makers as a less expensive alternative to direct program delivery. This fallacy results from the belief that, since the organization helps people to help themselves it should provide less direct service and, therefore, the costs of service delivery should decline. The problem is compounded by the fact that often people believe that, in order to become more leisure self-reliant, the agency should run the program and remove the burden of organization and planning from them. This is increasingly evident in a society which is now characterized by less leisure time (Shaw, 1990) and a concomitant rise in the importance given to leisure (Gregg & Posner, 1990). Moreover, among those not facing less leisure time (e.g., the elderly, the poor, etc.) theirs is a lack of resources to acquire the leisure experiences they desire. Research has shown that they are among the most constrained in their leisure (Searle & Jackson, 1985). Thus, facilitation does not necessarily connote doing less direct program provision. It may result in more. It is also important to note that when organizations have made the faulty assumption that facilitation would lead to decreased direct program services, they have found themselves juxtaposed between a lack of resources to carry out programs and the demand for more. This usually results in consumers finding alternative suppliers of the service they seek and loss of support from the political leaders or membership-elected board of directors for the programming function of the agency.

Numerous other approaches to programming have been discussed in the literature. These have been described by Carpenter and Howe (1985) and include the following:

- The *authoritarian* approach asserts that, because the recreation professional is trained in this area, he or she knows what others like;
- The *socio-political* approach argues that we must be attuned with the needs of special interest groups especially if they are well-connected to "city hall";
- The *reaction* approach is adequately described by the often stated claim that "the squeaky wheel gets the grease". In other words, the services are provided to those who have the loudest and most persistent requests;

- The *traditional* approach suggests that we offer what we have always offered because, if it worked in the past, it will work today;
- The *prescriptive* approach is best described by Murphy (as cited in Carpenter & Howe, p. 53) who wrote that "leisure programs are social instruments and should be provided in a manner that ensures that the social and personal needs of participants are met". Thus, there are a variety of recreation programming approaches that have been employed over the course of this century.

The facilitation method is clearly connected to the marketing approach because it is predicated on a bottom-up flow of information. The programmer works from the notion of what is desired by the members of the constituency that he or she serves and then attempts to mobilize the resources necessary to plan, develop and implement the program. As Rossman (1989) has noted, recreation programmers must be able to react to new initiatives and trends and use the process to their advantage to deliver the best product possible.

Theoretical Basis of Recreation Programming

It is important that we understand the benefits that accrue from recreation programs and appreciate the value of offering programs designed to meet those needs. Among the most often used models in studying the benefits of leisure participation is Maslow's (1970) model of the hierarchy of needs. This five part hierarchy was explained in Chapter Four and illustrated in Figure 4.1 (p. 66). It shows that, as people satisfy lower level needs, they begin to work on satisfying higher order needs. Leisure and recreation service providers have a role in helping individuals satisfy the three higher level needs and arguably can influence security needs as well.

SYMBOLIC INTERACTIONISM

Symbolic interactionism is one theoretical structure that is useful in understanding how individuals behave and why individuals behave in certain ways in recreation programs. Goffman's (1959) work on symbolic interactionism is the basis for much thought and subsequent development in this area. Blumer (1969, p. 4-5) summed the theory best in stating that symbolic interactionism:

> "sees meaning as arising in the process of interaction between people. The meaning of a thing for a person grows out of the ways in which other persons act toward the person with regard to the thing. Their actions operate to define the thing for the person. Thus, symbolic interactionism sees meanings as social products, as creations that are formed in and through defining activities of people as they interact."

As the research by Shaw (1985) and Samdahl (1988) suggested, leisure is a special meaning derived from social events in which individuals interact with each other and the objects of the event. Individuals interpret meanings differently and will react differently to the same stimulus. As a result, recreation programmers must allow for the participant to help shape the experience and facilitate their feelings of freedom the participant to help shape the experience and facilitate their feelings of freedom to choose. Clearly, rigidity in program structures is counter to the notion of symbolic interactionism.

SOCIAL EXCHANGE THEORY

Another perspective is offered by Searle (1991) in his examination of social exchange theory. Social exchange theory suggests that individuals will continue to engage in recreation programs as long as they derive the rewards from the experience that they seek (not necessarily the ones advertised), believe the program is worth the cost and the benefits exceed those costs (not only program fees but also babysitting costs, time to travel to the program, requirements for any special equipment, etc.). In addition, the program must be seen to have a high probability of providing the sought-after rewards and that they are as good as or better than those provided by other organizations. The social exchange approach substantiates the need for good assessment of the needs of prospective participants in order to design programs appropriately and it argues for adaptability in order to avoid a program design that is inappropriate for the needs of the participants. If individuals do not perceive that they are receiving fair benefits for their contribution to attend the program, then they will cease to engage in the activity offered by that provider. If there are no alternative providers, then the individual has little choice but to cease participation in that activity.

This discussion leads to the question of substitutability (Iso-Ahola, 1986). The concept of substitutability suggests that there are individuals who would engage in other activities in the absence of their most desired one. For example, a person may be prepared to participate in floor hockey if broomball was not available because of the similar physical demands, skills required, time involved, social aspects, etc. If substitution is viable, then programmers should explore this further with their clients to assess how they might more effectively meet their needs.

OPTIMAL EXPERIENCE

Csikszentmihalyi's (1990) research, described in Chapter Three in the discussion of optimal experiences, resulted in the notion of "flow". Flow is the match between an individual's ability and the challenge provided by the activity. As a result, leisure programs are often the best opportunity for individuals to experience "flow" and thus have an optimal experience. Csikszentmihalyi (1981) has suggested that recreation experiences become the litmus test against which all life pursuits are measured with respect to the level of satisfaction they create in the individual. Recreation programs have tremendous power to create positive experiences which are rewarding for people which in turn becomes the basis for their assessment of work benefits, family benefits, other relational benefits, and other aspects of their lives. The creation of an optimum match for the individual in a recreation program can be an influential event.

Leisure Education

Leisure education is a process designed to enable individuals to develop a satisfying leisure lifestyle. This is not a particularly new concept. Professor Charles Brightbill wrote about it in the 1950s in his book *Educating for Leisure-Centered Living*. He suggested that the school system and those in recreation must take on the responsibility of not just educating people so they can work effectively, but also so they can use their leisure effectively (i.e., in a satisfying manner).

Leisure education is a process. As such it is not a particular program or service but rather it represents something that should be incorporated into the program delivery system. The reason most public and not-for-profit agencies should address this issue is that part of their mission may be to reduce dependency on the system of service provision and enhance the individual's ability to manage his or her own lifestyle. Leisure education directly serves that interest.

Leisure education strives to achieve four objectives (Woodburn and Cherry, 1978). These are:

(1) to develop personal knowledge and understanding about leisure;
(2) to develop skills and personal resources for involvement in a wide range of leisure pursuits;
(3) to identify and assess personal leisure needs, interests and barriers and make appropriate lifestyle choices;
(4) to develop and express positive attitudes and clarify personal values relating to leisure.

With respect to objective number one, we need to be realistic in identifying our lifestyle aspirations and directions. In this context, we can then begin to understand the nature and significance of leisure in our lives. To this end, we need to become aware of the multitude of leisure resources so that choices are not made in the absence of sufficient awareness of alternatives. We also need to recognize the societal pressures that are continually influencing our leisure decisions. We need to understand the consequences of our actions and we need to understand how we learn best. Learning about leisure requires effort, curiosity, risk, pleasure, frustration, and success.

The second objective deals with the improvement of an individual's sense of perceived competence within the leisure domain. That is, the more you know the more you are able to perform well in different activities. This has direct consequences for an individual's willingness to risk and experiment with participation in a variety of activities. Moreover, the acquisition of a large repertoire of skills results in improved feelings of self-esteem and likely increases an individual's sense of control over his or her life. It is important to remember, with respect to improvements in psychological function, that this can be and often is domain-specific. That is, individuals may improve in leisure competence, self-esteem and locus of control but this does not necessarily transfer to other parts of their lives. One should be careful in stating the power of any particular activity with respect to changes in psychological well-being.

The third objective requires an individual to carefully assess his or her personal leisure needs and interests. Also required is an assessment of the constraints on his or her leisure. This is a process of individual needs assessment that is conducted with the same thoroughness that a leisure service professional should use in assessing the community's or a particular target market's needs. Essentially, this objective challenges the individual to gain an understanding of themselves in order to help themselves achieve a more satisfying lifestyle.

The fourth objective must be well-understood. The purpose of leisure education is not to shape values or attitudes. The purpose of leisure education is to help individuals to understand the values to which they subscribe, and to understand how those values influence their leisure choices. Attitudes are a powerful force with respect to changing behaviour, and the process of changing attitudes must be undertaken with great care Attempts to change attitudes should be focussed on helping individuals to recognize that a positive outlook toward leisure can open new vistas and opportunities for them.

Leisure education is an important process which is now being integrated into a wide variety of settings (see Chapter Nine on Recreation and Persons with Disabilities). Increasingly, leisure education has become a valuable service of recreation programmers and one that has the potential to contribute much to the quality of life that communities and individuals enjoy.

Issues in Recreation Programming

The provision of recreation programs is no longer a simple matter for public, not-for-profit, or commercial recreation service organizations. Such organizations are constantly being confronted with new issues to address in order to remain viable and relevant. Several are discussed here.

EQUITY IN PROGRAM SERVICE PROVISION

One of the issues that program planners face in the development and implementation of recreation programs is that of equity. Equity means fairness. The provision of parks and recreation services is influenced by the form of equity used in a particular organization. Thus, the question posed by equity is "who gets what?" (Crompton, 1985). Historically, the most popular form of equity has been that which is described as equal opportunity. In this model, each person receives approximately equal amounts and equal quality of services irrespective of the amount of taxes paid or of their need. Public parks and recreation services were provided on basis of *compensatory equity* at the beginning of the 20th century. This form of equity holds that services are provided to those most disadvantaged. That is, those who are in greatest need receive the greatest amount of service.

The third model of equity is referred to as market equity. In this model, services are provided on the basis of tax revenues provided or fees produced. This means that those who pay the most, get the most. This is the basis for private sector leisure services, in most cases, and for some in the not-for-profit sector such as golf and country clubs.

The final model that is used to achieve the appearance of equity is, indeed, not an equity model at all. It is the use of expressed demand in lieu of equity. That is, "the squeaky wheel gets the grease". According to this model, resources are provided on the basis of who is using them the most or who is most vociferous in their advocacy for services. Unfortunately this model receives a disproportionate share of attention as a means to deliver services because politicians tend to be sensitive to outspoken groups, especially if there is little opposition or if the opposition is not well-organized. This use of demand as a measure of equity is popularly used because it requires the least work and provides a convenient explanation for the decision.

In the allocation and distribution of leisure programs, equity will become an issue and increasingly there is pressure to adopt more of a market equity approach since it addresses the issue of financing in the most direct way. Compensatory equity has fallen from favour because of the costs it incurs.

These issues will reflect the philosophy and mission of the organization and will influence the prices that are established for services. Those organizations with a mandate to serve the disadvantaged or excluded groups may favour use of the compensatory equity model in their service delivery decisions. Commercial organizations would rarely opt for anything other than market equity model as an overall allocation strategy since ability to pay is critical for profitability.

The Role of the Agency's Philosophy in Programming

The development of the organization's mission is the process of determining what the general intent of the organization is. Why was it created? What business are we in? What do we seek to achieve? The mission must also keep in mind the interests of the people it is designed to serve, the interest groups which impact upon its activities and the individuals, collectives (e.g., United Way) or other organizations (e.g., government) which provide the necessary funding. Thus, the development of a mission statement is both an exercise in responding to the complex environment in which the recreation organization functions, and a means of communicating the values and beliefs of the organization in a rather straightforward and easy to understand manner. This helps the potential member, user or participant to determine if the organization would be a good fit with his or her own beliefs, needs and interests.

Defining the Leisure Products

As noted earlier, recreation programming has, in many leisure service agencies, become market-oriented. The marketing approach to recreation programming demands that programs and services be, first and foremost, designed to satisfy client group wants and needs. It is a demand-side orientation rather than a supply-side orientation to product development, placement, pricing and promotion (the 4 Ps of marketing). Figure 12.2 (from Crompton and Lamb, 1986), illustrates the temporal relationship between the assessment of wants and needs, the development of leisure products, and promotion of those products.

FIGURE 12.2
THE MARKETING CONCEPT

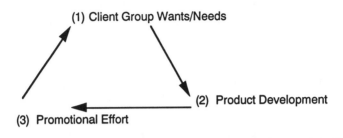

(1) Client Group Wants/Needs

(2) Product Development

(3) Promotional Effort

In contrast, some of the more traditional approaches to recreation programming begin with the development of the product, continue with its promotion, and then conclude with a hope that those products somehow satisfied the clients' wants and needs. On paper, this "selling" approach may not appear to be very different to the marketing approach but, in practice, the differences are significant.

What is it that the recreation programmer produces for the client? Is the recreation product a program, facility, or service? The recreation product, when viewed in the marketing context, is simply the satisfaction of client needs and wants. This may be referred to as a bundle of benefits or an experience that is usually facilitated by recreation programs, facilities, and services. The recreation programmer must be able to develop his or her product with this client group orientation (i.e., the marketing approach) in order to be successful in achieving the organization's mission and long-term goals and objectives.

NEED FOR STRONG RESEARCH

Murphy and Howard (1977) have suggested two important reasons for having research-based recreation programming. First, an assumed or supposed knowledge of a constituency's needs and interests is suspect because recreation as a profession does not have available a systematic, historic measurement of the impact of its services on which to base such assumptions or suppositions. Second, given the era of economic restraint in which we live, public accountability is much greater and it is difficult to justify expenditures for recreation on the basis of emotional appeals or based on what the recreation program planner just thinks the community wants. The decision-makers demand indisputable evidence of need and want to understand the potential impact of a service before allocating resources to it.

The message is clear. In an era of decreasing resources of all kinds and the increasing competition for those same resources, it is imperative that recreation programmers build in a high quality evaluation element into their program plans. The failure to do this will jeopardize the future of public and not-for-profit parks and recreation services. Commercial service providers have long understood that failure to achieve goals and objectives merits one decision—eliminate the program.

A useful summary of the reasons for doing evaluation research is presented by Lundegren and Farrell (1985, p. 2). They state that the purposes of evaluation research are:

1. to assess whether goals and objectives are being met,
2. to ascertain value and quality control,
3. to assist in decision-making (i.e., answer the "go/no go" question),
4. to aid in the development of a rationale for future action,
5. to demonstrate that a program is a legitimate, thereby, worthy of support,
6. to demonstrate accountability for a program to sponsors and agency administrators,
7. to aid in program revision (i.e., to improve a program),
8. to demonstrate and monitor program impact and effectiveness,
9. to contribute to the understanding of how programs increase leisure satisfaction and improve the quality of life for the participants, and
10. to weigh the benefits against the costs.

CHANGING DEMOGRAPHY

Recreation programmers must respond to the challenge presented by an increasingly older population and a declining number of children and youth relative to the entire population. Furthermore, for the next twenty years, the largest segment of society will be those who are middle-aged. They represent the major age group referred to as the baby boomers. The recreation programmer must consider the nature of the services and programs needed by this segment of the population and determine how it will provide or facilitate the delivery of those services and programs. In addition to responding to the quantity of baby boomers in the population generation, the astute recreation programmer will also recognize that, increasingly, they are the persons in governing positions.

While the older adults and baby boomers exert influence on the system by seeking more services, there is also a need to address the needs of the young adults (i.e., those individuals between 18 and 29 years of age). This generation of Canadians is sometimes referred to as Generation X (Coupland, 1991). These individuals often report feelings of disaffection with the excessive focus on the needs of the baby boom generation. In response, they seek their own identity and leisure programs to meet their unique needs.

SERVICES TO PERSONS WITH DISABILITIES

While the Decade of the Disabled declared by the United Nations (the 1980s) has come to a close, the progress made during that time for persons with mental and physical disabilities has been substantial. There is, however, still a need for greater integration efforts at all levels of recreation experiences, and programmers are increasingly faced with the challenge to ensure that integration also includes socialization and the development of friendships between individuals with a disability

and those without. The future will likely present more demands in this area as the process of deinstitutionalization initiated in the 1980s is replaced by efforts aimed at sustained independent living.

Summary

Recreation program planning is an important part of the leisure service delivery system. Over time, it has become increasingly sophisticated with the integration of marketing techniques and social science theory as a basis for understanding human behaviour. There are numerous issues facing service providers ranging from equity in service allocation to changing demographics. It is clear that research is important for sustaining financial support for recreation program services offered by agencies in the public, voluntary, and commercial sectors. The research drives the development of programs and allows for the effective use of resources to discover latent demand and to satisfy the demand that already exists. While programming is often the most "fun" activity in operating a recreation organization, it is clear that it takes more than a fun-loving leader and winning personality to ensure successful planning and delivery of recreation programs.

1. Describe the social significance of recreation programming.

2. Trace the evolution of recreation programming and be sure to highlight the major shifts in beliefs that accompanied each change.

3. Describe the limitations of Nash's model in a pluralistic society.

4. Why is marketing knowledge so important for recreation programmers?

5. Describe two other issues facing recreation programmers.

6. Describe leisure education and how recreation programmers can use this in their service activity.

References

Ajzen, I. & Fishbein, M. (1980). *Understanding attitudes and predicting social behavior.* Englewood-Cliffs, NJ: Prentice-Hall.

Babbie, E. (1989). *The practice of social research.* Belmont, CA: Wadsworth Publishing.

Blumer, H. (1969). *Symbolic interactionism.* Englewood Cliffs, NJ: Prentice-Hall.

Campbell, S. K. (1974). *Flaws and fallacies in statistical thinking.* Englewood Cliffs, NJ: Prentice-Hall.

Carpenter, G. M. & Howe, C. Z. (1985). *Programming leisure experiences: A cyclical approach.* Englewood Cliffs, NJ: Prentice-Hall.

Coupland, D. (1991). *Generation X.* New York, NY: St. Martin.

Crawford, D. & Godbey, G. (1987). Reconceptualizing barriers to family leisure. *Leisure Sciences, 9,* pp. 119-128.

Crompton, J. L. & Lamb, C. W. (1986). *Marketing government and social services.* New York, NY: J. Wiley and Sons.

Crompton, J. L. (1985). Marketing: Neither snake oil nor panacea. In P. Witt & T. Goodale (Eds.). *Recreation and leisure: Issues in an era of change (revised edition)* (pp. 175-194). State College, PA: Venture Publishing, Inc.

Csikszentmihalyi, M. (1981). Leisure and socialization. *Social Forces, 60,* pp. 332-340.

Csikszentmihalyi, M. (1990). *Flow: The psychology of optimal experience.* New York, NY: Harper and Row.

Gilhooly, D. (1991). Re-inventing the wheel. *Recreation Canada 49* (2), pp. 12-14.

Goffman, E. (1959). *The presentation of self in everyday life.* Garden City, NY: Doubleday and Co.

Gregg, A. & Posner, M. (1990). *The big picture.* Toronto, ON: Macfarlane, Walter & Ross.

Harter, S. (1978). Effectance motivation reconsidered. Toward a developmental model. *Human Development, 21,* pp. 34-36.

Henderson K. A., Stalnaker, D. & Taylor, G. (1988). The relationship between barriers to recreation and gender-role personality traits for women. *Journal of Leisure Research, 20,* pp. 69-80.

Henderson, K. (1990). The ethic of care: Leisure possibilities and constraints for women. In B. Smale (Ed.) *Proceedings from the Sixth Canadian Congress on Leisure Research* (pp. 345-349) Waterloo, ON: University of Waterloo Press.

Iso-Ahola, S. E. (1986). A theory of substitutability of leisure behaviour. *Leisure Sciences, 10,* pp. 203-215.

Jackson, E. L. (1988). Leisure constraints: A survey of past research. *Leisure Sciences, 10,* pp. 203-215.

Lundegren, H. M. & Farrell, P. (1985). *Evaluation for leisure service managers: A dynamic approach.* Philadelphia, PA: Saunders College Publishing.

Maslow, A. (1970). *Motivation and personality.* New York, NY: Harper and Row.

McFarland, E. (1970). *The history of public recreation in Canada.* Ottawa, ON: Canadian Parks/Recreation Association.

Rapoport, R. & Rapoport, R. N. (1975). *Leisure and the family life cycle.* Boston, MA: Routledge & Kegan Paul.

Rossman, J. R. (1989). *Recreation programming: Designing leisure experiences.* Champaign, IL: Sagamore Publishing.

Rotter, J. B. (1966). Generalized expectancies for internal versus external locus of control of reinforcement. *Psychological Monographs 80,* (1, Whole No. 609).

Russell, R. (1982). *Planning programs in recreation.* St. Louis, MO: The C. V. Mosby Company.

Samdahl, D. M. (1988). A symbolic interactionist model of leisure: Theory and empirical support. *Leisure Sciences, 1,* pp. 27-39.

Searle, M. S. & Jackson, E. L. (1985). Socioeconomic variations in perceived barriers to recreation participation among would-be participants. *Leisure Sciences, 7,* pp. 227-249.

Searle, M. S. (1987). *Leisure and aging in Manitoba.* Winnipeg, MB: Manitoba Culture, Heritage and Recreation.

Searle, M. S. (1991). Propositions for testing social exchange in the context of ceasing leisure participation. *Leisure Sciences, 13,* pp. 279-194.

Sessoms, H. D. (1985). Lifestyles and lifecycles: A recreation programming approach. In P. Witt and T. Goodale (Eds.) *Recreation and leisure: Issues in an era of change (revised edition)* (pp. 221-243). State College, PA: Venture Publishing, Inc.

Shaw, S. M. (1985). The meanings of leisure in everyday life. *Leisure Sciences, 7,* pp. 1-24.

Shaw, S. (1990). Where has all the leisure gone? The distribution and redistribution of leisure. In B. Smale (Ed.) *Proceedings from the Sixth Canadian Congress on Leisure Research* (pp. 1-5) Waterloo, ON: University of Waterloo Press.

Sneegas, J. J. (1986). Components of life satisfaction in middle and later life adults: Perceived social competence, leisure participation and leisure satisfaction. *Journal of Leisure Research, 18,* pp. 259-265.

Statistics Canada. (1989). *Family expenditures in Canada.* Ottawa, ON: Minister of Supply and Services.

Woodburn, R. & Cherry, C. (1978). *Leisure: A resource for educators.* Toronto, ON: Ministry of Culture and Recreation.

How Do You Rate?*

Is your leisure time producing the desired results? A wise use of leisure involves participating in all of the following four levels of activity: passive, emotional, active, and creative. If you are choosing several active and creative activities, you are not reaping the benefits available through your leisure hours.

The scope of recreational activities is as broad as life itself. However, for convenience in communicating about them, these activities have been classified into ten types. These ten types with an explanation of each, are as follows:

1. *Sports and Games*: Physical activities typified by tennis, basketball, gymnastics, bowling, swimming, skiing, softball, badminton, and hiking.

2. *Arts and Crafts*: Manipulative activities such as basket weaving, ceramics, cooking, knitting, leathercrafts, painting, plastic crafts, photography, and sculpturing.

3. *Drama*: Activities in which the participant is playing a part or observing others who are doing so. Activities vary from charades to follies, from marionettes to three-act plays, or from storytelling to play writing.

4. *Dance*: Social folk, square, tap, ballet, and modern and other forms of rhythmic expression.

5. *Music*: Glee clubs, choruses, quartets, bands, orchestras, operas, and solo work.

6. *Outing and Nature Activities*: Astronomy, camping, gardening, caring for pets, nature hikes, conservation, travelling, fishing, and hunting.

7. *Literary and Mental Activities*: Reading, debating, discussion, writing, mathematics, genealogy, public speaking, crossword puzzles, and study groups.

8. *Social Activities*: Those activities that two or more people do together in which the joy of being together is the primary motivating factor. Illustrative of these types are banquets, holiday parties, reunions, club meetings, church socials, and house parties. Most of the other types of activities may be used for "social" purposes.

9. *Collecting Activities*: Collectors items, from antiques to zippers.

10. *Service Activities*: Activities which give the individual satisfaction through helping other people. Activities range from helping a neighbour to serving as chairman of the school board.

Note: The reader is reminded that participation in the above types of activities may be on the passive, emotional, active and/or creative levels.

Self-evaluation Scale*

Check your leisure-time participation on the following chart to determine the quality of your recreational pursuits.

Opposite each type of activity check the levels of your *regular* participation as explained previously. Record the total score for each type of activity in the subtotal column and add those scores to get your grand total. Note that you may participate at all four levels for some activities and only one level or no levels for others. If you are not satisfied with your score, begin now to do something about it.
Evaluation Scale:

EVALUATION SCALE					
	Passive (1)	Emotional (2)	Active (3)	Creative (7)	Sub-total (15)
Sports and Games					
Arts and Crafts					
Drama					
Dance					
Music					
Outing and Nature					
Literary and Educational					
Social					
Collecting					
Service					
GRAND TOTAL					

176-260 Outstanding — Your potential and status seem outstanding, but perhaps you should devote more time to your job or relaxation.

140-174 Above Average — You seem to have achieved a balance between work and play.

85-139 Average — Your score indicates a fair status, but you may be one-sided or you may not be sufficiently creative.

55-84 Below Average — You are missing many of the good things life has to offer.

0-54 Poor — Wake up and live!

Note: Try filling out the evaluation scale as you would like it to read at, say, age 65. What needs to be done between now and then to get your score where you would like it upon retirement? Be specific as to the activities planned.

* How Do You Rate and Self-evaluation Scale reproduced with permission from I. Heaton, *How Do You Rate*, Brigham Young University Printing Services, 1960, pp. 6-8.

The State of the Profession

Overview

PURPOSE

The purpose of this chapter is to provide an overview of the issues associated with the move toward achieving professional status for those who work in leisure services. The chapter will describe some of the principal organizations that exist to promote leisure in Canada and assist those in the field (both volunteer and paid employee). We will also briefly describe some of the organizations that exist internationally, and review the state of university and college education in leisure.

LEARNING OBJECTIVES

At the completion of this chapter, you should be able to:

1. describe the relevant changes that have occurred in the leisure service field,

2. describe the issues associated with the movement to gain professional status,

3. describe the history and current state of national and provincial organizations,

4. describe the more notable international organizations in the field and identify their focus, and

5. describe the status of higher education in leisure in Canada.

The State of the Profession

The development of leisure services in Canada has come through the efforts of a combination of volunteers and individuals employed by leisure service agencies. Many of the first paid employees of leisure service agencies were professionals from other fields. At the turn of the century, it was not uncommon to find persons with backgrounds in social work, education, and physical activity among the leaders of the recreation field. Over time, educational programmes emerged which were designed to train Canadians in the field of recreation. McFarland (1970) notes that there were a few academic programmes housed in education, social work, and other disciplines to provide trained professional leadership. In the early 1960s, degree programmes focused on recreation emerged at the University of British Columbia and the University of Alberta. Today, there are recreation degree programmes available in seven of the ten provinces, and diploma programmes in eight of the ten provinces. However, questions concerning the advancement of leisure services to the level of a profession remain. Is recreation a profession or is it an area of employment comprised of a multidisciplinary group of individuals? Is there a unique body of knowledge that constitutes recreation? How do you transform what was a social movement designed to improve living conditions, youth development, and the quality of life, into a profession? Finally, what advantages are there for those who receive services from leisure services agencies by its workers receiving professional status? The purpose of this chapter is to address those questions and describe the state of the field in Canada.

From Social Movement to Profession

As explained in Chapter Two, the recreation or leisure services field had its beginning in the playground movement of the late 1800s and early 1900s. In its early stages, the concern was with promotion of healthy development of children and reduction of delinquent behaviour among youth. There was also another movement initiated in Eastern Canada to develop more urban parks and provide open space for aesthetics and certain forms of activity. All of these efforts were to improve the quality of life for Canadians and they were especially focused on rapidly growing urban areas.

Later, and especially following World War II, the need for trained individuals to provide leisure services became more apparent. Local governments expanded their involvement in service provision, provincial governments expanded their recreation departments and parks operations, and the federal government enhanced the national park system. The federal government also had a growing fitness and amateur sport department which included a unit called Recreation Canada Directorate (Westland, n.d.). As a result, more individuals could find employment in leisure services and more universities and colleges recognized the opportunity to offer degree and diploma programmes to prepare leisure service workers and promote a more complete understanding of the concept of leisure and its role in society.

The result of this development is that today, despite some shrinkage in the number of degree and diploma granting programmes, there is a vibrant community of well-trained practitioners working in the field. Despite recessionary times, there has continued to be a market for new graduates from recreation curricula. There is also a strong network of scholars working in the field of leisure. Many are, of course, affiliated with recreation departments at universities and colleges, but others are in departments such as sociology, geography, philosophy, psychology, urban planning, environmental studies, and landscape architecture.

The combination of multidisciplinary interests, roots in a social movement, and the evolution of specific degree programmes in recreation have given rise to advocacy for maintenance and promotion of the multi-faceted orientation of the field while others assert it is time to identify those working in the leisure services field as a unique group with distinct skills and knowledge. Those seeking distinction generally support the idea of professionalization.

WHAT IS A PROFESSION?

A profession is said to having many characteristics which distinguish it from other fields of employment. Sessoms (1991) wrote an article for *Recreation Canada* on the experience of U.S. leisure services practitioners in seeking status as professionals. He summarized the four qualities that a field of employment must have in order to become a profession.

- There must be recognition by the public of its importance to the welfare of the public: a *social mandate.*
- There must be acceptance by both those who practice and those who receive the service that the practitioner needs specialized knowledge and training in order to perform the service correctly.
- There must be a foundation of professional organizations which assume responsibility for the control and destiny of the profession.
- There must be a body of knowledge and programmes of formal preparation to impart that knowledge to those who wish to practice (p. 21).

Furthermore, a profession is characterized by a code of conduct or ethics and a programme of accreditation of university programmes to ensure that necessary knowledge is imparted by individuals appropriately suited to this task. These are the characteristics of a profession. The question remains: Should those who work in leisure services aspire to such status?

THE DEBATE

McGill and Hutchison (1991) noted that many of the assertions of gains made through the achievement of professional status could be challenged. Perhaps the root of the debate concerning whether leisure service practitioners should become professionals is in the first item that Sessoms (1991) noted concerning a social mandate. Associated with this is the question of whether the establishment of the field as a profession will enhance services to individuals and groups in whatever setting they may find themselves.

The answer has yet to free itself from the intense debate on the subject. Unfortunately, neither position taken by the debaters is well-supported by independently collected and analyzed evidence. On one hand, McGill and Hutchison (1991) and others (cf. Witt, 1991) have questioned whether professionalism does anything more than increase the control of the provider of the service and diminish the control of the consumer. Does a professional model assert a contrary view to the one of facilitation described in the chapter on programming or the theoretical positions of symbolic interactionism and social exchange which require a sensitivity to the needs of the person experiencing the program? Sessoms (1991) has argued that professionalism is a means of securing better quality services and programs through ensuring that the individual providing the services meets certain standards and adheres to a certain code of conduct. It would no longer be a control issue, but rather an opportunity to ensure that the professional is better able to understand the theoretical aspects of programming and service delivery and, therefore, able to be more sensitive to the needs of the individual. Citing another advantage of professionalization, Semple and Briks (1988) suggested that the recreation professional working in a team environment with other professionals may be able to best maximize service delivery. Thus, in their assessment, the leisure service professional can promote the multidisciplinary aspect of the field by being distinguished from others but working collaboratively with them. This debate will continue for the next several years. A recent policy discussion by the Canadian Parks/Recreation Association led to the conclusion that this issue "needed more study". However, many provincial organizations are moving toward or have established the framework for professional certification (e.g., British Columbia, Saskatchewan, Manitoba, Nova Scotia, Ontario).

Associations of Leisure Service Practitioners and Volunteers in Canada

In Canada, there are a number of organizations which exist to promote recreation, parks, or some aspect of them at both the national and provincial levels. The increased number of individuals who work in the field is, in part, reflected by the growth of organizations designed to serve their interests. On a national level there is the Canadian Parks/Recreation Association (CP/RA), Canadian Association for Leisure Studies (CALS), Canadian Association for Health, Physical Education and Recreation (CAHPER), and the Canadian Intramural Recreation Association (CIRA). In addition, there is another national organization which assists professionals through the support, conduct and dissemination of research. This is the Canadian Fitness and Lifestyle Research Institute (CFLRI). Finally, there is the National Fitness Leadership Advisory Committee which is supported by government and other national associations to promote the development of fitness leadership in Canada.

CANADIAN PARKS/RECREATION ASSOCIATION (CP/RA)

The Parks and Recreation Association of Canada (PRAC) was formed nearly fifty years ago (in 1945) and, in 1969, the name was changed to the Canadian Parks/ Recreation Association (Mcfarland, 1970). The original national organization emerged from the membership of the Ontario Parks Association and was initially focused more on parks than recreation matters (the Ontario Parks Association became defunct with the advent of the PRAC but was reorganized in 1953 and still operates today). However, the focus on parks soon changed and the association is, today, the major body representing recreation and park practitioners working in the public sector and in particular, municipal settings. The CP/RA's mission is:

... the enhancement of quality leisure lifestyles and environments for all Canadians through the efforts of its membership and allies in advocacy, education, information sharing, policy development and other national initiatives (CP/RA Strategic Plan, 1992).

Membership is open to governments, commercial organizations, agencies and individuals who are committed to this mission.

The CP/RA became more effective in asserting itself as the national organization representing parks and recreation after 1969. It was in that year, following the annual conference in London, Ontario, that the association received support from the federal government, established a national office with a full-time executive director and changed the name of the national publication from *Parks and Recreation in Canada to Recreation Canada*. The main reason for this name change was to make it bilingual (Drysdale, n.d.).

In 1969, The CP/RA also tried to establish the Recreation Institute of Canada which would be an organization solely for individuals working in the parks and recreation field. It was to be a professional organization. Its first chairman was Cor Westland who was Director of Recreation Canada in the federal government until 1976. At the time he became chairman of the Institute was a professor of recreation (known as "recreology" at the time) at the University of Ottawa. The Institute's activities were to support the development of individuals working in the field in order that they might become more proficient and have a network of contacts to use as a resource. The Institute published some monographs but was unable to garner much support and ceased to exist several years later (McFarland, 1970).

Today, the CP/RA has its head office in Ottawa in the National Sport and Recreation Administration Centre. This is also the place where all national sport governing bodies are housed and organizations such as CAHPER, CIRA, and CFLRI. The CP/RA publishes *Recreation Canada* five times annually, publishes a national newsletter called RecreAction, co-sponsors a futures newsletter called Leisure Watch Canada with Rethink Group (a private consulting firm), sponsors an annual conference, acts as an advocate of parks and recreation with the federal government (e.g., was active in the 1992 national referendum on the constitution to ensure that recreation was included in the proposed social charter), supports provincial initiatives, has an annual awards program honouring individuals and organizations, provides support for an individual to enhance their professional development through the Harry Boothman bursary, establishes national policies to guide their actions and present to governments and others to encourage positive development of leisure services, works with other national and international associations, and engages in other activities in support of parks and recreation development in Canada.

CANADIAN ASSOCIATION FOR HEALTH, PHYSICAL EDUCATION AND RECREATION (CAPHER)

The Canadian Association for Health, Physical Education and Recreation (CAPHER) evolved from its forerunner, the Canadian Physical Education Association (CPEA), which was established in 1933 (Gurney, 1983). The CAHPER was established in 1947 when the CPEA voted to change its name. In its early years, CAHPER made attempts to be active in supporting recreation development. This was especially true in the period of the late 1950s and early 1960s when Elsie McFarland was Vice-President of Recreation. She initiated a survey of members, the results of which suggested that there should be greater attention to recreation matters. Together with an initiative by the Parks and Recreation Association of Canada, McFarland began to examine how the two associations could cooperate and collaborate. Despite the best of intentions, a collaborative relationship never really developed and CAHPER was never able to successfully define the role of recreation in the association (Gurney, 1983). In 1975, CAHPER eliminated the role of Vice-President, Recreation and no demand has been expressed by the membership for more activity in this area. In all likelihood, the R in CAHPER was muted by the concurrent development of the Canadian Parks/Recreation Association. Nonetheless, individuals interested in physical activity and its role in leisure may find membership in CAHPER appropriate to their interests.

CANADIAN INTRAMURAL RECREATION ASSOCIATION (CIRA)

The Canadian Intramural Recreation Association (CIRA) was established in 1977. Its mandate is to promote the development of intramural and recreational programs at all levels of the educational system. In 1982, financial support was received from the federal government department of Fitness and Amateur Sport to augment the original funding supplied in the formative years by Labatt's Breweries of Canada. This allowed for the hiring of a full-time executive director in its Ottawa head office and put the association on a developmental path which has seen it grow significantly over time. CIRA's primary clients are teachers and students throughout the education system. The association provides resource information, an annual conference, participates in advocacy activity and provides other educational courses (CIRA, 1987). A 1993 decision of the federal government has paved the way for the merger of CIRA with CAPHER, thus reinforcing the school athletics and physical education focus of CAPHER and placing intramural recreation and sports in the context of physical education.

THE CANADIAN FITNESS AND LIFESTYLE RESEARCH INSTITUTE (CFLRI)

The Canadian Fitness and Lifestyle Research Institute (CFLRI) grew out of the federal government initiative in 1981 to conduct a national survey on the fitness levels of Canadians. This research effort is known as the Canada Fitness Survey. In December of 1985, the association which was originally established to conduct the survey was incorporated as the Canadian Fitness and Lifestyle Research Institute (CFLRI). In creating the organization, the federal government provided funds in order for it to assume the role of providing financial support to researchers interested in lifestyle and fitness throughout Canada, to conduct research itself, and to distribute the results of that research to practitioners, the public and researchers. The mission of the CFLRI is:

> to enhance the well-being of Canadians through research and the
> distribution of information on physically active lifestyles to the
> public and private sectors.

In 1988, with support from the Campbell Soup Company, the CFLRI launched a follow-up study of the 1981 survey called the Campbell's Survey on Well-Being in Canada. The Institute is an important resource for practitioners throughout the leisure services field. It is an important national resource for research in the areas of its focus and provides another dimension to the advocacy for leisure services in Canada.

CANADIAN ASSOCIATION FOR LEISURE STUDIES (CALS)

The Canadian Association for Leisure Studies (CALS) was established in Edmonton in 1981. The association brings together researchers from academic and professional settings to promote the study and understanding of leisure. Researchers come from such diverse backgrounds as Geography, Sociology, Environmental Studies, Philosophy, Psychology, and of course, Leisure Studies. The Association hosts the Canadian Congress on Leisure Research once every three years and publishes the proceedings of that event. This research organization provides an important vehicle for leisure researchers to interact and develop the knowledge that forms the basis of the field of practice.

PROVINCIAL ASSOCIATIONS FOR LEISURE PRACTITIONERS AND VOLUNTEERS

Each of the provinces and territories in Canada has a provincial recreation and park association. There is no formal linkage among these associations nor between the provincial and national associations. Rather, each operates independently within its own constitution and by-laws. Table 13.1 lists the provincial and territorial recreation and park associations in Canada. Table 13.2 lists other provincial associations in Canada that have some role with respect to leisure service practitioners.

These organizations provide a wide range of services to their members. Some of these include, but are not limited to, an annual conference, lobbying of public policy decision-makers, newsletter, magazine, buyer's guide, specialty workshops, joint membership with CP/RA, job bulletins, and scholarships. Some of the variability in services can be attributed to different levels of resources available to each association. The size of the membership and the provincial government policy regarding funding of provincial recreation associations influences the resource base dramatically and the services that a particular association can provide. Some, such as the British Columbia Recreation and Parks Association, have three full-time and two part-time staff while Manitoba Parks and Recreation Association has one staff member and Prince Edward Island and the Northwest Territories have no staff. The criteria for membership also vary as does the cost. For example, in Manitoba it costs $60.00 (in 1992) to join the association and the criteria is "any individual prepared to support the objectives of the association". In Alberta, an individual membership is for persons employed in leisure services or individuals interested in the field and costs $107.00 (in 1992). The association in Newfoundland and Labrador also accepts any individual interested in or working in the field of leisure services as a member. They were charged $50.00 per year in 1992. In Ontario, individuals do not belong to the Parks and Recreation Federation of Ontario. Rather, they belong to a member association of the federation such as the Ontario Recreation Society, Society of Directors of Municipal Recreation in Ontario, or the Ontario Recreation Facilities Association. In total, there are 13 member associations of the Parks and Recreation Federation of Ontario.

Provincial associations often encourage membership for individuals who are supporters of the leisure services field but not employed in it. As a result, different arrangements exist in each province and some have given rise to other associations. For example, in Saskatchewan, the focus of the Saskatchewan Parks and Recreation Association is with lay members and promotion of the field in general. The Saskatchewan Recreation Society (SRS) was established to provide a forum for professionals to interact. The SRS policy on membership in the society excludes lay members. Similarly, full membership in the Society of Directors of Municipal Recreation Directors of Ontario is exclusively for individuals employed full-time in recreation, have a certain number of years of experience and meet other criteria established by the society. On the other hand, the members of the Ontario Recreation Facilities Association (ORFA) are municipalities. The ORFA was originally the Ontario Arenas Association until 1990 when it changed to its present name (ORFA, n.d.).

TABLE 13.1
PROVINCIAL AND TERRITORIAL RECREATION AND PARK ASSOCIATIONS IN CANADA

British Columbia Recreation and Parks Association
Alberta Recreation and Parks Association
Saskatchewan Parks and Recreation Association
Manitoba Parks and Recreation Association
Parks and Recreation Federation of Ontario
    (comprised of 13 member associations)
Association Québécoise des Directeurs/Directrices du Loisir Municipal
Recreation Association of Nova Scotia
Recreation and Parks Association of New Brunswick
Association des Travailleurs en Loisir du Nouveau Brunswick
Prince Edward Island Recreation Association
Newfoundland and Labrador Parks and Recreation Association
Northwest Territories Recreation and Park Association
Recreation and Parks Association of the Yukon.

TABLE 13.2
OTHER PROVINCIAL AND TERRITORIAL ASSOCIATIONS IN RECREATION AND PARKS

Alberta Association of Recreation Facility Personnel
Alberta Therapeutic Recreation Association
Alberta Fitness Leadership Certification Association
Saskatchewan Recreation Society
Manitoba Recreation Facilities Association
Manitoba Fitness Leadership Development Association
Ontario Recreation Society
Association of Aquatic Personnel of Ontario
Ontario Fitness Council
Ontario Municipal Recreation Association
Ontario Parks Association
Ontario Recreation Facilities Association
Society of Recreation Directors of Municipal Recreation of Ontario
Ontario Research Council on Leisure
Recreation Council on Disability in Nova Scotia
New Brunswick Fitness Council

International Associations for Leisure

In addition to these national and provincial associations, there are also numerous international associations to which many Canadians belong. These include the National Recreation and Park Association (NRPA) based in the United States, the World Leisure and Recreation Association (WLRA) which is affiliated with the United Nations and is headquartered in Canada, the Travel and Tourism Research

Association (TTRA) (which has a Canadian chapter), American Alliance of Health, Physical Education, Recreation, and Dance (AAHPERD), American Therapeutic Recreation Association (ATRA), National Intramural-Recreational Sports Association (NI-RSA), and the Resort and Commercial Recreation Association (RCRA).

AMERICAN ALLIANCE OF HEALTH, PHYSICAL EDUCATION, RECREATION, AND DANCE (AAHPERD)

The largest of these organizations is American Alliance of Health, Physical Education, Recreation, and Dance (AAHPERD) with the National Recreation and Park Association next in line. The AAHPERD is made up of many different associations such as the American Association for Leisure and Recreation, American Association of Health Education, and National Association for Sport and Physical Education, among others. The American Association for Leisure and Recreation has become increasingly more active in the past ten years with publishing books and reports, ensuring that the *Leisure Today* insert in the alliance's magazine is prepared for spring and fall publication, and offering sessions at the Alliance's annual conference, among other activities. AAHPERD has a large historical association with the National Education Association in the United States and as such, has a large membership base of teachers. As a result of the more recent initiatives from the American Association for Leisure and recreation housed within AAHPERD, more recreation practitioners have chosen to belong.

NATIONAL RECREATION AND PARK ASSOCIATION (NRPA)

The National Recreation and Park Association was formed in 1966 when a number of different organizations merged to create it. The NRPA is also made up of member organizations called societies. There is the National Therapeutic Recreation Society, American Park and Recreation Society, Society of Park and Recreation Educators, National Student Branch, National Society of Park Resources, and the Armed Forces Recreation Society. Each of these societies has its own board of directors, but each is subject to the policies established by the board of trustees for the association. The NRPA provides many services including a national convention, several publications (*Parks and Recreation Magazine, Journal of Leisure Research, Therapeutic Recreation Journal, Trends, Grist, Design*, etc.). In recent years the NRPA has moved aggressively into the certification of practitioners in leisure services. Those in nontherapeutic environments seek certification as a Certified Leisure Professional (Sessoms, 1991) while those in therapeutic recreation may be certified by an independent organization called the National Council for Therapeutic Recreation Certification. In both cases, certification requires meeting certain educational and experience criteria and successful passing of a standardized examination. In addition, the NRPA has worked with the American Association for Leisure and Recreation (AALR) to develop a national council on accreditation of university curricula. As a result, there are specific standards established for university curricula to meet in order to be accredited by the joint NRPA/AALR accreditation council. The NRPA has had an impact beyond its borders as many Canadians have been involved with the association from serving on its Board of Trustees to being honoured with several of its prestigious awards. The NRPA is an important resource for individuals working or volunteering in the field.

TRAVEL RELATED ASSOCIATIONS

The other associations all have a role to play and perform different functions. The Travel and Tourism Research Association is, according to its membership brochure, "devoted to improving the quality and scope of travel and tourism research and marketing information". Members are researchers and professors in the field of travel and tourism, small businesses, large corporations, and students.

The Resort and Commercial Recreation Association was founded in 1981 and has members who are recreation and activity professionals working in resorts, campgrounds, vacation home communities, theme parks, cruise lines, universities and other related commercial recreation enterprises.

WORLD LEISURE AND RECREATION ASSOCIATION (WLRA)

The World Leisure and Recreation Association (WLRA) was established in 1956 as the International Recreation Association (IRA) and has consultative status with the United Nations. Over the years, the WLRA (and IRA before it) performed many tasks from providing recreation services to United Nations forces stationed in the Gaza Strip in the Middle East to conducting an international symposium on leisure and aging at the United Nations headquarters in New York City (Westland, 1987). The association's purpose, according to Robert Wilder (1987) has been:

to serve as a catalyst, to bring together the leaders, from every field of human service, who believe in the positive benefits of recreation for individuals, for their societies, and for promoting understanding and peace between nations and cultures (p. 4).

The association is the link between and among countries throughout the world and their practitioners and volunteers who seek to improve the quality of life through leisure services.

UNIVERSITY AND COLLEGE EDUCATION IN LEISURE SERVICES

There are numerous universities and colleges providing educational programmes in leisure services throughout the country. Most degree programmes are four years in length and require a semester long field-work placement as a minimum work experience component of the curriculum. Although there is no formal accreditation process in Canada for university curricula in leisure and recreation, most universities employ a process of regular internal review followed by reviews by external experts. This process ensures that the quality of curricula is sustained. Among the universities, most degree programmes are found in the Faculty or School of Physical Education and Recreation (e.g., Alberta, Manitoba, Dalhousie, New Brunswick, Victoria, Brock) while some are in the Faculty of Arts (e.g., Ottawa, Concordia) and still others are housed in different administrative units. The University of Waterloo, which is the largest degree programme in Canada with 13 faculty members is housed in the Faculty of Applied Health Sciences while Acadia University's recreation degree programme is located in the business school.

College programmes exist from coast to coast, from Malaspina College on Vancouver Island to Arctic College in the Northwest Territories and Newfoundland and Labrador College of Trades and Technology. Most programmes last a minimum of two years. In some cases these programmes are complete diploma programmes such as Mount Royal College in Calgary which provides training for those seeking entry- level positions in community and therapeutic recreation. On the other hand, Red Deer College's programme is a university transfer programme with the first two years being transferred to the University of Alberta or other universities such as the University of Manitoba.

The difference between college and university programmes lies in the long-term career focus a student has. The college programmes can provide excellent training for entry level positions and in some cases for more technical positions such as arena or swimming pool operator. The university programmes are aimed at providing the student with the skills to move upwardly through the leisure service organization to higher levels of responsibility and management. As a result, many college graduates work for a while and then return to university to extend their education and enhance their long-term career potential.

If you are a student interested in a career in leisure services you should seek out the university and/or college nearest you to examine the possibilities. In addition, you should contact your provincial association and join as a student member. All associations have student member categories. Finally, if you do choose to pursue studies in leisure and recreation, then seek out volunteer experiences and summer employment to augment your repertoire of skills and abilities that are necessary to be competitive in the job market upon graduation.

Summary

This chapter has discussed the issues surrounding the move towards professional-ization in the leisure services field in Canada. Some of the arguments for profession-alization include the potential for better quality service, better training, improved theoretical development, more control through professional standards, and raised stature when involved in interdisciplinary work. Arguments against professional-ization include the potential for reduced client control of service delivery, and a perceived lack of need or advantage in seeking professional status. The various international, national and provincial associations to which a leisure service practi-tioner might belong were described and it was suggested that, together, they provide a voice for the field and offer a full range of services for the professional.

STUDY QUESTIONS

1. What is the difference between a profession and a field?

2. How might the achievement of professional status for leisure service workers make them better able to serve their clients?

3. What would you include in a Code of Ethics for Leisure Service Professionals?

4. Given your particular interest in leisure services and your province of residence, what associations should you join? Why?

5. In addition to pursuing formal postsecondary education and training, how should you prepare for a career in leisure services?

References

Canadian Intramural Recreation Association. (1987). *The first ten years*. Ottawa, ON: CIRA.

Drysdale, A. (no date, mimeo). *Twenty-five years: Canadian Parks and Recreation Association*.

Gurney, H. (1983). *The CAHPER Story*. Ottawa, ON: CAHPER

McFarland, E. (1970). *The history of public recreation in Canada*. Ottawa, ON: Canadian Parks/Recreation Association.

McGill, J. & Hutchison, P. (1991). Pitfalls of increased professionalism in the field of leisure. *Recreation Canada, 49*(3), pp. 25-30.

Ontario Recreation Facilities Association, Inc. (no date, mimeo). *Arenas to Facilities— Our History*.

Semple, G. & Briks, M. (1988). The recreation professional and the multi-disciplinary approach to helping. *Recreation Canada, 46*(1), pp. 44-46.

Sessoms, H. D. (1991). Certifying park and recreation: The American experience. *Recreation Canada, 49*(3), pp. 21-24.

Westland, C. (no date, mimeo). *Recreation leadership in Canada*. A paper presented to the First World Conference of Experts on Leadership for Leisure.

Westland, C. (1987). I.R.A.—W.L.R.A. 1956-86. Thirty years of service. An historical perspective. *World Leisure and Recreation, 29*(1), pp. 9-13.

Wilder, R. (1987). President's Message. *World Leisure and Recreation, 29*(1), 4.

Witt, P. (1991). Gaining professional status: Who benefits? In Goodale, T. & Witt, P. (Eds.) *Recreation and leisure: Issues in an era of change (3rd ed.)*. (pp. 263-274). State College, PA: Venture Publishing, Inc.

Chapter Fourteen 14

Issues

Overview

PURPOSE

The purpose of this chapter on issues is to focus attention on circumstances and changes in Canadian society that might affect or be affected by leisure services. It is intended that your consciousness of and concern in matters relating to these issues will be heightened, and that you will view leisure services as being within the range of solutions that are appropriate to specific social problems. In addition, this chapter should stimulate thinking about the future, particularly as it relates to the role of leisure in our lives and the way that leisure services in Canada will be managed and delivered.

LEARNING OBJECTIVES

After studying the material presented in this chapter, you should be able to:

1. identify important issues that influence leisure opportunities and services in the community,

2. identify current events and circumstances that are and/or will become important and relevant to leisure service delivery in the future, and

3. anticipate and prepare for the leisure opportunities and constraints that may be presented to you in the future.

Issues

The early proponents of recreation in Canada saw it as a tool to use in addressing some of the problems experienced by a struggling society in an emerging nation. Recreation was viewed as a facilitator of social contact and cultural exchange. It was seen as a way to instill corporate, community and national pride, and it was believed to provide educational and health benefits to participants. Recreation was seen first as a commercial opportunity and, eventually, as a social responsibility. It has always had supporters who present it as part of the solution to the personal and collective problems that concern us most.

The simplicity of a newly confederated Canada has given way to the complexity of a modern, prosperous nation, but with this "progress" have come additional social, economic and environmental challenges. Several that are of contemporary and/or future interest and are of direct relevance to our discussion of leisure services in Canada will be examined in the following pages.

The Aging Population

Since confederation, the median age of the Canadian population has increased almost ten years, and there are now more of us that are over 30-years-old than there are children, teenagers and young adults. Figure 14.1 illustrates this dramatic rise in the median age.

FIGURE 14.1
MEDIAN AGE (IN YEARS) OF CANADIAN POPULATION SINCE 1880
SOURCE: STATISTICS CANADA, NOVAK (1988)

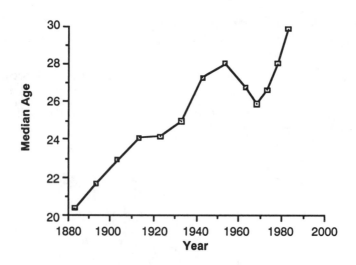

As the baby boomers (that disproportionately large number of people born between 1946 and 1961) get older, the median age will continue to rise and could, by the turn of the century, be as high as 33. Not only is the median age increasing, but the proportion of older Canadians (65 years of age or older) in the population is expected to be an unprecedented 17 percent by the year 2021. Figure 14.2 shows how the proportion of older Canadians in the population has changed since the beginning of the 20th century. It also illustrates the projected growth of that proportion into the first quarter of the next century.

FIGURE 14.2
PERCENTAGE OF CANADIANS WHO WERE AND WILL BE 65 YEARS OF AGE AND OLDER
SOURCE: STATISTICS CANADA
(FIGURES FOR 2001 AND 2021 ARE ESTIMATES)

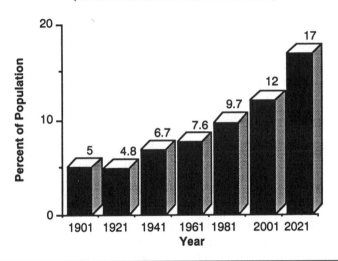

The implications of an aging society are significant for all providers of social and commercial services. Leisure service providers must recognize the impact that this change will have on their roles, responsibilities, and opportunities. For example, the decreasing relative size of children and youth segments of the population should lead to a re-evaluation of the traditional child and youth-orientation of many leisure service organizations. This means that some recreation programs and services for juvenile population segments may have to be reduced or eliminated in order to re-allocate resources to programs and services for more mature segments. It also means that recreation practitioners will need to upgrade their skills, and that professional associations and educational institutions will need to adjust curricula and profes-sional development and training programs to better equip leaders and workers for service to an older client base. In addition, many recreation facilities will need to be redesigned and modified to accommodate the interests, needs and limitations of older adult users. The popular recreational activities of a younger population will likely change as we grow older, and the leisure service provider will need to have the market assessment and product development skills to keep up with these changes. We must be prepared to support the new forms of leisure and recreational activity that the old Baby Boomers will create.

As those Baby Boomers retire, their demand for leisure goods and services will expand beyond the current periods of peak demand. More flexibility in personal schedules will allow leisure service agencies to offer their services during the day because more people will be available at that time. The evening peak demand period now experienced in many recreation facilities may become more manageable as the alternative scheduling potential grows. Increased free time and schedule flexibility should also enhance the opportunity to develop more volunteers for community recreation programs and service activities.

Leisure service providers in the public sector should also plan to respond to a probable situation where there will be fewer income earners and taxpayers to support a larger dependent population that is both demanding and politically powerful.

The Family

The average number of people in a Canadian family is less now than it was in the early 1960s. Statistics Canada figures show that, in 1961, there were an average of 3.9 persons in the family. By 1986, that average was down to 3.3 persons and, in 1991, it was estimated to be only 2.9 persons. More than a third (38 percent) of the 6.8 million families in Canada are two-person families, and 11 percent of the entire population are unattached individuals. The 1986 Canadian census revealed that 12.7 percent of the nation's families were single-parent households. Of those single-parent families, 17.8 percent had a lone male parent and 82.2 percent had a lone female parent. In 42.7 percent of the single-parent families, there were 2 or more children at home. Slightly more than half (54.6 percent) of Canada's families are made up of husband-wife couples with children at home.

These statistics demonstrate that, even though there are many traditional "Mom, Dad and kids" families, providers of leisure services must consider the circumstances of many other family structures in order to properly serve the community. It should also be remembered that, while there are many two-parent families, it is often the case that the household is a blend of families from previously dissolved marriages. Single-parent families, two-parent blended families, childless families, multiple-generation families, and traditional nuclear families should all contribute to and be a part of our understanding of family.

Recognizing the different family structures that are common in society allows the providers of leisure services to respond to the different needs, opportunities and constraints that segments of the population may have. For example, children from single-parent families may be constrained in participation in leisure programs that require a great deal of parental support if that lone parent has other children to attend to or is temporally or financially disadvantaged. Likewise the recreation opportunities for single parents may be limited, when compared to opportunities that are available to parents who have a supportive spouse or greater economic advantage. Appropriate attention to family recreation needs requires that we think of all types of families when developing programs and delivering leisure services.

The Poor

In 1991, the average family income in Canada was $53,131. The mean income was substantially lower ($46,742) which means that approximately 70 percent of the families in Canada have a below-average income. In addition, almost a million families (representing 14.3 percent of the population) have low incomes (i.e., depending on the size of the family and the community in which they live, an amount somewhere below $20,000). There are also many families whose household income levels are quite high. As illustrated in Figure 14.3, just over one third (33.5 percent) of Canadian families received incomes in excess of $60,000 during 1991.

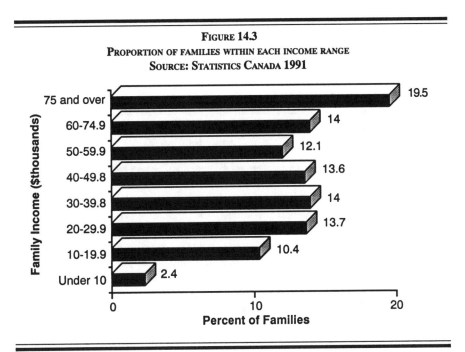

FIGURE 14.3
PROPORTION OF FAMILIES WITHIN EACH INCOME RANGE
SOURCE: STATISTICS CANADA 1991

While these family income statistics are helpful in understanding the potential financial advantage of different segments of our society, a more dramatic description of the opportunity gap between the poor and the rich can be presented in a comparison of family wealth within income classes. Wealth is a better indicator of financial constraint and opportunity with respect to leisure services because it puts family income into the context of debt, family size and accumulated assets. Figure 14.4 shows how increases in family income contribute to proportionally greater increases in family wealth.

With respect to income, there may be a seemingly small difference between some families, but the wealth and the ability of each family to dedicate resources to family recreation and leisure pursuits is likely to differ more significantly than the small income differences might otherwise suggest. Differences in wealth distinguish between the rich and the poor.

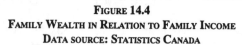

FIGURE 14.4
FAMILY WEALTH IN RELATION TO FAMILY INCOME
DATA SOURCE: STATISTICS CANADA

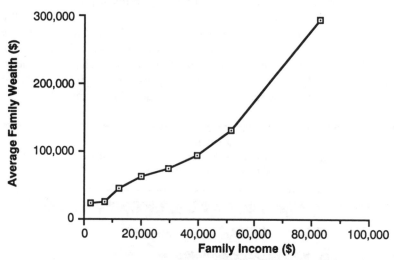

Providing appropriate leisure services for the poor is and will continue to be a challenge to public policy-makers and to the leisure service profession. Of particular concern are those individuals who Lahey (1991) identified as the "new poor" (i.e., those people whose poverty has recently extended to the point where it creates new social imbalances). Lahey described three groups of new poor; children living in poverty, the working poor, and the frail elderly living in the community. For these groups of individuals, leisure services need to provide more than just opportunities to pass time, but should help to build self-esteem, develop supportive social networks, and teach self-reliance skills. Lahey also suggested that the therapeutic benefits of recreation services should be delivered through a home-based, chronic care model which means that leisure service providers should not simply offer a one-time program and sit back waiting for the poorer segment of society to come rushing through the doors to sign up.

In responding to the needs of the poor, the leisure service profession must focus on identifying and satisfying needs, and on delivering programs and services in the most appropriate way. This will require special consideration and planning with respect to resource allocation and distribution, pricing, accessibility, location of facilities, programs and services, and product development that is based on providing leisure benefits of most worth to the economically disadvantaged. In addition, traditional measures of consumer demand will need to be revised to reflect the needs of those who are unable to express them through normal market-based media such as paying the admission price or program registration fee.

Unemployment

Related to the challenge of addressing the leisure needs of economically disadvantaged members of our society is the opportunity that leisure service providers have to assist the unemployed. The national unemployment rate is highest for males in general and for the 15-24 year old age group of both sexes. The national rate of unemployment in 1992 averaged 11.2 percent and the rate for unemployment among young Canadians was consistently 3 percent or 4 percent higher (Statistics Canada, 1992).

The obvious implications of unemployment for leisure services relate to the increased temporal resources that are available to those without work, and the decreased financial resources that would likely limit their leisure opportunities. It would be an oversimplification to assert that, just because a person is unemployed, he or she has more leisure time. Many unemployed individuals spend long hours every day searching for employment, retraining, or worrying in an unleisurely way. For them, unemployment is nothing like leisure and time without a job is not free time. There are others, however, who are able to see and enjoy opportunities to pursue leisure interests while waiting for or creating employment situations. Their leisure interests may include volunteer leadership in a recreational setting, or they may be interested in participating in programs offered by community recreation agencies.

Unemployment is often accompanied by reduced financial ability. In developing and using special recreation programs and services to reduce the stress of unemployment, leisure service providers must be constantly aware of the combined social stigma and financial hardships that burden this client group. As with other special populations discussed throughout this book, the unemployed have particular leisure needs and circumstances to which leisure service organizations must be prepared to respond.

Crime and Violence

In all likelihood, social control and crime prevention were touted as benefits to be expected from the initiation of many of the earliest public recreation programs in Canada. Proponents of recreation have continued to boldly declare its value in stemming the tide of juvenile delinquency and crime in the community and, it appears, most public policy-makers are inclined to accept the claim. Until recently, however, there has been very little Canadian research that has supported the suggested link between crime prevention and leisure opportunity. Winther (1989) documented recreation's role as an agent of social change in remote northern communities and described recreation services as a "powerful social force" which "fulfills a multitude of roles" (p. 20). One of the roles described by Winther is that of standing as a socially acceptable substitute for criminal behaviour. Empirical support for this position has been offered in a study on the impacts of recreation services in northern Manitoba communities and reserves (Searle, Mactavish, Adam-Sdrolius, Brayley, & Winther, 1992).

Increases in Criminal Code offences were recorded in all provinces and territories except the Yukon during the 1980s and first years of the 1990s. Since 1981, the violent crime rate in Canada has been steadily increasing at an annual average rate of 5 percent, and all provinces and territories contributed to this trend. Homicides accounted for only 0.3 percent of all violent crimes reported by police in 1991. Most violent crimes involved assault (without a weapon), and a large share (11.7 percent) of them were sexual assaults (Statistics Canada 1991). These trends in criminal behaviour and the benefits identified from recreation programming in communities where crime rates are high emphasize the need for more use of recreation as a means of social control through individual and community development. If, however, the goal of a recreation program is to reduce or control crime, it should be designed and operated in such a way as to achieve that goal. This requires skilled program planners and leaders which, in turn, requires post-secondary training programs and curricula to develop this specialized skill in the students.

Multiculturalism and Racial Intolerance

Unlike the United States which is often described as a melting pot of cultures, Canada is best described as a cultural mosaic. Public policy has consistently defended the idea that differences within the nation are good for it, and the protection of the variety of cultures brought by "new Canadians" is an important duty of governments at all levels (Dabydeen, 1991). Table 14.1 illustrates the cultural diversity of Canada and shows that there are other important ethnic populations besides the British, French, and Aboriginal Peoples.

TABLE 14.1
SIZE OF MAJOR ETHNIC POPULATIONS IN CANADA (STATISTICS CANADA, 1986)

Major Ethnic Category	Population	Percent of Population
Aboriginal peoples	711,720	2.34
Arab origins	103,550	0.34
Black origins	260,335	0.86
British origins	12,371,485	40.72
Caribbean origins	81,160	0.27
Eastern European origins	1,886,585	6.21
East and Southeast Asian origin	688,485	2.27
French origins	8,123,360	26.74
Latin, Central and South American origins	50,030	0.16
Northern European origins	690,925	2.27
Pacific Islands origins	10,350	0.03
South Asian origins	314,035	1.03
Southern European origins	1,705,170	5.61
West Asian origins	51,590	0.17
Western European origins	3,335,080	10.98

Violent confrontations and outbursts like those experienced in Montreal, Halifax, and Toronto in the early 1990s remind us that, in spite of Canada's official multicultural position, there is racial intolerance and a significant amount of unwillingness by some people to accept the contribution that diversity makes to the fabric of Canadian society.

Leisure services can be helpful in sustaining the cultural mosaic of the community. In a study of the City of Ottawa's approach to providing leisure services to its ethnic communities, Bolla, Dawson and Karlis (1991) observed that ethnospecific recreation is important to most ethnic populations, and that ethnic communities, regardless of their size or heterogeneity, develop their own cultural and recreation infrastructure. Support for maintenance and expansion of this infrastructure was seen as an acceptable role for mainstream municipal recreation agencies.

Recreation organizations can also play an important part in promoting multicultural exchange and discouraging racism. The Heritage Days celebration in Edmonton and Winnipeg's Folklorama festival are examples of leisure events designed to display the cultural diversity of those communities and to help those who attend to appreciate the contribution that people from many nations have made to the quality of life they enjoy.

Multiculturalism also presents some unique challenges to leisure service organizations. For example, some patriarchal subcultures may unconsciously or otherwise thwart the efforts and limit the success of leisure service organizations in extending services to women (Carrington, Chivers & Williams, 1987). Providers of leisure services must seek to understand the impact of culturally determined leadership structures on the ability of specific members of the society or family to receive and benefit from those services.

In addition, structural barriers to participation in recreation programs and use of recreation facilities may be related to cultural conditions. Barriers such as physical distance due to voluntary ethnic clustering, lack of awareness due to language and communication difficulties, and lack of transportation due to culturally based fear of public transit, or gender roles with respect to driving often affect the response of particular ethnic groups to worthwhile leisure service initiatives (Kew, 1981; Dembrowski, 1988). A leisure service organization that is sensitive to multicultural issues will ensure that policies and procedures are established to reduce such barriers.

The existence or perceived existence of racial or ethnic discrimination practices by leisure service personnel can sometimes constrain participation in recreation programs by an ethnic community (Bolla et al, 1991). Clear indications of non-discrimination should be made whenever there is a possibility that an ethnic group in the community may feel the leisure service provider does not understand nor care about its cultural norms, interests and requirements. Incidentally, that clear indication needs to be more than just a sign in the lobby that professes "acceptance of all people regardless of race, religion, etc."—it needs to be demonstrated in the way the organization serves its clients.

Environmental Protection and Sustainable Development

In all that we do, there is an increasing awareness of the need to progress and develop without inappropriately harming any part of the local or global environment. Canada is home to the World Centre for Sustainable Development and Canadians support the idea that any development should cost no more than the effort that is required to keep it sustainable. That effort is worthy of both policy-makers and professionals who are involved in the support and delivery of leisure services.

Fox (1991) presented the field with a challenge when she declared that "In the midst of despair, fear, uncertainty and change, the park and recreation profession can become a vision and voice of life-sustaining values such as protection of the natural areas and the environment, respectful connection between all living beings, and maintenance of quality, health-giving leisure activities" (p. 28). Fox added that "for all our concentration and fascination with management principles, marketing strategies, and satisfying the client, we are, in the final analysis, an idealistic profession and it is time we included an ethic of respect and protection for the ecosphere in our mission" (p. 30). That ethic should result in more sensitivity being exercised in the planning, construction and operation of parks and recreation facilities. It should result in the advocacy of environmental protection through recreation programs and services. It should result in an emphasis in leisure activity that "lifts the human spirit" rather than promotes mindless consumption and materialism. The ethic of respect and protection should, above all else, instill in each of us a sense of responsibility for the well-being of our children and the generations of Canadians that follow them.

Health

One of the most important financial issues facing provincial governments in Canada is the need to control health care costs. Some governments have tried to control costs by limiting health professional salaries and reducing hospital budgets. While a certain amount of success can be achieved through this retrenchment strategy, a more beneficial approach to cost control is to invest in mechanisms that reduce the demand for health care services.

The 1986 paper titled *Recreation Strategies for the Promotion of Health* prepared by the Alberta Government for the annual meeting of the provincial Ministers of Recreation and Sport indicated that 75 percent of illnesses are attributable to lifestyle choices and environmental influences, while only 25 percent are attributable to biological sources. The paper also suggested that lifestyle-related illness are preventable and could be reduced by the promotion of healthy behaviours which would include balanced recreational activity. Thus, recreation was recognized as having potential to control health care costs.

National advertising campaigns and programs such as Participation and Active Living frequently stress the health benefits of engaging in a balanced set of leisure activities. They suggest that recreation promotes physical, psychological, spiritual and social health by helping us to develop cardiovascular endurance and muscle strength, cope with stress, maintain a sense of purpose in life, and be able to get along with and enjoy social interaction.

A specific preventative role for recreation in reducing the demand for health care services was articulated by Iso-Ahola and Crowley (1991) who linked substance abuse in adolescents to boredom in leisure. Recreational activity, it was suggested, can be positive if "behaviours are alternatives to drugs that fill free time, alleviate boredom, and make adolescents feel good about themselves" (p. 260). In addition to preventing health problems by providing alternatives to unhealthy behaviour, recreation can help in the curative side of the substance abuse problem. The therapeutic treatment of substance abusers often includes recreational activity for diversionary purposes, recreational activity in support of a positive learning environment, and recreational activity as a coping skill development exercise (Francis, 1991).

Constitutional Reform and Political Upheaval

Attempts by federal governments since the early 1980s to consolidate support for the Canadian Constitution have provided several opportunities for the advocacy of recreation and the promotion of leisure as a right of citizenship. In the failed attempt to achieve a national consensus on the 1992 Charlottetown Accord, the federal government of the day proposed to transfer jurisdiction of recreation, tourism, and several other services to the provinces. Instead of continuing to recognize the primacy of the provinces in leisure services while maintaining the right to offer national programs, the federal government was giving sole responsibility for recreation to the provinces and suggesting that it would play no role in such matters. The constitutional reform package was rejected by a national referendum, but not on the issue of the transfer of responsibility for leisure services. It is likely, therefore, that future reform efforts will resurrect this idea and once again put recreation in political limbo. In the meantime, several important questions need to be addressed (Balmer, 1992). For example, what body will provide the "national voice" for recreation in Canada if the federal government divests itself of this function? From where will funding for truly national projects come? How can exchanges of recreation information, innovation and insight across Canada be facilitated? Who will advocate for the recreation interests that remain in the federal system (e.g., National Parks)?

General disenchantment of the public with politicians and the political system has characterized the final decades of this century. The democratic right to require change has been exercised and new governments have been established to help us realize our dreams for a "better" Canada. With change comes upheaval and uncertainty as well as further disenchantment with new governments struggling, with limited success, to solve old problems. Recreation and leisure services are subject to the buffetings of political storms but, so far, have maintained the ability to stay afloat as a buoy in a somewhat turbulent harbour.

Aboriginal Peoples

As illustrated in Table 14.1, (page 252) aboriginal peoples constitute 2.34 percent of Canada's population. Many live in remote northern communities where recreation resources and services are not as developed as they are in "white" communities, but are considered to be just as important if not more so. Efforts by federal and provincial governments to establish community recreation structures to serve the needs of aboriginal peoples have led to a better understanding of the opportunities and challenges that are unique to this part of Canadian society. A Manitoba initiative was designed to train native leaders to be a recreation resource to their own communities within the context of their own culture. A two-year comprehensive study of the impact of that initiative (Searle et al., 1992) identified several important issues to be addressed when planning for and providing leisure services for aboriginal peoples. With respect to the development and training of aboriginal recreation leaders, it was recommended that alternative curricula be developed with a sensitivity to cultural issues and learning processes that may be different within the native community structure. It was also noted that traditional leadership structures in native communities may not provide the same support for young recreation leaders as is provided in other cultures that adhere less to the age hierarchy leadership model. Unique challenges face the trained, but young, recreation professional when dealing with the more mature, revered elders who control the resources and influence opinions in the community. Other seemingly insignificant behaviours also need to be considered in a cultural context for the effective planning and delivery of leisure services to aboriginal peoples. These include the actions of and meanings given to such things as eye contact, instructional directives, and advisory boards.

Rural Depopulation

In the Atlantic provinces, settlement of rural areas peaked as the first decade of this century drew to a close. Not long afterwards, rural areas in Central Canada also ceased to grow due to new settlement. It was not until the economically depressed 1930s that Western Canada's trend of people moving onto the land was reversed and rural residents looked to the cities for employment and opportunity. Rounds (1991) described the population of rural areas as changing from the early local communities centered on a country store, church, and school to regional "hub" communities with larger towns as service centres. He studied more recent rural and urban population statistics and concluded that the next stage of population is currently in progress; namely, the stage of rural depopulation.

It should be noted that depopulation of rural areas is accompanied by aging of the remaining population. It's the younger people that are moving out of the truly rural areas, and those that are left are getting older as individuals and as a population.

The implications of rural depopulation for leisure services are many. The traditional growth-oriented approach to planning, for example, no longer applies in rural settings. The focus on facility planning should, logically, change from building new facilities and adding new programs to reusing existing facilities and scaling down current program offerings. Of course, facility and program resources should also be evaluated with respect to their applicability to the interests and needs of older users.

Rural residents enjoy access to more outdoor recreation resources, and their leisure activity choices often relate to the availability of those resources and associated opportunities. In the urban recreation environment, the person or family that moved from the farm or small community may find very little to match the outdoor-oriented activity interests they have cultivated.

Another recreation impact of rural depopulation is a diminished tax base to support the public recreation system in rural communities. Apparently fixed costs such as those for utility services in curling rinks could easily become unbearable for the reduced population, and public pressure may force the closure or limited operation of many recreation facilities.

Fiscal Limitations

To say that the 1990s will be characterized by fiscal restraint in public, private and commercial sector activities is to state the obvious. The national debt continues to grow despite official belt-tightening and increasing taxation. That debt (and the cost of servicing it) will not disappear because of the loosening of government purse strings and the infusion of major sums of money into social services. Hard times are to be with us for many years.

Fiscal limitations in the delivery of leisure services require adjustment on the part of leisure service providers, and tempered expectations on the part of consumers. Leisure service organizations are encouraged to "do more with less" and have, since the late 1970s, strived for that goal using creativity and a variety of tested marketing practices. After more than a decade of fiscal restraint, it must be accepted that sometimes the appropriate response to having less is doing less. An acceptable compromise objective might be to do the same with less or, as the popular bumper sticker suggests, work smarter, not harder.

In striving for greater efficiency in service delivery, leisure organizations need to review and consider alternative delivery systems. For example, some public libraries which maintain several branch libraries in suburban areas have had to close some or all of those branches because of reduced budgets. Using duplicate resources and employing technology could make it possible for the library system to be reestablished at minimal cost and with minimal reduction in service. The duplicate resources to be utilized are the school libraries which could house the public library's children's collection and be opened to the public. Technological adaptations might include installing computer terminals in the school library, through which catalogues could be searched and books ordered for delivery to the school on the next day from a single centralized library facility. In this example, the leisure experience of browsing would be reduced, but community access to the books would be maintained.

Greater efficiency in leisure service organizations can also be achieved through organizational reform. Most organizational structures have too many levels of management and could appropriately be flattened (i.e., have the number of levels of authority or control between the chief executive officer and the non-supervisory worker reduced).

Fiscal limitations also require providers of leisure services to give proper attention to revenue generation activities. This means that they must employ a variety of suitable pricing strategies and ensure that legally expropriated funds (i.e., taxes) are fully justified. In the public sector, it is especially important that consumers of recreation services are assured that taxes and fees collected for those recreation services go towards maintenance of that service.

Technology

If you or a friend has purchased a piece of electronic equipment lately, you probably don't want to be told this, but it's no longer the latest innovation. Technology is advancing at such a rate that the already short time required to get most new products to the market is long enough for a newer, improved version to be developed. What we marvel at today we take for granted or consider obsolete in the near future. Consider, for example, the impact of plastic in your life or, more specifically, in your leisure. You are probably wearing something made of plastic, you may be sitting on something plastic, you likely ate using something plastic, and the sounds you hear around you are probably being channeled through a plastic encased device. Many of your frequently used leisure items are made with plastic (e.g., toys, electronic equipment, cars, sports equipment, videos, tools, etc.). We take plastic for granted, but there's a good chance that someone in your family (perhaps a parent or grandparent) remembers what it was like to live in a world with no plastic.

The Royal Bank Reporter occasionally devotes an issue to a discussion of how technology affects our lives. In 1989, this widely distributed publication identified several technological wonders that serve as good examples of how technology will impact our leisure in the future. They are described in Table 14.2.

There are two general responses to technological advancement and its intrusion into our leisure lives. One response is to embrace it gleefully and buy all the high tech "toys" one can find to use in making fun. The second response is to seek escape from the synthetic environment of technology and pursue natural environments and natural experiences. Leisure service providers need to be prepared to facilitate both responses.

Expectations of Government

In time, the Canadian public has come to demand quality services from its governments. More recently, however, the demand for quality service has been coupled with a demand for relief from the burden of personal income and property taxes. This apparently contradicting set of expectations is commonly held and is no less applied to public leisure services than it is to other government services. More than ever, governments and public agencies are required to be accountable to their consuming publics.

Quality service is less a function of financial resource availability than it is a function of organizational and professional attitude. The old adage that "if it's government, it's not as good" has no basis in the competitive leisure service market and the public settings where the consumer's needs are most important. Quality service does not necessarily require higher taxes and may, in all probability, contribute to a more financially sound operation of the service.

TABLE 14.2
TECHNOLOGICAL WONDERS THAT COULD IMPACT ON LEISURE

Technological "Wonder"	Description
Videophone	A device which sends and receives images over phone lines so you and your party can both talk and see each other at the same time.
HDTV (High Definition Television)	A flat wall-sized screen that will entertain you with sharper and brighter images and top-quality stereo sound.
Teleshopping	Selection and purchase of goods through an in-home terminal. Payment will be made using a debit-card and the item(s) will be delivered to your home.
The Electronic Car	Equipped with a video map display that uses satellite tracking to show you where you are and how to get to where you're going.
The Smart House	One wiring cable and an array of micro-compressors will allow appliances, security systems, and entertainment devices to communicate with each other, outside services, and you.
Voice-Activated Cellular Phone	No bigger than a pencil, and powerful enough to use in a cellular environment, this device will allow you to reach out and touch just about anyone at any time.

These are just examples and it is possible that even they have become obsolete in the time between the writing of this book and your reading of it.

Planning for the Future

A popular television show which aired in the late 1960s presented a view of the way experts believed life would be in the 1970s and beyond. One show in the series focussed on leisure, and offered some exciting predictions about leisure opportunities and attitudes in the future. For example, it was suggested that, by the year 2000, the average worker in North America would spend only 22 hours of each week on the job in full-time employment. In addition, that average worker would receive 25 weeks of paid annual vacation and could retire with full pension benefits at age 38. Experts interviewed on the show predicted that, by 1980, many people would own and use personal hovercraft which they could purchase "just about anywhere" for only $1,500. They also talked of a lunar space station which would accommodate regularly scheduled shuttle-loads of tourists who choose a more exotic destination than the Caribbean which, they predicted, would be highly accessible because of a $50 air bus service from most points in Canada and the United States. With the advantage of hindsight, it is easy to scoff at the warped foresight of these experts. For that reason, we have followed the advice to either make no specific predictions about the future or predict only for a future that begins ten years after we expect to have died of old age. That way nobody can tell us that we were wrong!

Quite deliberately and without apology, our discussion of the future deals with generalities. It is designed to prepare us to think about what might happen and what might be relevant to this introduction to leisure services in Canada. In reviewing the literature about the future, it becomes clear that most predictions are based on the following assumptions: (1) the absence of major war or catastrophic global event, (2) correct estimation of earth's resource inventory, (3) constant human behaviour in situations like the present, and (4) a continued valuing of leisure.

Balmer (1991) made several propositions to focus attention on the trends that will likely have the greatest impact on the parks and recreation field in the 1990s. He proposed that:

1. consumptive forms of recreation will fall into disfavour,
2. there will be a greater desire for and tolerance of allowing urban parkland to be restored to more natural states,
3. human-powered movement will be more popular,
4. adultism will challenge the foundations of public recreation,
5. the eco-experience will be sought after by more people,
6. passive pursuits will rise in favour to match physical recreation,
7. highly structured activity will become less appealing while informal, flexible individual activity will rise in popularity,
8. home will become a more comfortable place for Canadians to spend their leisure hours,
9. recreation programs will increasingly be designed as preventive social services, and
10. recreation programs will regain lost stature as ideal opportunities to develop the leadership needed in tomorrow's Canada.

The face of leisure services in Canada is changing and will continue to change in the future. The changes that are predicted here are based on observation of current conditions in the economy, the political arena, and the state of the leisure service profession. They are also based on population trends and social directions that are measurable. There is undoubtedly good news and there is most certainly bad news in the future, but Dr. Emmett Brown (a fictional time traveller in the popular 1980s movie series *Back to the Future*) said it best when he counselled his young friends that "The future hasn't been written yet. The future is what you make it."

Summary

Throughout this chapter we have highlighted numerous issues which face leisure service organizations and professionals and those which may be influenced by leisure services. The range of issues is quite extensive including: demographic changes related to age, rural depopulation, ethnicity, and family structure; social pressures associated with decreasing racial tolerance, increasing numbers of poor persons, rising crime, and unemployment; environmental challenges; health issues; and, political change due to the recognition of aboriginal rights, constitutional pressures and fiscal limitations. The future is a challenging one for all of us and in particular, the leisure service professional.

STUDY QUESTIONS?

1. Describe how the changing age patterns of our society will impact upon leisure service organizations.

2. In Chapter One we asserted that there is a growing role for leisure in health care systems. What have you learned from this chapter to substantiate that assertion?

3. Consider the historical development of leisure services in Canada from 1900 to 1990. Do you see any patterns emerging?

4. What would be the impact of no federal government role in leisure services? Look back at the discussion in Chapter Five on the emergence of a national policy before you respond.

5. Given that the population is aging, the family structure is substantially different than the norm of 30 years ago, and some of the other social pressures that exist today, do you think that the way we define leisure will change? How?

6. What are the challenges for those charged with preserving our natural resources in the coming years?

7. How does the rise in recognition and respect for aboriginal rights influence future natural resource management?

8. Is there a danger in emphasizing the economic value of leisure over the social value when discussing the issue of rural depopulation?

9. What strategies would you employ to help design a leisure service agency respond to the needs of Canadians in the year 2010?

References

Balmer, K. (1991). Is there a future for public sector parks and recreation? *Recreation Canada, 49*(2), pp. 16-24.

Bolla, P., Dawson, D., and Karlis, G. (1991). Serving the multicultural community: Directions for leisure service providers. *Journal of Applied Recreation Research, 16*(2), pp. 116-132.

Carrington, B., Chivers, T., and Williams, T. (1987). Gender, leisure and sport: A case study of young people of South Asian descent. *Leisure Studies, 6*(3), pp. 265-279.

Dabydeen, C. (1991). Municipalities and race relations: Partnership in action. *Recreation Canada, 49*(4), pp. 16-17.

Dembrowski, K. (1988). *Survey on recreation for ethnic older adults.* Toronto, ON: Ontario Ministry of Tourism and Recreation.

Fox, K. (1991). Environmental ethics and the future of parks and recreation. *Recreation Canada, 49*(2), pp. 28-31.

Francis, T. (1991). Revising therapeutic recreation for substance misuse: Incorporating flow technology in alternatives treatment. *Therapeutic Recreation Journal 25*(2), pp. 41-48.

Iso-Ahola, S. & Crowley, E. (1991). Adolescent substance abuse and leisure boredom. *Journal of Leisure Research, 23*, pp. 260-271.

Kew, S. (1981). *Ethnic groups and leisure.* London, UK: The Sports Council and Social Science Research Council.

Kunstler, R. (1991). There but for fortune: A therapeutic recreation perspective on the homeless in America. *Therapeutic Recreation Journal, 25*(2), pp. 31-40.

Lahey, M. (1991). Serving the New Poor: Therapeutic Recreation Values in Hard Times. *Therapeutic Recreation Journal, 25*(2), pp. 9-18.

Novak, M. (1988). Aging and Society: A Canadian Perspective. Scarborough, ON: Nelson.

Rounds, R. (1991). The population context for recreation planning in rural western Canada. *Recreation Canada, 49*(3), pp. 11-14.

Searle, M. S., Mactavish, J., Adam-Sdrolius, H., Brayley, R. E., & Winther, N. R. (1992). *An Assessment of the Impact of the Northern Recreation Director Pilot Project.* A Technical Report for Manitoba Culture, Heritage and Citizenship and Manitoba Northern Affairs.

Winther, N. R. (1989). Recreation: An agent of social change in remote northern communities. *Recreation Canada, 47*(5), pp. 20-23.

OTHER BOOKS FROM VENTURE PUBLISHING

The Activity Gourmet
by Peggy Powers

Adventure Education
edited by John C. Miles and Simon Priest

Assessment: The Cornerstone of Activity Programs
by Ruth Perschbacher

Behavior Modification in Therapeutic Recreation: An Introductory Learning Manual
by John Dattilo and William D. Murphy

Benefits of Leisure
edited by B. L. Driver, Perry J. Brown and George L. Peterson

Beyond Bingo: Innovative Programs for the New Senior
by Sal Arrigo, Jr., Ann Lewis and Hank Mattimore

The Community Tourism Industry Imperative—The Necessity, The Opportunities, Its Potential
by Uel Blank

Dimensions of Choice: A Qualitative Approach to Recreation, Parks, and Leisure Research
by Karla A. Henderson

Doing More With Less in the Delivery of Recreation and Park Services: A Book of Case Studies
by John Crompton

Evaluation of Therapeutic Recreation Through Quality Assurance
edited by Bob Riley

The Evolution of Leisure: Historical and Philosophical Perspectives
by Thomas Goodale and Geoffrey Godbey

The Game Finder—A Leader's Guide to Great Activities
by Annette C. Moore

Great Special Events and Activities
by Annie Morton, Angie Prosser and Sue Spangler

Internships in Recreation and Leisure Services: A Practical Guide for Students
by Edward E. Seagle, Jr., Ralph W. Smith and Lola M. Dalton

Leadership and Administration of Outdoor Pursuits, Second Edition
by Phyllis Ford and James Blanchard

Leisure And Family Fun
by Mary Atteberry-Rogers

The Leisure Diagnostic Battery: Users Manual and Sample Forms
by Peter A. Witt and Gary Ellis

Leisure Diagnostic Battery Computer Software
by Gary Ellis and Peter A. Witt

Leisure Education: A Manual of Activities and Resources
by Norma J. Stumbo and Steven R. Thompson

Leisure Education II: More Activities and Resources
by Norma J. Stumbo

Leisure Education: Program Materials for Persons with Developmental Disabilities
by Kenneth F. Joswiak

Leisure Education Program Planning: A Systematic Approach
by John Dattilo and William D. Murphy

Leisure in Your Life: An Exploration, Third Edition
    by Geoffrey Godbey

A Leisure of One's Own: A Feminist Perspective on Women's Leisure
    by Karla Henderson, M. Deborah Bialeschki, Susan M. Shaw and Valeria J. Freysinger

Marketing for Parks, Recreation, and Leisure
    by Ellen L. O'Sullivan

Outdoor Recreation Management: Theory and Application, Third Edition
    by Alan Jubenville and Ben Twight

Planning Parks for People,
    by John Hultsman, Richard L. Cottrell and Wendy Zales Hultsman

Private and Commercial Recreation
    edited by Arlin Epperson

The Process of Recreation Programming Theory and Technique, Third Edition
    by Patricia Farrell and Herberta M. Lundegren

Quality Management: Applications for Therapeutic Recreation
    edited by Bob Riley

Recreation and Leisure: Issues in an Era of Change, Third Edition
    edited by Thomas Goodale and Peter A. Witt

Recreation Economic Decisions: Comparing Benefits and Costs
    by Richard G. Walsh

Recreation Programming And Activities For Older Adults
    by Jerold E. Elliott and Judith A. Sorg-Elliott

Research in Therapeutic Recreation: Concepts and Methods
    edited by Marjorie J. Malkin and Christine Z. Howe

Risk Management in Therapeutic Recreation: A Component of Quality Assurance
    by Judith Voelkl

A Social History of Leisure Since 1600
    by Gary Cross

The Sociology of Leisure
    by John R. Kelly and Geoffrey Godbey

A Study Guide for National Certification in Therapeutic Recreation
    by Gerald O'Morrow and Ron Reynolds

Therapeutic Recreation: Cases and Exercises
    by Barbara C. Wilhite and M. Jean Keller

Therapeutic Recreation Protocol for Treatment of Substance Addictions
    by Rozanne W. Faulkner

A Training Manual for Americans With Disabilities Act Compliance in Parks and Recreation Settings
    by Carol Stensrud

Understanding Leisure and Recreation: Mapping the Past, Charting the Future
    edited by Edgar L. Jackson and Thomas L. Burton

Venture Publishing, Inc
1999 Cato Avenue
State College, PA 16801